ART FOR THE WALL
FURNITURE
& ACCESSORIES

15

The Designer's Sourcebook

GUILD SOURCEBOOKS
Madison, Wisconsin
USA

Published by
GUILD.com™
931 East Main Street
Madison, WI 53703 • USA
FAX 608-227-4179
TEL 608-257-2590
TEL 877-284-8453
info@guild.com
www.guild.com

Administration
Toni Fountain Sikes, President
Michael Monroe, Artistic Advisor
Katie Kazan, Chief Editorial Officer
Nathan Turnbull, Trade Resource Coordinator
Linda Seebauer, Administrative Assistant
Laura Marth • Paula Cosby, Assistant Artist Coordinators

Production, Design, Editorial
Ann Schaffer, Production Artist
Scott Maurer, Production Artist
Nikki Muenchow, Editorial Manager
Dawn Barker, Editorial Staff
Leslie Ferrin, Writer
Susan Troller, Writer

DNP America, Inc., Printer

Artist Coordinators
Reed J. McMillan, Director of Artist Marketing
Carol Chapin • Michelle Spude • Jennifer Stofflet
Anna Trull • Anne Wilder

Distribution
Distributed to the trade and art markets worldwide by
North Light Books, an imprint of F&W Publications, Inc.
1507 Dana Avenue • Cincinnati, OH 45207
TEL 513-531-2222 • TEL 800-289-0963

ISBN (hardcover) 1-880140-42-X ISBN (softcover) 1-880140-43-8
Printed in Hong Kong

Cover Art: Marie V. Mason, *Women's Circus Band*, acrylic on canvas, 48" x 58", and *Red Dog*,
acrylic on canvas, 58" x 48". Details from artwork by Marie V. Mason also appear throughout
this book. See page 117.

TAKING STOCK:
15 YEARS OF GUILD SOURCEBOOKS

Eight or nine years ago, *Art Calendar* magazine paid us a great compliment when they called our publications "the industry standard in artist sourcebooks." High praise, indeed! We thanked *Art Calendar* and grabbed the phrase for our tagline.

But the sober side of praise is obligation, and with this 15th anniversary edition of *The Designer's Sourcebook*, we look back to see how well we've served the art and design communities. To do this, we've used the ultimate measure: What new artwork exists in the world because of **GUILD** Sourcebooks? Where is it located, what does it look like, who made it, who bought it, who commissioned it?

Our featured essay, beginning on page 10, describes a number of **GUILD**-inspired commissions. Others are described — and shown — in the one-page features sprinkled throughout the book. In every case, these projects elevate their settings. We hope they'll serve to inspire new generations of artwork through **GUILD** Sourcebooks.

Still, after 15 years of ink and paper, we're very excited about our new venture on the Internet.

GUILD.com, which opened to the public in March 1999, offers contemporary art and fine craft for direct sale to consumers. As with **GUILD** Sourcebooks, **GUILD**.com allows artists to display and sell their work in a product of exceptional standards. Artwork shown both in the sourcebooks and on the website is juried by an advisory board headed by Michael Monroe, former curator-in-charge of the Smithsonian Institution's Renwick Gallery.

Of special interest to design professionals is a section of **GUILD**.com specifically for artists who undertake commissioned projects. Please take time to visit (http://www.guild.com) and let us know what you think! Whatever the medium, we're determined to remain "the industry standard."

TABLE OF CONTENTS

FEATURES

Fifteen Years of GUILD Sourcebooks   *10*

Our featured essay celebrates 15 years of building ties between artists and design professionals.

Commission Stories

GUILD advertisers share their sourcebook successes.

Profiles of GUILD sourcebook Users

Interviews with design professionals who use GUILD Sourcebooks to commission art for their projects.

TABLE OF CONTENTS

ARTISTS

Artists by Section

TABLE OF CONTENTS

RESOURCES

Artists by Section

FURNITURE

LIGHTING

ACCESSORIES

PEDESTAL SCULPTURE

MURALS

ART FOR THE WALL

PAINTINGS & PRINTS

PHOTOGRAPHY

(listing continued)

ARTISTS BY SECTION

TEN GREAT WAYS

to use *The Designer's Sourcebook 15*

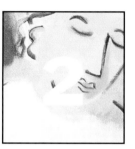

WHAT'S NEW? Specifically, what's new in the last 15 years courtesy of the artists and design professionals who get together through GUILD Sourcebooks? Read the answer in our featured essay (see pages 10-15) and in the one-page illustrated articles sprinkled throughout the book.

QUALITY CONTROL. This book begins with an assurance: these artists are reliable and professional. Featured artists in GUILD Sourcebooks have been juried in on the basis of experience, quality of work, and a solid reputation for working with architects and designers.

DESKTOP DIRECTORY. GUILD Sourcebooks are designed for quick reference, as well as leisurely browsing. The "Index of Artists and Companies" is a comprehensive listing, so it's easy to find a current phone number or check product information. Your rolodex may grow stale; *The Designer's Sourcebook* is fresh each year.

DO IT ONLINE. GUILD.com's new Trade Resource Program is a great supplement to GUILD Sourcebooks. Log on to www.guild.com and click the "Trade Resource" button. Registered trade professionals can purchase art at a discount, post project listings, request artist recommendations, and much, much more.

MOTIVATION. *The Designer's Sourcebook* is a great resource for client meetings. Clients have been known to reach levels of extreme excitement upon viewing the artistic possibilities showcased here.

INTRODUCING GUILD.com. We love paper and ink, but we love the Internet, too. GUILD.com features artists from GUILD Sourcebooks in a special section; look for the "Commission Center." While you're there, take time to window shop or place an order from an extraordinary selection of contemporary artworks.

TELL US. We're always interested in feedback about GUILD Sourcebooks and the GUILD.com website. Is there a feature you'd like added to the online Trade Resource Program? A way we can make your life easier? Call our dedicated Trade Resource staff toll free at 1-877-565-2002, or e-mail us at tradeinfo@guild.com.

GO AHEAD AND CALL. If something intrigues you while perusing *The Designer's Sourcebook* — a shape, a form, an exotic use of the commonplace — please, give the artist a call. Serendipity often leads to a wonderful creation.

ARTISTS THEN AND NOW. Many of the artists whose work you see here are also represented in earlier GUILD publications; look for references on artists' pages. You can order most of these early volumes through our main office; call 1-877-344-8453 for order information.

LET US HEAR FROM YOU. This volume of *The Designer's Sourcebook* is filled with information about great design projects. We love hearing about these projects, and love to show them off in our sourcebooks. Let us know about *your* most recent triumph ... perhaps we'll feature it in next year's edition.

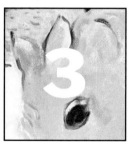

FIFTEEN YEARS OF GUILD SOURCEBOOKS

Susan Troller

A good idea makes sense. It has a kind of persuasive logic. It tends to get people nodding in agreement, because they can see how it could improve the way things are, or the way things are done.

A great idea changes everything. Even if it makes observers shake their head in doubt and skepticism at first, a ground-breaking idea thrives on challenges, cuts its own paths, and, ultimately makes it an exercise in imagination to remember the way things were before. It stands as a clear marker dividing Before and After.

GUILD Sourcebooks appears to be such an idea.

Times Have Changed

As GUILD Sourcebooks (formerly THE GUILD) celebrates its 15th anniversary and moves into the 21st century, it would be easy to forget what was before. Today we are all riding a tumultuous wave of information and communication that is, quite literally, changing everything. The way we work. Where we work. The expectations we have about time and distance. The way we relate to each other. Although this communications explosion could not have been predicted in 1985, the idea behind THE GUILD — the burning belief that artists and design professionals ought to be knit into a rich, symbiotic community — was already positioned to take advantage of it.

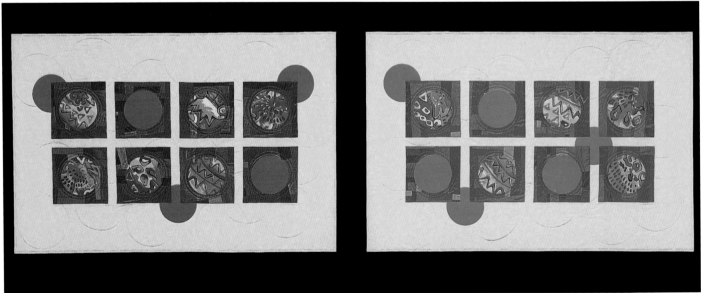

Robin Cowley, *Spheres*, 1998, art quilt, Circuit City headquarters, Richmond, VA

Don Tuttle Photography

Kathy Bradford, sandcarved glass wall, 1998, Vilar Center for the Arts, 33' × 8' × 4"   Foaad Farah

urban area, on back country roads and in dozens of artists' communities, there were people breathing new life and imagination into ancient crafts and creating amazing art.

Her idea was as simple as it was novel: to bring artists and design professionals together for their mutual benefit, and for the satisfaction and delight of their clients. She took a deep breath, began THE GUILD, and never looked back.

Was GUILD Sourcebooks a great idea? Only time will truly tell. But, for many artists and design professionals, it certainly has changed everything.

The Source of Information

Currently, GUILD Sourcebooks produces two annual publications that are the leading provider of information on commissionable artists in North America. Since its inception 15 years ago, THE GUILD has published more than 350,000 books. More importantly, literally thousands of new art commissions have been generated through matching design professionals with artists through GUILD contacts. Both artists and design professionals have come to rely on GUILD sourcebooks as an important element in how they do business. It is not overstating the case to say that GUILD Sourcebooks has been an important factor in today's renaissance of fine American crafts by creating and promoting a broad national and international market that supports artists.

In the design fields, the information revolution has transformed and greatly abbreviated our notions about deadlines and turnaround times. FAX machines, CAD, modems, e-mail, the Internet and overnight mail have all combined to turn the pressure to high. But good design does not always prosper when "think time" is eliminated from the immediate-need schedules of the instant information age.

With this increased speed and complexity of communication, both artists and design professionals have found a more urgent need to cut through the clutter of irrelevant information, to get to the point more quickly and, most importantly, to have a way of identifying reliable professionals in their fields.

Foretelling the Future

When Toni Fountain Sikes began THE GUILD back in 1985, she was an art administrator with a passionate vision. She knew artists whose talents weren't being well-utilized. She saw architects and designers who couldn't find the brilliant and highly skilled artisans they needed to introduce appropriate, original art into their work. She recognized that much of the contemporary built environment was remarkably dull and featureless because it was widely assumed that true craftsmanship in a wide variety of media was dead. But she also knew that in every

Making Connections

Sharon Devenish, president of Devenish Associates, one of the leading independent commercial interior design firms in the Midwest, says she relies on GUILD sourcebooks for an outstanding pool of art and artists for her clients. "I would simply not know about many of these artists if they were not accessible through THE GUILD," she says. In addition, Devenish uses the sourcebooks to enhance plans she has for specific sites, and to help a client understand what might be possible in a given area. "I also like to just paper-clip things I especially like, but have no current need for. I use these ideas as part of the creative process; something that I can consider over time, and when the right project and client come along, I know where to turn."

Kathy Bradford works in a studio at home in a small town in the mountains outside of Estes Park, Colorado, but her work can be found all over the United States. A glass artist with a broad background in other media, Bradford attributes most of her larger, challenging commissions to contacts that have come through THE GUILD.

"I've been at this almost 25 years, and from the get-go my ambition has been to do meaningful work — larger, significant pieces that are unique and are sited where they have an impact on the people who see them. The fact is, I like working by myself in a

Jeff G. Smith, resurrection window, 1998, St. Albert the Great Catholic Church, Austin, TX

small studio. I don't want to do production work, and I don't particularly want to manage other people, although I enjoy collaborations from time to time.

"THE GUILD helps give an an artist like me — independent, working mostly alone — the credibility to compete successfully on large projects virtually anywhere. My Web site and THE GUILD are my connections with the world. I don't have a storefront, I don't do shows, I don't even show much work in galleries right now. But I've got commissions through the year 2001. We really do live in the age of long-distance communication, and I've found that it's not necessary to live in New York or Philadelphia to do work there."

Meeting Objectives

Fellow glass artist and westerner Jeff Smith agrees. After two decades in the city, Smith is currently in the process of moving his studio from Dallas to West Texas. A Texan who has done commissioned work from Saudi Arabia to Hawaii, Smith also uses GUILD Sourcebooks as his main marketing tool.

"When I began Architectural Stained Glass, Inc. over 20 years ago, I was literally pounding the pavement, looking for work. I've come light years since then, and THE GUILD has been a great help."

Smith continues, "One of the best things about THE GUILD, say as compared with a listing in the phone book's business section, is that your potential clients are already preselected to some extent. For example, I don't do traditional stained glass — no men in robes or that sort of thing. It's a waste of a client's time, and mine, if they call with that kind of need. With THE GUILD, they can see what I do, and if they choose to call me, it's because they already like what they've seen."

Although Smith is especially attuned to creating architectural glass for churches, chapels and synagogues, his commissions over the years have ranged from schools and libraries to restaurants and palaces. "Of course the commissions that come through THE GUILD are great, but I rely on it for more than just getting inquiries from potential clients. The reprints are the backbone of my marketing portfolio, along with magazine articles. The combination has been very effective.

"If you want to know the truth, I think I'm like many, many artists who find the whole sales effort of marketing art pretty difficult — almost distasteful. That's an important reason why I find THE GUILD so valuable. When you're trying to maintain artistic integrity and still pay the electric bill, it's a good feeling to respect the market you're reaching. You have a sense of confidence that you'll be able to work well with your client, and work the details out without much trouble. All of this contributes to a generally creative atmosphere. It allows me to concentrate on my work and on continuing to explore new and interesting directions in art."

Smith cited his work on a resurrection window for St. Albert the Great Catholic Church in Austin, Texas, as an example of a recent project where the collaboration between artist and client went especially well.

"This commission provided an ideal context for an essentially achromatic palette of colorless and white glasses. My enthusiasm about such a palette has grown in recent years. When I was contacted by the client, they had already seen a similar commission in a previous GUILD edition, so they were already on the 'right page' and we could move easily ahead from there."

Satisfactory Commissions

Fiber artist Robin Cowley, who lives in the San Francisco Bay area, creates art quilts with strong graphic images and highly

E. Joseph McCarthy, tropical fish tile collage over working aquarium, 1999, Tampa International Airport, 3' x 60'

André Banville

effective and imaginative use of color. Interested in art and sewing all her life, seven years ago Cowley quit her day job as a partner in managing construction jobs so she could concentrate all her talent and energy on her artwork. She now has a host of corporate and private clients.

Several recent commissions that came through GUILD Sourcebooks are particularly satisfying to her, for different reasons.

"I got a call from the United States State Department. Someone in their interior design area had seen my work in THE GUILD, and they were interested in a similar piece for the U.S. Embassy in Armenia. It all worked out, and now I have a quilt in Armenia!"

Cowley also got a call from an architectural firm inquiring about her work for a commission for Circuit City's corporate headquarters in Richmond, Virginia. The committee process, Cowley explains, was quite exacting and time-consuming, but then the project moved quickly and easily toward completion.

"Of course I'm pleased to have my work displayed in the headquarters of a high-profile company. I'm happy that the clients have been so enthusiastic about my art, and that's been very positive for the architect as well. And finally I'm very satisfied that we worked so successfully through the committee process, arriving at a size and price everyone was happy with."

These days, Cowley has a steady flow of commissions, and three or four inquiries each month from THE GUILD. But she is quick to point out that her first successes did not come easily or automatically. "When I was just starting out I went to the Design Center in San Francisco, to see if I could show my work. No one would talk to me! So I peeked in the interior designers' offices, and I saw that most of them had copies of THE GUILD. I decided then and there that's where I needed to be, so that's what I worked toward. And now the designers call me! So many people have access to THE GUILD, and they use it."

Building Business

Like Robin Cowley, tile artist Joe McCarthy of Custom Tile Studio in western Massachusetts is good at business as well as art. For 18 years, he and a staff of ceramic artists have been creating highly regarded custom murals for art consultants, architects and major design firms. If you ask him what still stirs the creative fires, he'll say he most loves a project where he is challenged artistically, and where he gets to try something new. That's why a recent commission through GUILD Sourcebooks made a special impression.

The public art project involved a collaboration between the Tampa Aquarium and the Tampa International Airport to install a large aquarium in the redesigned airport. A design firm that consulted with the airport authority contacted McCarthy's firm to submit a proposal after seeing one of their realistic tropical fish tile murals in the sourcebooks.

"During the two-day juried process, I presented two models: One of my realistically represented tropical fish scenes that I've been executing for a number of years; in the the other, I used an exciting new technique I call 'tile collage,' which involves a water-jet cutting process used to precision-shape the tile. There are actually three different layers to the completed mural, which measures 60 feet long by 3 feet high. Even though it all had been carefully preplanned, this new technique made creating this piece seem like spontaneous combustion for me. It was exhilarating to see it all come together as I explored a new artistic process. I'm working on another 'tile collage' piece now and couldn't be happier," McCarthy explains.

McCarthy, a GUILD artist for over 10 years, believes most of his large-scale projects have come through GUILD contacts. "THE GUILD is becoming more and more well known," he says. "The response rate from the books is excellent, and the response rates from our GUILD mailings are terrific. I'm dealing with triple the number of projects in the last two years as in the previous eight years."

Transcending Works

When an artist's passion for a project has been set on fire, the results can be more than just aesthetically pleasing. For fiber artist Laurie dill-Kocher and sculptor Bruce Wolfe, recent commissions from GUILD Sourcebooks allowed them to create work that transcended their usual highly skilled work, entering a realm of warmth and spirit that they both consider quite remarkable.

Dill-Kocher is a full-time studio artist who has taught at the Rochester Institute of Technology-School for American Crafts and has been featured in the *New York Art Review*. For her, a tapestry completed last year for the Jewish Association for the

Aging, Weinberg Village was especially meaningful. The artist says all her work these days is in some sense spiritual, but this project, *Tree of Life*, was special because the imagery in the tapestry combined the symbolism of the Torah, the Menorah and the Tree of Life.

"I worked with art consultant Marcia Rosenthal on this project, and that by itself was a pleasure. She just made everything go so smoothly, helped cut down on any uncertainty and created such a good marriage between the client and me as the artist. There's nothing better than working with a really good consultant," dill-Kocher says.

The project itself was equally pleasing to the artist because the client asked her what she would most like to do as a tapestry for a very high-traffic area at their site. "I could think of probably three or four things right off the top of my head. They were open and receptive. I was finally able to produce a subject close to my heart. It was a wonderful experience."

Paying Tribute

Bruce Wolfe is a sculptor and artist who has created highly visible projects for celebrities and large corporate clients. He has sculpted the likeness of people like George Schulz, and his illustrations grace advertising for many well-known American brand icons, including Levi's jeans, Celestial Seasonings Tea and Indiana Jones movie posters. Even with experience in all these projects, he found a recent GUILD commission to be somewhat unusual — and rewarding.

He was recommended to client Dennis Farrey by another California sculptor and GUILD advertiser, Archie Held, who had seen and admired Wolfe's work in THE GUILD. Farrey, a California businessman, was looking for a representational sculp-

Laurie dill-Kocher, *Tree of Life*, 1998, wool tapestry for the Jewish Association for the Aging, Weinberg Village 24" x 72"

Bruce Wolfe, bas-relief of Ben Kalberer, 1999, bronze, Hazelton, ND, 3' x 7'

tor who could capture the spirit and warmth of someone he remembered fondly from his youth in North Dakota. The man, Ben Kalberer, had been dead for over 20 years, and his only likenesses came from a handful of family snapshots. But Farrey was donating $1.5 million to help build a state-of-the-art high school in the town where he grew up, and he wanted people never to forget Kalberer, a benefactor to his community who inspired Farrey's gift to his hometown. Farrey sought no recognition for himself, only the opportunity to name the gymnasium for Kalberer and to create a permanent monument to Kalberer's generosity.

So Wolfe went to work and created a bronze bas-relief, 7 feet tall and 3 feet wide and mounted on a naturally cleaved piece of slate. Installed outside the new gymnasium, Ben Kalberer's likeness will preside over generations of North Dakota high school students, reminding them to think of others, to give to those in need, and to give back to their communities. In addition, two small statues of Kalberer based on Wolfe's bas-relief will be awarded annually to one adult and one student who have contributed to the community.

"This was an amazing project," Wolfe says. "The absolute center of it was the notion of trying to perpetuate and inspire goodness in a place. Dennis Farrey is the most wonderful, thoughtful client I think I've ever had. He invited me and my wife to the school's dedication, and we were honored to go. It may have been December in North Dakota, but it was one of the warmest, most moving American events I've ever been part of. Ben Kalberer's family was there, and they were so touched, and sent me gifts they had made themselves when I got home. Incredible."

Changing Lives

Would these commissions — so satisfying to the designers, their clients, and the artists — have come about without GUILD Sourcebooks? Would the American fine crafts movement have found and nurtured so many new hands and visions without THE GUILD's assistance? We like to think that GUILD Sourcebooks has made a difference in many lives in the past 15 years — that it does stand as a dividing line between the past and a better future.

As the pace of information exchange and communication continues to accelerate, GUILD Sourcebooks is still anticipating the future, encouraging increased contact between artists, architects, designers, consultants and clients. The goal remains that great GUILD idea: to promote the dialog, collaboration and connections which foster the creative spirit in all of us. The ideal result, of course, is art — and relationships —that make the world a more beautiful place.

Susan Troller frequently writes about the arts and families.
She is currently at work on a book about dreams and grief.

A Sampling of Successes

Some of the artists who have sold work through GUILD Sourcebooks:

Peggy Mach, bronze sculpture for Villanova University, Villanova, PA • **Jill Casty**, painted steel sculpture for Lewis Homes, Rancho Cucamonga, CA • **Ulrika Leander**, handwoven wall piece for St. Mary's Hospital, Huntington, WV • **Jonathan J. Clowes** and **Evelyn J. Clowes**, atrium sculpture for Royal Caribbean International Cruise Lines, Oslo, Norway • **Bruce Howdle**, ceramic mural for Wichita Mountain Wildlife Refuge, near Lawton, OK • **Robert Boucher**, cast concrete sculptural facade for Christie's Los Angeles, Beverly Hills, CA • **Paul Friend**, stained glass for private residence, Cherry Hill, NJ • **Bill Hopen**, bronze sculpture for Adorers of the Blood of Christ, Wichita, KS • **Polly Gessell**, large glass panels for Spago, Beverly Hills, CA • **Peter Handler**, conference tables for the president of Nickelodeon • **Marjorie Tomchuk**, works on handmade paper for a Japanese designer • **Kathleen Sharp**, art quilt for Kaiser Permanente, Martinez, CA • **Susanne Clawson**, mixed-media work for American Airlines, Dallas, TX • **Michael Anderson**, large steel sculpture for Wisconsin Manufacturers and Commerce, Madison, WI • **Trena McNabb**, acrylic on canvas painting for Association for Supervision and Curriculum Development, Owings Mills, MO • **Ted Jonsson**, stainless steel sculpture for SAP Labs, Inc., Palo Alto, CA • **James T. Russell**, stainless steel sculpture for Motorola Corporation, Beijing, People's Republic of China • **Joan Schulze**, fabric collage for Spieker Properties Gateway Center, San Jose, CA • **Paul Sable**, acrylic atrium sculpture for Lucent Technologies, Altamonte Springs, FL • **Michael D. Bigger**, welded steel sculpture for Brazos Valley Arts Commission, College Station, TX • **Marilyn Henrion**, art quilt for Dana Farber Cancer Institute, Boston, MA • **Douglas O. Freeman**, seven bronze sculptures for City of Tokyo, Japan • **Koryn Rolstad**, atrium sculpture for Meriter Hospital, Madison, WI • **Elle Terry Leonard** and **Josh Johnson**, ceramic relief mosaic for Tampa International Airport, Tampa, FL • **George Peters**, fiberglass atrium sculpture for Tokyo Bay Hilton, Tokyo, Japan • **Robert Pfitzenmeier**, atrium sculpture for American Family Insurance, Madison, WI • **Margaret Oldman**, sandcarved glass scene for *Bridget*, yacht in Alameda Marina, CA • **John DeVlieger**, mural for Russian Tea Room, New York, NY • **Shawn Athari**, glass arrowheads for Washington State Ferries • **Christina Spann**, custom lighting fixtures for Hyatt Regency Hotel, Phoenix, AZ • **M.A. Klein**, mixed-media fiber collages for the Library of Congress, Washington, DC • **Suzanne Donazetti** and **Kenneth Payne**, folding screens for Alexandria's, San Francisco, CA • **Martha Chatelain**, paper sculpture for Tokyo hotel/restaurant • **Alonzo Davis**, acrylic on linen work for Anderson Consulting, Northbrook, IL • **Joel A. Schwartz**, courtyard gate for Johnson residence, Palm Springs, CA • **Anne Marchand**, oilbar on paper work for executive offices of All First Bank of Maryland, Baltimore, MD • **Marcia Hewitt Johnson**, art quilt for American Airlines, Dallas, TX • **Gloria Zmolek**, handmade paper quilts for Kelsey Seabold Clinic, Houston, TX

FEATURED ARTISTS

FURNITURE

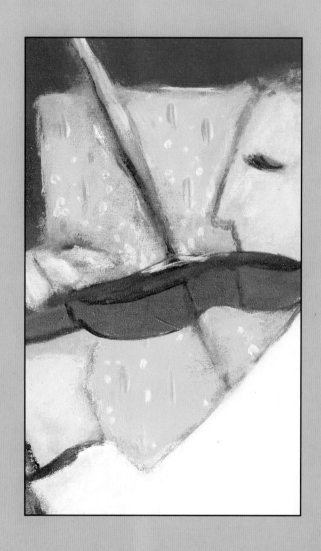

Jonathan Benson

Jonathan Benson Furniture
104 Haozous Road
Santa Fe, NM 87505
TEL 505-473-9172
FAX 505-473-9109
E-Mail: jbenson7@usurf.com
Web: www.bensonfurniture.com

Jonathan Benson's work is functional, sturdy and fluid. His fascination with the materials he uses is always evident in his work. Whether combining fine-figured veneer surfaces with roughly textured burl and polished marble, or creating contrasts with color and form, his work has vibrant energy that will complement any environment.

Benson's designs are often inspired by the landscape and colors of the southwestern United States where he lives. He has been making furniture for nearly 25 years, and his pieces are in numerous private collections nationally and internationally. His complete line of furniture is available in most woods.

A *Faultline*, red elm burl, maple, 48"L

B *Pedestal*, fiddleback makore, maple burl, marble, 42"H

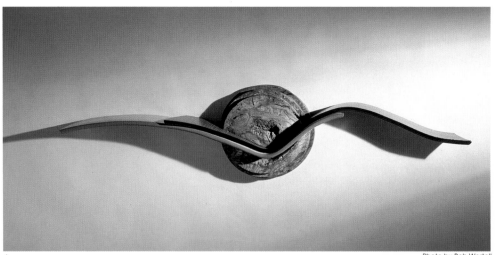

A

Photo by Bob Wortell

B

Photo by Bob Wortell

Black Wolf Design

Terry Sweeney
1611 Chase Drive
Omro, WI 54963
TEL **920-685-8550**
FAX **920-685-8551**
E-Mail: **terry@blackwolfdesign.com**
Web: **www.blackwolfdesign.com**

At Black Wolf Design, experience blended with ambition produces a wonderful variety of wood furnishings ideally suited for the home or office. Superior craftsmanship and the demand of excellence makes every piece produced a work of art.

Although Black Wolf Design has just introduced its first line of furniture, custom orders are welcomed. The design team and talented staff look forward to working with interior designers and architects. For price quotes or design questions, please call.

A *Black Wolf Signature Series Chest,* hard maple and stainless steel, 30"H x 44"W x 20"D

B *Signature Series Entertainment Center,* flame red birch, stainless steel, 76"H x 44"W x 28"D

A

Photo by Phil Weston Graphics

B

Photo by Phil Weston Graphics

Custom Steel Ltd.

Nancy Coutts
Wayne Benton
81 Hamburg Turnpike
Riverdale, NJ 07457
TEL **973-835-0010**
FAX **973-835-1342**
E-Mail: **uma@erols.com**
Web: **www.customsteelltd.com**

Design team Wayne Benton and Nancy Coutts combine their artistic skills as metal artists and designers. For ten years, they have been producing unique "ultra-modern antiques" for both commercial and residential interiors.

Their designs stretch around the globe and have been recognized with a number of awards. Recent installation sites include the New York Society of Security Analysts in the World Trade Center, New York City, and the U.S. Embassy in Ottawa, Canada. Each commission is unique to the needs of the client in both form and function.

The team designs and hand builds specifically for each environment, specializing in fabricated steel design. Glass, stone and wood, among other media, are used in conjunction with the steel, which is either 304 series stainless steel or various mild steel materials. They offer simple clear lacquer, hand-painted finishes or chemical patinas appropriate for indoor or exterior applications.

Choose from a portfolio of designs or help design an ultra-modern antique appropriate for your space.

A *Comfort Zone*, bed

B *Two Fly Through*, glass and stainless steel cabinet

C *Backstock*, cabinet

D *It's 4 O'clock Somewhere*, bar

E *Kick It Out*, steel and glass dining table

A   Photo by JB Grant

C   Photo by JB Grant

D   Photo by JB Grant

B   Photo by JB Grant

E   Photo by JB Grant

Robert L. Cooper

Cooper Woodworking
302 South Second Street
PO Box 278
Grimes, IA 50111
TEL 800-828-3666
TEL 515-986-2222
FAX 515-986-9393
E-Mail: **cooperia@netins.net**
Web: **www.cooperwoodworking.com**

Wood artist Robert Cooper has been enjoying success in Des Moines for nearly 26 years. He now produces custom-made and limited-edition furniture. With the inspiration of Iowa's landscape, he creates his pieces by combining modern design theories with skilled woodworking.

His recent works are made of woods found locally combined with many exotic foreign types. He often adds materials like metal or leather and incorporates imaginative coloring and staining techniques. His forms deal with the relationship between contrasting and complementing materials and styles.

His custom furniture is in demand by corporate, commercial and residential customers. He has recently done work for World Food Prize and was featured in *Better Homes & Gardens* and *Iowa Architect.*

A   *Deco-Buffet,* purple heart, bird's eye maple, leather

B   *Wine Showcase,* bubinga, champher, steel

C   *Armoire,* ebonized maple, steel, simulated paduek

D   *Tribal Entryway,* left: rough-sawed walnut, bird's eye maple, steel; right: mahogany, paduek

A

Photo by Bill Nellans

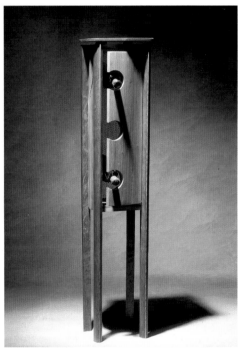

B

Photo by Bill Nellans

C

Photo by Bill Nellans

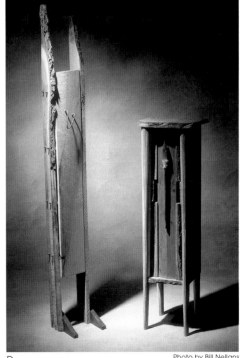

D

Photo by Bill Nellans

Michael Creed

Craft Artist
2129 Broadway Street
Lynchburg, VA 24501
TEL **804-845-6452**
E-Mail: **MichaelCreed2129@hotmail.com**

Combining fine craft skills and a vivid imagination, Michael Creed creates unique furniture and functional sculptures. Primarily working by commission, he produces pieces for homes, offices, churches, schools, regional art centers and children's museums.

In the expectation of becoming valued antiques, all of his pieces are solidly made using the finest materials and finishes.

SHOWN: *Ramesses Retreat*, a library ladder/chair exploring the Exodus through visual narrative, © 1999, ebonized walnut, leather, brass, 62"H

Photo by Robert DeVaul

Photo by Robert DeVaul

Michael Creed

Craft Artist
2129 Broadway Street
Lynchburg, VA 24501
TEL 804-845-6452
E-Mail: **MichaelCreed2129@hotmail.com**

Henley Hornet's Crocodile Book-A-File, shown here, is a mobile-kinetic book cart commissioned for the library of Henley Middle School in Crozet, VA. Made to hold and bring attention to the newest library books, the "Book-A-File" resulted from a design collaboration between Creed and the entire sixth-grade class of 200 students. The hornet mascot turns on a vertical axis by cranking the propeller.

SHOWN: *Henley Hornet's Crocodile Book-A-File*, © 1997, aniline dyed birch, curly maple, laminated colorwood, papier mâché, paint, steel mechanicals, 72"L

Photo by Michael Bailey

Glenn de Gruy

Glenn de Gruy Woodworks
11630 Jeff Hamilton Road
Mobile, AL 36695
TEL 334-633-5765

Glenn de Gruy has been building custom furniture for 30 years. His training was in building authentic reproductions and restoring antique furniture using traditional hardwoods, cabinetmaking joinery, and hand-rubbed lacquer finishes.

Currently, he uses mixed media and a variety of faux and painted finishes. Craft remains emphasized. The furniture is made to last for generations.

De Gruy works to client specifications, and is often called on to build beds as well as a variety of other furniture. Prices upon request; installation available.

Also see this GUILD sourcebook:
THE GUILD: 4

A Solid mahogany king-sized bed, 76"W x 80"L x 86"H

B Crotch mahogany and gold leaf table, 30"H x 7'Dia

A

Photo by Thigpen Photography

B

Photo by Thigpen Photography

Jeff Easley

215 Eighth Avenue South
PO Box 502
Wellman, IA 52356
TEL **319-646-2521**
TEL/FAX **319-628-4766**
E-Mail: **JEasley811@aol.com**

Flexibility with designs, dimensions and wood choices are hallmarks of Easley's art furniture and wall sculptures and are highly valued by those whom he has worked with in the past. All woods are their natural colors and are non-endangered. Visual support is available upon request.

Selected commissions include:
US West corporate offices
Gannett corporate offices

Also see these GUILD sourcebooks:
Designer's: 12, 13, 14

A *Available Space*, wall sculpture, © 1999, 72"H x 34"W

B *Buffet*, © 1998, 34"H x 70"W x 17"D

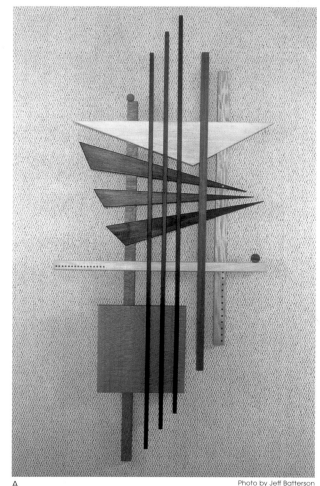

A

Photo by Jeff Batterson

B

Photo by Jeff Batterson

A few years ago, I visited Dr. Eugene Tardy, a very well-known plastic surgeon in the city of Chicago, for treatment of a breathing problem. The doctor was in the process of remodeling and refurbishing his waiting room. During my follow-up visits, I showed him my work in *The Designer's Sourcebook 6,* and he and I discussed the creation of a unique piece of art. The piece, a table, would be the focal point of his office and also memorialize the theme of his practice: metamorphosis.

The metamorphosis theme came from the fact that Dr. Tardy specialized in rhinoplasty; his surgery changed not only the form, structure and function of a patient's nose, but created beauty where none existed before. We agreed that a table exhibiting a butterfly within a female profile would be the perfect symbol to exemplify this theme.

The table shown took three months to construct. The base is made of wood set with ceramic tiles. The tiles are surrounded by mosaic chips and rods; colors are coordinated with the colors of the room. The top of each base is inlaid with beveled mirror, and the tabletop is a very large and heavy piece of one-inch-thick plate glass.

The imagery shows both sides of a female profile. When pushed together, the two profiles become a butterfly — the idea being that you walk into the office looking one way (a caterpillar) and leave ultimately as a butterfly.

— **NH**

Nancy Heller

COMMISSIONING AGENT: Dr. Eugene Tardy

TITLE: *Metamorphosis*

DESCRIPTION: Table, wooden base with ceramic relief murals and inlaid mirror

SITE: M. Eugene Tardy, Jr., M.D., Head & Neck Polasurgery Ltd., Chicago, IL

Julie Ferber

Julie Ferber Studio
85 South Broadway
Nyack, NY 10960
TEL/FAX **914-353-1904**
E-Mail: **jferberstudio@aol.com**

"I hope to express the fascination and magic I feel when I create, evoking the playfulness and wonder within us all."

— Julie Ferber

Julie Ferber combines the spirit of childhood with the careful hand of an artist to create timeless pieces of painted furniture. Using intense color and whimsical patterns to express her heart and soul, Ferber brings out the personality of each piece, making every creation unique. Her work is magical and filled with joy.

Commissions and inquiries are welcome.

Prices available upon request.

A *Child's Jungle Rocker*, 1999, hand-painted maple

B *Child's Lady Bug Game Table and Chair Set*, 1999, hand-painted maple

A

Photo by Stephanie Violette

B

Photo by Stephanie Violette

John Hein

John Hein, Studio Furnituremaker
105 Featherbed Lane
Hopewell, NJ 08525
TEL **609-466-8122**
E-Mail: **jhein@pluto.njcc.com**
Web: **pluto.njcc.com/~jhein**

John Hein designs and builds elegantly restrained hardwood furniture with a purity of form that emphasizes the aesthetic qualities of the materials. A traditional respect for nature combined with a contemporary structure result in fluid, spare pieces of furniture in which the intrinsic quality of precious woods and their grains are allowed to stand out.

SHOWN: *Felicity's Cabinet*, walnut, maple, mahogany, wenge, cocobola, rosewood, Gabon ebony, 70" x 41" x 10.5"

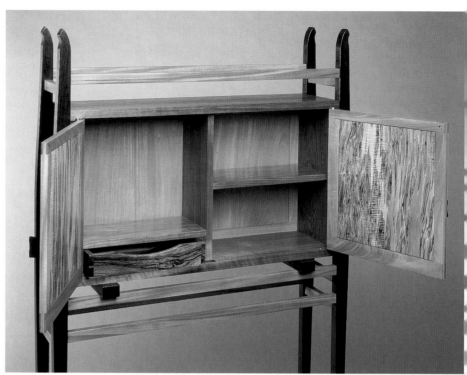

Photo by Ross Stout

Photo by Ross Stout

Freefall Designs

Suzanne Donazetti
Kenneth Payne
PO Box 797
Carrizozo, NM 88301
TEL **505-648-2313**
E-Mail: **suz@nm.net**
Web: **www.freefalldesigns.com**

Suzanne Donazetti and Kenneth Payne work together to create abstract images in copper. Donazetti gilds and paints the copper using transparent inks and iridescent pigments, and weaves it in graceful curves. Payne designs and builds the supporting structures of wood or copper. Pieces are lightweight and coated to ensure low maintenance.

Their vibrant artworks are commissioned and collected nationally. Commissions range from large public art and corporate installations to smaller residential wall pieces. Galleries include Expressions in Fine Art in Santa Fe, NM, and Palm Desert, CA; and Galleria Silecchia in Sarasota, FL.

Commissions are welcome. The artists enjoy working with clients on color preferences, shapes and sizes for specific sites. Additional information is available upon request.

Also see these GUILD sourcebooks:
Designer's: 9, 12, 13, 14
Gallery: 1996

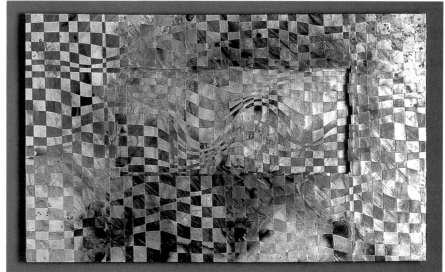

Layered wall sculpture, gilded, painted, woven copper, 18" x 30" x 1"   Photo by George Post

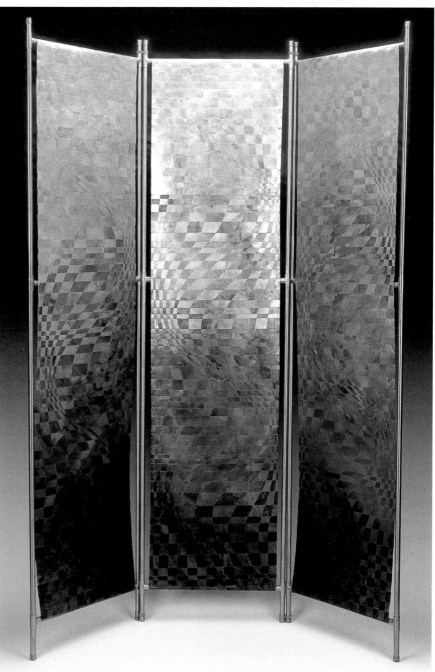

Folding screen, gilded, painted, woven copper, 4.5' x 6'   Photo by Jerry Anthony

Dr. Gindi

c/o Susan James
6 Souhegan Street
Milford, NH 03055
TEL 603-598-2846
E-Mail: **Dr_Gindi@yahoo.com**

Dr. Gindi's chair objectivations — expressions of the spirit in gesture, words and art — are the starting point of an emotional journey toward culture.

The German-Egyptian art designer Dr. Gindi, currently based in Beijing, has been sensitized to other cultures by numerous stays and travels abroad.

She is used to wandering in cultures, immersing herself in their inner lives while emotionally processing these impressions. The chairs are a tangible product of her own emotional culture.

These objectivations reflect a unique style, capturing the spirit of Chinese culture while incorporating a personal aestheticism.

The Emperor, Son of Heaven, shown at right, is safeguarding the harmony between heaven and earth. The interaction of his palace's structure and colors is drawn from ancient Chinese astronomy.

The *Double Happiness* chair, shown below, has a design based on the written Chinese character "double happiness," used especially for weddings. The joy of conjugal life should last forever.

A *Double Happiness*, 48"H x 44"W x 20"D

B *The Emperor*, 60"H x 20.8"W x 24"D

A

B

Mind2Matter Studios

Jon Mark, Creator
Charlie Eskew, Project Coordinator
964 Watkins Street
Atlanta, GA 30318
TEL/FAX 404-713-5821
E-Mail: creator@mind2matter.com
Web: www.mind2matter.com/gallery/

Jon Mark, an artist capable as a sculptor and a painter from abstract to fine art, departs from traditional interpretations to manifest his vision in practical designs for the future. Jon Mark's extensive knowledge of materials and methods provides a broad platform upon which he designs and creates futuristic furnishings and artistic pieces. Born in fairy tales, they endure as you grow.

The line shown is titled *Circa Futura*. Pieces in this line are created as one-of-a-kind, or numbered-and-signed limited editions. All creations in the *Circa Futura* lineage may be viewed at the web gallery listed above.

Commissions are considered.

A *Ice Lilies,* lamp with cobalt, resin and steel, 30"H

B *Continental Shelf,* table with acrylic or glass and steel, 28"H

C *Birth of a Fable,* table with solid maple burl top, aluminum leaf and steel, 33"H

A

B

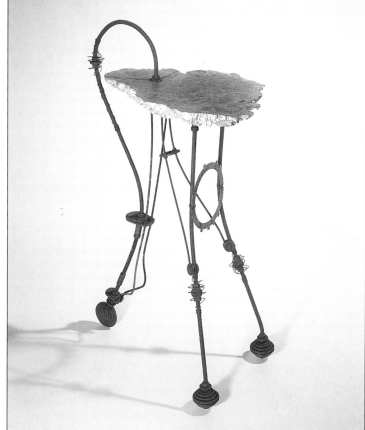

C

Warren Carther

COMMISSIONING AGENT: Swire Properties, Ltd. in conjunction with Corporate Art Associates, Ltd.

TITLE: *Chronos Trilogy*

DESCRIPTION: Three monumental glass sculptures: *Vestige* (shown), 27' x 16' x 4'; *Sea of Time*: 100' x 27' x 6'; *Approach of Time*, 40' x 12' x 1½'

SITE: Swire Properties, Ltd., Hong Kong

Chronos Trilogy is a suite of three monumental glass sculptures. Each sculpture represents a particular facet of time: past, present and future. The conceptual perspective relates to the passage of time in Hong Kong, a phenomenon of energy and movement found only in the city of the dragon.

The tallest piece within the *Chronos Trilogy*, *Approach of Time*, rises from the ground floor and pierces through an opening in the first floor to a height of 40 feet. The longest work, *Sea of Time*, was created with undulating convex and concave curves and stretches 100 feet through the lobby. The weight of all three sculptures totals 25 tons.

The project began with a letter from Mr. James Cavello of Corporate Art Associates, Ltd. in New York City. James requested more information about my work, visuals on previous projects and a detailed explanation of my technique and medium. James and his partner, Margarite Almeida, had seen a large-scale project I had completed in the Canadian Embassy in Tokyo while referencing a GUILD sourcebook and said they found the work extraordinary.

Corporate Art Associates, Ltd., an art and appraising firm, specializes in artwork that is site specific. The company had been contacted by Swire Properties, Ltd. of Hong Kong, a company seeking artist submissions for a flagship building in a new office complex. Swire was considering three sculptures to be placed within the two-story glass enclosed lobby. The company had already reviewed hundreds of artist submissions and Corporate Art Associates, Ltd. presented artists to Swire as well. The final artist selection included myself and two other sculptors. After the presentation, I was selected as the artist to create all three works.

The response to *Chronos Trilogy* has been tremendous. Currently, other art commissions are being planned in Asia and the United States.

— **WC**

Markian Olynyk

Markian Studios Inc.
2776 West 10th Avenue
Vancouver, BC V6K 2J9
Canada
TEL **604-738-9791**
FAX **604-738-9722**

Markian Olynyk has been designing and creating custom art glass since 1977. Recently, he has expanded his studio's focus to include a line of half-inch tempered glass screens in various styles.

Versatile design, innovative techniques. Prestigious installations worldwide.

Clients include:
Vancouver International Airport
Private residence of Mr. William Gates
World Trade Center
Bank of Hong Kong
Renfrew Public Library
Selkirk Financial-Chicago
US Bank
Air Canada
Shaughnessy Hospital

Also see these GUILD sourcebooks:
Architect's: 9, 15

A *Earth* series screen

B *Zelenka* series screen

C *Toccata* series screen

A

B   Photo by Joaquin Pedrero

C   Photo by Joaquin Pedrero

William Poulson

W. Poulson Glass Studio
PO Box 705
1318 Oak Court
Arnold, CA 95223
TEL/FAX 209-795-5365

William Poulson's unique folding screens and lamps are inspired by the Asian masters of *ukiyo-e* (wood block prints) and *sumie* brush painting. As a third-generation woodworker, Poulson's remarkable craftsmanship is expressed in unsparing attention to detail.

More than 20 years ago, Poulson joined his skills in cabinetry and furniture making with his newfound love for art glass to create stunning functional art that combines the beauty and softness of wood and the brilliance of glass. His numerous public and private art glass commissions incorporate his original designs based on nature themes.

Please call or write for prices.

A Table lamp, sculpted wood, slumped glass, 27" x 19.5"Dia

B Limited-edition folding screen, sculpted cherry, art glass, 70" x 60" x 12"

C Dining table, black walnut, fused glass, 29" x 78" x 50"

D Dining table chair, 48" x 18" x 22"

A

Photo by Mike Rothwell

B

Photo by Robert Arnold

C

Photo by Robert Arnold

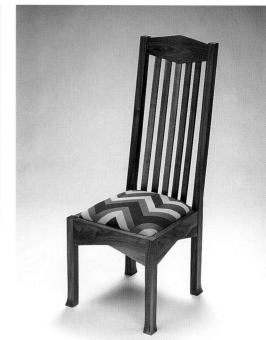

D

Photo by Robert Arnold

Henry B. Richardson

One Cottage Street
Easthampton, MA 01027
TEL **413-527-1444**
E-Mail: **Henry@henryrichardson.com**
Web: **www.henryrichardson.com**

The sound of breaking glass calls to mind images of destruction. In Henry Richardson's studio, however, broken glass is the element of creation. Richardson uses fractured glass to create sculptures and furniture that are prized for their originality and craftsmanship.

Richardson has exhibited work at the Holsten Gallery in Massachusetts, the Heller Gallery in New York, and the Longstreth Goldberg Gallery in Florida. He has worked successfully with architects and designers, and his work can be found in numerous corporate and private settings.

A *One Man's Passion,* 1999, fractured flat glass, solid, 20"H x 14"W x 16"L

B *Acker Coffee Table,* 2000, fractured flat glass, hollow, 18"H x 22"W x 52"L

A

B

Once again GUILD sourcebooks have come through – Architectural Ceramics' page in *The Architect's Sourcebook* attracted the eye of Kelly Taafee of Kelly Taafee Designs, Inc. In the fall of 1998, I was asked to submit slides for a public arts project commissioned by Hillsborough County Aviation Authority for the City of Tampa, Florida. The site was the Tampa International Airport, highly visible and right in my own backyard.

I wanted the piece to stand out, to be remembered. Two of Architectural Ceramics' specialties, relief and mosaic, were combined to win the commission after a lengthy run of committees, interviews, and maquettes.

The piece is entitled, *El Movimiento del Mar*, (*The Movement of the Sea*) and boasts 280 square feet of relief mosaic made from Architectural Ceramics' own line of handmade ceramic tile. Three-dimensional fish, crabs, and squid colorfully romp through 70' x 4' of mosaic water. The Florida sea life depicted swim and shimmer in the light. In fact, the piece itself is like sunlight on water.

It's wonderful to pretend to be just another traveler at the airport, watching my fellow travelers going about their business, often stopping to watch the sea creatures going about theirs.

— EL

Architectural Ceramics

COMMISSIONING AGENT: Hillsborough County Aviation Authority for the City of Tampa, FL

TITLE: *El Movimiento del Mar*

DESCRIPTION: Relief mosaic made from handmade tile; 280' sq.; 70' x 4'

SITE: Tampa International Airport, Tampa, FL

Ed Archie NoiseCat

Neo-abOriginal Art
5259 Harbord Drive
Oakland, CA 94618-2512
TEL **510-601-7336**
FAX **510-595-7336**
E-Mail: **ed@noisecat.com**
Web: **www.noisecat.com**

Contemporary sculptor Ed Archie NoiseCat has worked with the structures and motifs of the Northwest Coast since shortly after he graduated from the Emily Carr College of Art and Design in 1986. Since leaving his Salish homelands, NoiseCat has grown to appreciate the arts and architecture of other indigenous peoples around the world.

NoiseCat's work evokes the rich history of his ancestors in the Pacific Northwest. It builds on that region's tradition of great carvers of the past and present, yet it has a style, intensity and exacting level of craftsmanship all its own. NoiseCat joins the structural forms of the Northwest Coast longhouse with traditional Japanese and Northwest Coast native tools to create one-of-a-kind and limited-production furniture.

Designers' inquiries and commissions are welcomed.

Birth of Thunder, 1999, cherry, maple, glass, abalone, 24K gold leaf, 40" x 40" x 16"

Photo by Sibila Savage

4 Bears, 1999, mahogany, walnut, yellow cedar, abalone, glass, 72" x 40" x 34"

Photo by Sibila Savage

Homecoming, walnut, yellow cedar, paua shell, glass, 60" x 32" x 16"

Photo by Sibila Savage

Betsy Krieg Salm

American School-Girl Art
9235 Schier Road
Interlaken, NY 14847
TEL 607-387-5330
E-Mail: info@betsykriegsalm.com
Web: www.betsykriegsalm.com

To the best of her knowledge, Betsy Krieg Salm is the only artist in the world presenting "American School-Girl Art" as a genre. She decorates fine period reproduction furniture and accessories using watercolor and ink, as was done 200 years ago by young women in the "academies."

Her collection includes sewing and work tables, face screens and boxes. Her pieces stand among some of the finest collections of antiques and folk art in the world.

Commissions are welcomed.

A Sabre-leg sewing stand (detail)

B Bracket foot, single drawer "work" box, 5"H x 15.75"W x 9.5"D

C Sabre-leg sewing stand, 30"H x 24"W x 18"D

A

B

C

Rosebud Studio

Wendy Grossman De Segovia
141 Pantherkill Road
PO Box 432
Phoenicia, NY 12464
TEL **914-688-9823**
FAX **914-688-7326**
E-Mail: **rosebudstudio@aol.com**
Web: **www.guild.com**
Web: **www.rosebudstudios.com**

Rosebud Studios specializes in pique assiette mosaics, using a technique that artist Wendy Grossman calls "painting with plates."

Incorporating china she finds in antique markets, or utilizing china of the client's choice, whether found or inherited, Grossman works so that designs and patterns emerge. Other found objects, including mosaic tiles, marbles, *objets d'art* and mirrors are often included in her one-of-a-kind pieces.

Grossman has more than 25 years of experience as a painter and fabric designer. She has now turned her talents toward designing unique vases, mirrors, nightstands and end tables. Her work can be seen in private and public spaces nationwide, from nurseries to entranceways, from waiting rooms to living rooms.

Completed work is available; commissions are welcome. Contact the artist for more information.

Green Summer Table, © 1999, broken china and tile, 14"D x 21"W x 26.5"H

Photo by Steffany Rubin Photography

Pink Mandala Table, © 1999, stained glass, 12"Dia x 23.5"H

Photo by Steffany Rubin Photography

Blue Geisha (top view), © 1999, broken china and glass, one of a set, 22"Dia x 21"H

Ines Smrz

6474 North Garden Grove Lane
Glendale, WI 53209
TEL   414-352-7160
E-Mail: **ismrz@execpc.com**
Web: **www.guild.com**
Web: **www.smrz.homestead.com**

Ines Smrz's innovative screens are freestanding wooden bas-relief that are sculpted to create an interesting sense of depth and dimension.

Acrylic paints and stains are used to enhance the intricacy of the design, and each is lacquered for durability. The average height is six feet and the average width is seven feet. A wide variety of themes can be commissioned. Prices range from $7000 to $20000.

A *Putting on the Glitz II,* 6'H x 7'W

B *Serengeti,* 6'H x 9'W

A

B

Theodore Box Designs

Theodore Box
PO Box 2325
Vineyard Haven, MA 02568
TEL **508-696-6126**
FAX **508-696-8431**
E-Mail: **info@tedbox.com**
Web: **www.tedbox.com**

Ted Box's art is in private collections the world over. Each piece of art furniture is designed to accommodate climactic variations without losing its precise functional properties.

For further examples of his extraordinary work — and to commission custom pieces — please contact the artist for more information.

A *Ripple Table*

B *Neptune's Armoire*

C *Curved Rolltop Desk*

A

Photo by Charles Utz

B

Photo by Steve Rodgers

C

Photo by Bob Schellhammer

JOHN MUDGETT

Industrial Designer/Interior Space Designer

When John Mudgett plans space for the very large, very complex projects his firm designs and builds, he is always keenly aware of the need to humanize the environment. "We are one of only a handful of design firms in the country that specializes in large scientific complexes. Given the nature of our projects, we have a special challenge to make the environment appealing and hospitable."

Trained as an industrial designer, Mudgett runs his firm's interior design group, and advocates using artists as part of the professional design team. "We encourage clients to use original art both on a monumental scale and in more modest ways," he explains. "When art is woven throughout a space, it adds tremendously to the environment."

A recent project involved glass artist Paul Housberg's vision for the new cafeteria building at Pfizer Central Research in Groton, Connecticut. The cafeteria was located in what had been an employee walkway through a grove of trees.

"We wanted to capture the spirit of changing light and seasons and movement," Mudgett recalls. "Without being literal, we wanted the large dining area to feel as much like a forest as possible.

"I looked through THE GUILD and was immediately impressed by Paul's work. I felt this person could work with the kind of gesture we had in mind. And he did. His idea—to create four large walls of glass at the compass points and attach a season to each—was sheer brilliance."

Both the collaborative process and the final result are everything Mudgett could have hoped for. "Each panel is 11 feet wide by 12 feet high and weighs about 5,000 pounds. The space is spectacular, the art and artist were an integral part of creating it, and the client loves it. In fact, they've published a little booklet to hand out to people who ask about it. It's been a great success."

Photo by Cliff Moore

CAROL KODIS

Interior Designer

For Carol Kodis of Kodis Associates, art is not something that stands apart from architecture or design. Kodis brings art and artists into her plans from the very beginning of a project. Her Massachusetts space planning and interior design firm works primarily with commercial and corporate office design accounts, with a sprinkling of residential projects.

"I prefer to incorporate art work into the basic design of the space," she says, "to add imagination and support the image the client wants to develop. It's best to do that right from the start."

Kodis's design for the new corporate headquarters of Pegasystems, in Cambridge, is a case in point. Her challenge was to develop an office environment suitably creative for this fast-growing, high-tech software firm, while also enhancing Pegasystems' image with clients, including some of the world's largest banks.

The centerpiece of her award-winning design was a reception area featuring acid-etched glass by GUILD artist Duncan Laurie of Degnan/Laurie Studios. Large glass panels, set into two arched doorways, highlight a striking promenade leading from the reception area. "We did many things throughout the space that were distinctly Pegasystems," Kodis recalled. "Artwork is an elegant, sophisticated way for a corporate client to develop a unique identity."

Kodis uses GUILD sourcebooks to find both artists and inspiration. "As a resource, they are particularly helpful," she says, "because they show installations and give us a context. This is often more useful than seeing individual pieces in a gallery. It helps us think early on about how to incorporate the artist's work into a project.

"I urge designers and architects to explore working relationships with a variety of artists. The interplay of ideas between the client, designer and artist expands and enriches the dimensions of a project."

Photo by Yoke Wong

LIGHTING

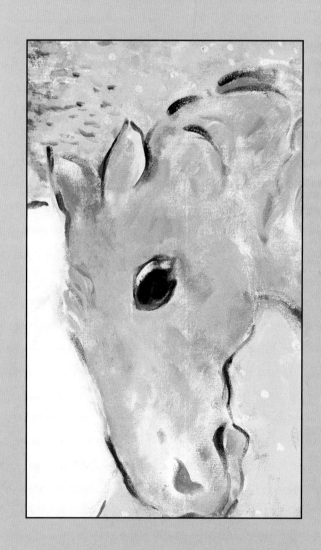

Nina Paladino Caron
Michael K. Hansen

California Glass Studio, Inc.
1815 Silica Avenue
Sacramento, CA 95815
TEL 916-925-9322
FAX 916-925-9370
E-Mail: ninapaladino@cgsglass.com
Web: www.cgsglass.com

Michael K. Hansen and Nina Paladino Caron have been studio partners for 24 years, founding California Glass Studio in 1977. They have created lighting for home as well as commercial use. The chandeliers and wall sconces are custom-made, born out of the free-form bowls that have become their signature works in glass.

The chandelier in seafoam, mauve and purple is called *Oasis,* while the green, peach, red and amethyst chandelier is named *Rain Forest.* The wall sconces pictured are from the *Rain Forest Series.*

Michael and Nina's glass art is included in private and corporate collections nationally and internationally. Their work has been on loan to the embassies in Norway and Switzerland through the Art in Embassies Program.

Also see these GUILD sourcebooks:
THE GUILD: 4, 5
Designer's: 6, 7, 8, 9, 14

Photos: Rick Waller/New Media Vision

Barbara Fletcher

Paper Dimensions
17 Powerhouse Street #318
Boston, MA 02127
TEL 617-268-8644
FAX 978-670-5290
E-Mail: Paper3d@hotmail.com
Web: www.paperdimensions.com

Fletcher has been working with paper for over 10 years and has utilized its texture, color and durability in new and surprising ways.

The luminescent sculptures below show the beautiful texture of the paper and are carefully crafted around lampshades with bases that take a low-watt bulb. The paper is sprayed for extra durability. Wall-mounted sculptures, such as the one shown at right, are also available, either lit or unlit.

Public collections include St. Margarets and Massachusetts General and Children's Hospital, Boston, MA.

Other works from ornaments to larger hangings, mobiles and pedestal pieces are available. Prices range from $6 to $500.

Also see these GUILD sourcebooks:
THE GUILD 1, 5
Designer's: 6, 7, 14

Fish, unlit cast paper, 26"L x 18"H x 5"D

Photo by Jan Bindas

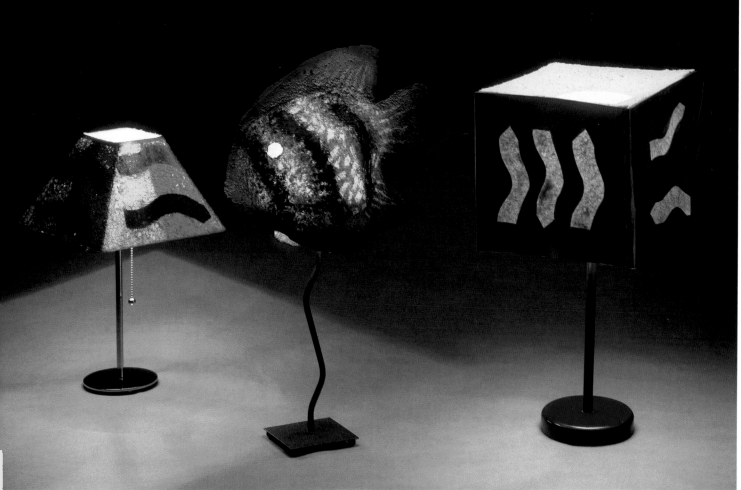

it cast paper lamps, left: 20"H, 10" x 10" x 8" shade; center: 23"H x 14"W x 6"D; right: 23"H, 10" x 10" x 10" shade

Photo by Jan Bindas

Labyrinth Designs

Christine Dregalla
Keith Brzozowski
1412 Swissvale Avenue, Firehouse #2
Pittsburgh, PA 15221
TEL **412-242-8789**
E-Mail: **LabLamps@aol.com**

Paper artist Christine Dregalla and woodworker Keith Brzozowski have combined their crafts to create the *Column Lamp,* a unique idea in atmospheric lighting.

When the lamp is off, the beauty of its turned hardwood elements and the tactile interest of its shade are emphasized. Standing six feet tall, the architectural form is contrasted by its human scale, bringing a surprising intimacy.

When the lamp is on, the sculptural solidity of the unlit lamp is replaced by an animated glow. The internal illumination reveals its translucent character and speaks to the dynamics of its natural materials.

The *Column Lamp* shade, made of traditional kozo and abaca fibers, is remarkably resilient, easily maintained and available in a full palette of colors. A variety of turned hardwoods also are available to complement existing decor.

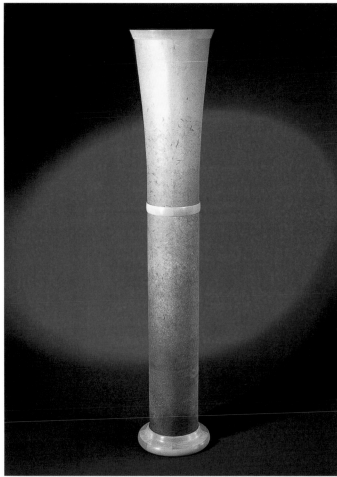

Autumn Fire, Column Lamp, handmade paper, maple, 71" x 13"Dia   Photo by Rob Long

Sea Levels, Sandstone and *Forest Canopy, Column Lamp* grouping   Photo by Rob Long

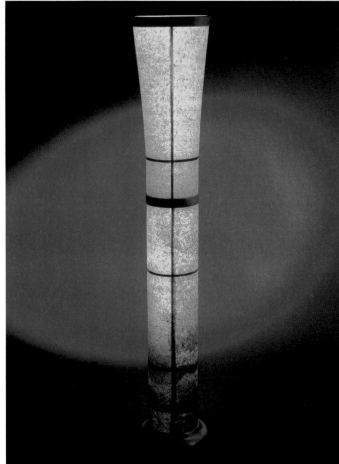

Autumn Fire, Column Lamp, handmade paper, maple, 71" x 13"Dia   Photo by Rob Long

Peter Mangan

634-A Guerrero Street
San Francisco, CA 94110
TEL 415-431-7060
TEL 830-833-2843
E-Mail: mangankk@infinex.com

Peter Mangan creates sculptural lights that engage the viewer and illuminate a space. Glass and metals combine, resulting in unique and contemporary pieces. He enjoys making chandeliers, wall sconces, floor lights, sculptures and panels.

Mangan has worked as an artist for more than 20 years and exhibits internationally. He has created lighting for numerous restaurants, homes and businesses.

A *Sazerac*, restaurant chandeliers, glass and metals, each: 5' x 5' x 5'

B *Building of the Pyramid*, chandelier, glass and metals, 36" x 36" x 23", 26" sq. at the top

A

B

Edie Morton

172 Howard St. NE, Studio A
Atlanta, GA 30317
TEL **404-377-1134**
E-Mail: **ediemorton@aol.com**

Poetic, ethereal and organic qualities are found in Edie Morton's light diffusion sculpture and luminaires.

In her transformation of various woods, porcelain, gold and silver leaf, Japanese papers and fabrics, one may experience the interconnectedness of all life.

Morton's high quality of craft and attention to detail create a balance between the materials and her art through which she pays homage to the world around us.

A Sconce, 1998, mixed media, 60"H x 15"W x 11"D

B Chandelier, 1999, holly, Japanese paper, metal, gold and silver leaf, 101"H x 48"W x 96"D

A   Photo by Paul Dingman

B   Photo by Kevin Ames

Angelika Traylor

100 Poinciana Drive
Indian Harbour Beach, FL 32937
TEL 321-773-7640
FAX 321-779-3612
E-Mail: angtraylor@aol.com
Web: www.angelikatraylor.com

Specializing in one-of-a-kind lamps, autonomous panels and architectural designs, Traylor's award-winning work can be recognized by its intricate, jewel-like composition.

Often referred to as having painterly qualities, Traylor's works — such as the exquisite lamp and charming autonomous panel shown here — reflect an original and intensive design process, implemented with meticulous craftsmanship and an unusually beautiful selection of glass.

Her work has been featured in many publications, and she has been recognized in seven different *Who's Who* reference books.

Please inquire for more information on available work, commissions and pricing.

Also see these GUILD sourcebooks:
THE GUILD: 2, 3, 4, 5
Designer's: 7, 8, 9, 10, 11, 12, 13, 14
Architect's: 6

Photo by Randall Smith

Photo by Randall Smith

"I believe a work of architecture is more than just an enclosing shelter."

PHILLIP FRUCHTER

Architect

Architect Philip Fruchter advocates integrating meaningful art into architecture, but cautions that it should be a carefully planned element central to the design, rather than a decorative afterthought.

"We prefer to integrate art into our projects, rather than use it as an appliqué," he explains. This means planning ahead. It also means working with artists who can come into a project early and understand the demands of an architectural construction schedule.

Fruchter, one of three partners at Papp Architects in White Plains, New York, is also a glass artist with a number of sculptural glass installations to his credit. As such, he endorses the use of art within the architectural design.

"I believe a work of architecture is more than just an enclosing shelter, and art and fine crafts can be effectively combined with the design to bring spirit and energy to the project," he says.

Fruchter worked with GUILD artist Katherine Holzknecht on an ambitious three-story, three-building, multi-tenant complex with over 175,000 square feet of space. The design included many long corridors which were created with a series of niches to add visual interest and to provide a space suited to original artwork. Fruchter's firm approached Holzknecht based on her work shown in THE GUILD.

"When she provided portfolio materials, it was clear she had the vision, quality and craftsmanship we were looking for," he says. The artist created a series of five related sculptural pieces using a natural wood grid, brightly colored dowels, raw aluminum sheets and woven wire. Collectively titled *Symbiosis*, the pieces were produced and delivered on schedule, and remain highly respected works of art several years after installation.

"At the time we began working with Katherine, some people questioned whether it was prudent to work with an artist in Washington state when our project was located in New York. That proved to be no problem, however. She was very business-like, and extremely sensitive to commercial construction demands and architectural schedules. We accomplished what we had in mind; we were pleased and the client was pleased."

Photo by George E. Peirce

"These artists provide the kind of work that elevates a design project into the realm of the memorable,"

BARBARA ELLIOTT

Interior Designer

With 25 years of international interior design experience, Barbara Elliott of Concord, California, was no stranger to large-scale, complex projects when she began working on a John Q. Hammond hotel down the coast at Seaside. Elliott, who often uses original art in her award-winning projects, designed a dramatic focal point in the hotel's central foyer by using colorful ceramic floor tile commissioned from a firm in Mexico. Unfortunately, as the construction deadline approached, a problem became evident.

"I knew that the construction schedule couldn't be altered, and it was clear that the supplier was simply not going to get the tile to us as promised. I was as disappointed as I was frustrated," Elliott explains.

"The very day we realized that we couldn't use our original plan, my copy of THE GUILD arrived. I was leafing through the pages, and saw George Fishman's ceramic work pictured. It was beautiful, and looked just like what I had in mind."

Elliott called the Florida artist, explained her predicament, and noted that the deadline was impos-

sible and the budget uncompromising. Fishman agreed to take on the challenge. He prepared the mosaic, premounted the tiles for easy installation, and meticulously packed the work for shipment. Then, en route to California, disaster nearly struck again.

"Somehow, the shipper dropped the package," Elliott recalls. Instead of a premounted mosaic, the

designer had many beautiful fragments. Again she called Fishman, who got on a plane, set up a temporary studio in the hotel's construction zone and went to work.

Remarkably, the tile work was in place on time, and a terrific success with the client. "George is so talented and energetic," Elliott says, "and he was such a wonderful team player. I'd highly, highly recommend working with him."

Elliott's positive experiences with GUILD artists didn't end with Fishman.

"I have also been delighted to work with Christina Spann. Her lighting designs add a wonderful, imaginative touch. Like George, she's flexible, accommodating and comes through beautifully on a tight schedule. Both of these artists provide the kind of exciting, high-quality work that elevates a design project into the realm of the memorable."

Photo by Russ Fischella

Victor Chiarizia

Fruit of the Fire Glass
17 Main Street
Talcottville, CT 06066
TEL **860-647-7071**
FAX **860-647-0780**
E-Mail: **glassblower@compuserve.com**
Web: **www.victorchiarizia.com**

Victor Chiarizia explores sculptural shapes in glass while combining fluid forms with spirited colors. The artist's work is represented nationally in galleries and exhibited in public and private collections throughout the United States.

Chiarizia is a multi-talented glass artist with more than 25 years of glass blowing experience. He has successfully completed numerous commissions for architects, designers, corporations and individuals. When working closely with clients and drawing upon his extensive technical command of glass, he brings vision to form.

Commissions are welcomed. Portfolio and additional information available upon request.

A *Aurora,* 21"H x 6"W

B *Gondola,* 18"W x 9"H

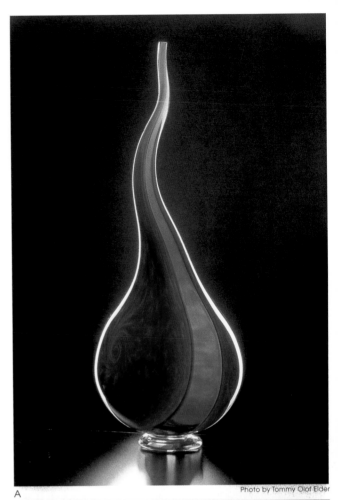

Photo by Tommy Olof Elder

A

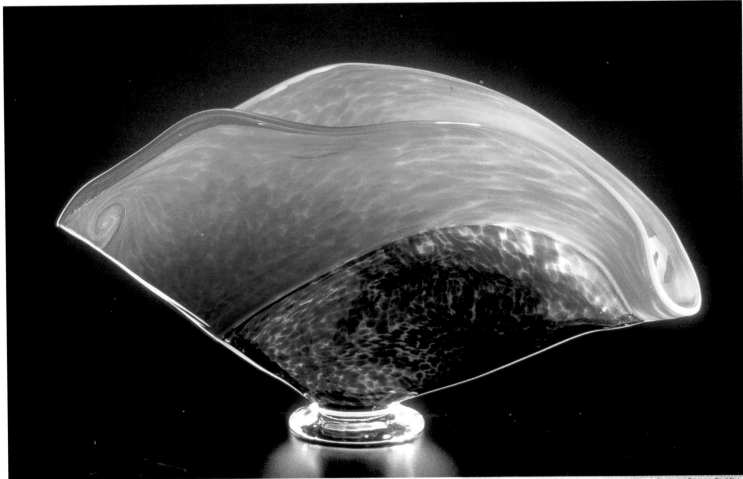

Photo by Tommy Olof Elder

B

Deborah Goldhaft

Fire & Ice Glass Studio
11933 SW Cove Road
PO Box 2292
Vashon, WA 98070
TEL **206-463-3601**
FAX **206-463-1859**
E-Mail: **deborah@fireiceglass.com**
Web: **www.fireiceglass.com**

Deborah Goldhaft's glasswork blends elements of geometric and scientific design, anthropology and feng shui. Working in glass since 1981 has given her skill in creating three-dimensional images with unusual depth and visual interest.

Goldhaft offers custom-designed carved and etched glass for the designer or architect whose demands require impact. Specializing in double-sided deep carving and innovative uses of etched mirror, she works with clients who prefer personal involvement and one-of-a-kind value. This studio can satisfy the most eclectic taste.

Also see these GUILD sourcebooks:
Designer's: 11, 12, 13, 14
Architect's: 12, 13

A *Time Keeps on Slipping, Lamp Plate Techtonic Series #1*, 1999, etched plate glass, maple, 18" x 16"

B *Feng Shuei Village and Linear City*, 1995, etched plate glass, 18" x 22"

C *Stradbroke Dreaming*, memorial for Hollins Crompton, 1992, etched plate glass, 8" x 10"

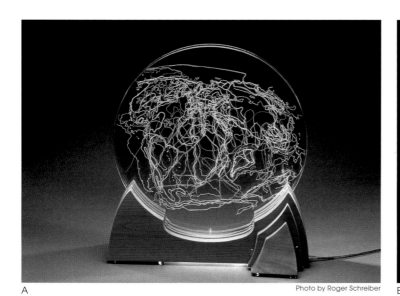

A
Photo by Roger Schreiber

B
Photo by Michael Rosenberg

C
Photo by Michael Rosenberg

Pamela Segers

1061 Ashwood Green Way
Snellville, GA 30078
TEL 770-985-9170

Pamela Segers has been airbrushing on clay for over 20 years. Her clay figures and platters can be made for the wall or a pedestal.

Her style is unique and her dedication to crafts-manship is immediately obvious. She believes her pottery can be visually challenging as well as useful. Many of her clay figures are birdhouses. Her most immediate concern is to make her images personal and stimulating enough to draw the viewer in for a closer look.

Segers' pottery has been featured in *Clay Times* magazine, *NICHE* magazine, *Airbrush Action* magazine, and the Amaco catalog and poster. She was a 2000 NICHE award winner.

A Thrown airbrushed platter, 5" x 22" x 22"

B Slab-built airbrushed fish, 14" x 21" x 5"

A

Photo by Bart's Photography

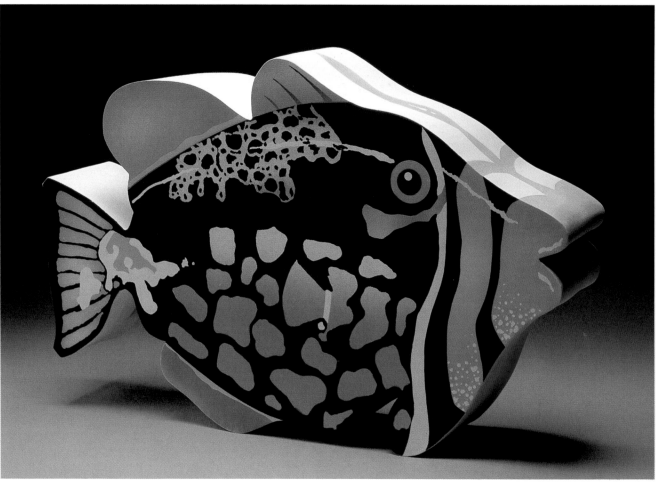

B

Photo by Bart's Photography

Binh Pho

Wonders of Wood
48W175 Pine Tree Drive
Maple Park, IL 60151
TEL **630-365-5462**
FAX **630-365-5837**
E-Mail: **Toriale@msn.com**
Web: **www.wondersofwood.net**

A master of unique finishes and textures, Binh Pho is a Chicago-based artist who works primarily with wood. He combines color, dye and metal leaf gilding to create commanding, primitive art forms. His works have been included in major juried shows and are also in private and corporate collections.

The magnificent skyline of Chicago at sunset has inspired the *Cityscape* series. This piece has received overwhelming reception by the public and art collectors alike. Therefore, he has expanded the series to include other major cities around the world, such as New York, Seattle and Paris.

A *Chicago,* reverse side detail, 1999, maple and lacquer dye, 12"D x 11"W x 5"H

B *Chicago,* front view, 1999, maple and lacquer dye, 12"D x 11"W x 5"H

C *New York,* 1999, maple and lacquer dye, 14"D x 11"W x 5"H

A

B

C

Sandra Christine Q. Bergér

COMMISSIONING AGENT: Art Holdings Corporation

TITLE: *Arctic Ice*

DESCRIPTION: Custom-cast glass sculpture, 23"H x 11"W x 11"D, 55 lbs.

SITE: Thermo King Corporation World Headquarters, Minneapolis, MN

GUILD Sourcebooks provides the forum to showcase work that leads to commissions. *Prismatic Ice* appeared in *The Designer's Sourcebook 13* and caught the attention of Leslie Palmer-Ross of Art Holdings Corporation. Leslie wanted a sculpture that was "icy," unusual, and appropriate for her client, Thermo King, a global leader in refrigeration, heating units and temperature control systems. Thermo King was remodeling its corporate headquarters and wanted a special piece of artwork for the reception area in the president's office suite. Having seen the *Prismatic Ice* series, Leslie made the connection for what was to become *Arctic Ice* — a wonderful commission.

In early 1999, Art Holdings Corporation requested information about my sculptures and costs. Next, they sent a letter outlining the scope of the work and an architect's rendering of the site. Finally, they requested a full-scale model. After making seven variations, I submitted what my studio team and I believed was the best model of *Arctic Ice*.

To our surprise, the client was less than enthusiastic. They thought the model was too "glacial" and instead wanted the "tip of the iceberg." We developed another model, presented a sample of the cast-glass modules to be used, and received the approval to begin fabrication of a 23" high, asymmetrical sculpture. Because our client asked that we extend beyond the limits of our experience, we responded by developing new techniques for achieving challenging art.

Arctic Ice took five-and-a-half months from casting to final sculpture. It was composed of 18 solid blocks of custom-cast glass carefully assembled to capture the illusion of frozen water. As a metaphor for Thermo King, the sculpture suggests both molten glass and super-cooled firm liquid.

— SCQB

Tuska Inc.

Seth Tuska
147 Old Park Avenue
Lexington, KY 40502
TEL 606-255-1379
FAX 606-253-3199
Web: www.tuskastudio.com

Tuska Inc. represents the work of fine artist John R. Tuska (1931-1998). The studio offers reproductions of one of the artist's most engaging works: *Illuminates*, cutworks of the human form engaged in the motion of dance, suspended on open screens.

Each screen is hand-assembled to order in custom dimensions and materials, ranging from natural materials such as woods, steel, aluminum or bronze to contemporary polymers.

Each screen is meticulously executed and rendered in exceeding detail. True craftsman quality makes them ideal for use as window or wall hangings, room dividers, gates, shutters, landscape decorations or other custom applications.

SHOWN: *Illuminates Dance 1,* 1999, smoked acrylic on wooden frame, 6'H x 3'W

Photo by Lee Thomas

David Woodruff

Woodruff Woods Studio
192 Sonata Drive
Lewisville, NC 27023
TEL **336-945-9145**
FAX **336-945-3896**
E-Mail: **pdwoods@worldnet.att.net**

The turned wood artistry of David Woodruff is a three-dimensional interplay of color, wood grain, form and space, promising the pleasure of new discovery.

The major objective in his artistry is the continuous evolvement of methods for revealing nature in wood. He states, "My challenge in the creation of each 'one-of-a-kind' piece is developing that form which reveals and pays homage to the infinite variety of nature."

Woodruff's works use woods with mineral, metal and fossil bone as occasional contrasting inlay materials. The diversity and museum quality of each unique piece mirrors his lifelong passion for wood and wood artistry.

Woodruff's creations and commissions reside in private, corporate and selected gallery collections.

Commission inquiries welcomed.

Olive Vase, 2000, olive wood, ebony, 5"W x 12"H

Untitled, spalted oak burl, 1999, 4.5"H x 12"W

Caldera, 2000, big leaf maple burl, 7"H x 19" x 23", can be wall mounted

Photos: McNabb Studio

Nancy J. Young
Allen Young

02 Martingale Lane SE
Albuquerque, NM 87123
TEL 505-299-6108
FAX 505-299-2238

Nancy J. Young creates durable wall art in hand-cast paper. These pieces can be hung in a framed or unframed format. Also, they may be patinated to resemble metal.

Together, Nancy and Allen create three-dimensional sculptural pieces.

Commissions accepted. Prices from $200 to $3000. Information upon request.

Selected commissions include IBM, AT&T, American Express and the U.S. State Department for embassies in New Guinea and Venezuela.

Also see these GUILD sourcebooks:
THE GUILD: 3, 4, 5
Designer's: 6, 7, 8, 9, 10, 11, 12, 13, 14

A *Convocation,* hand-cast paper, bronzed and patinated, 21"H x 40"W

B Hand-cast paper vessel, bronzed and patinated, 8.5"D x 38"Dia

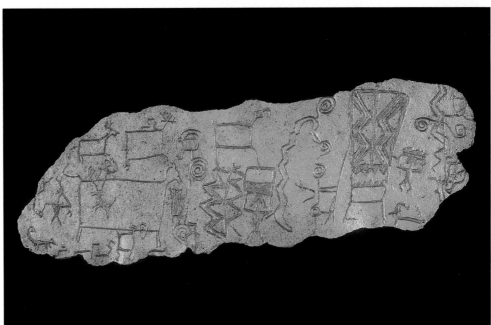

A   Photo by Pat Berrett

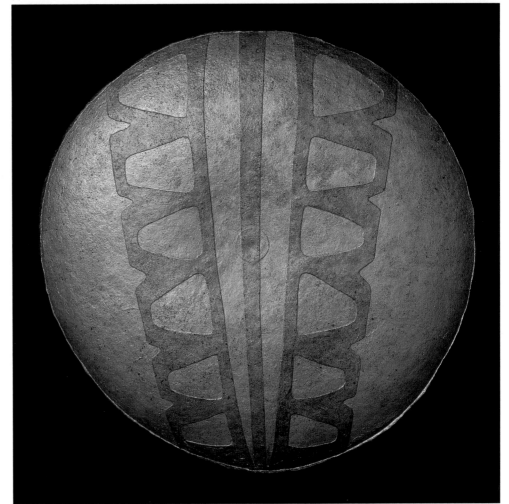

B   Photo by Pat Berrett

PEDESTAL SCULPTURE

George Beckman

Kinetic Innovations
55 Eastpoint Way
Moneta, VA 24121
TEL 540-721-4097
TEL 919-677-0530
E-Mail: **vangeo@mindspring.com**

Over the past decade, George Beckman has created hundreds of unique kinetic sculptures. That body of work now enhances institutions and private residences worldwide. Themes of flight, music, and freedom radiate from his mirror-finished stainless steel pieces. They captivate whether in motion or at rest.

Beckman blends graceful forms and intricate kinetic elements to interplay in visual flowing rhythms when the piece is set in motion. The creative synergy delights and fascinates the viewer. "Fine art should have the potential to stir our emotions and exhilarate our senses. When my work elevates that potential to reality, I've achieved my artistic goal," he states.

Beckman's work is exhibited in museums, design centers and fine art galleries. Completed work is available, and commissions are invited. Prices start at $3000.

Ecstasy, 1999, polished stainless steel, 77" x 34"

Photo by Tim Stamm

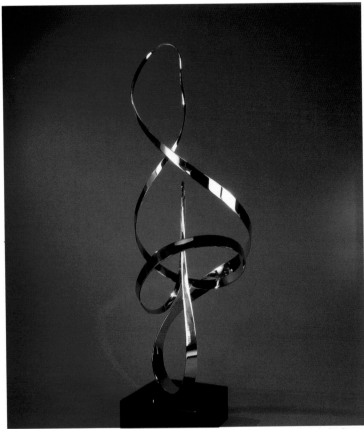

Shadow Dancer, 1999, polished stainless steel, 50" x 23"

Photo by Tim Stamm

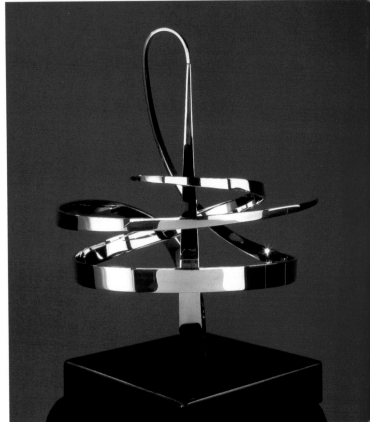

Galaxy, 2000, polished stainless steel, 20" x 14"

Photo by Tim Stamm

Sandra C.Q. Bergér

Quintal Studio
100 El Camino Real #202
Burlingame, CA 94010
TEL 650-348-0310
FAX 650-340-0198

For over 20 years, glass artist Sandra Bergér has been creating fragile art — limited editions, one-of-a-kind sculptures and architectural works.

Solid modules of custom-cast glass form these "icy" sculptures from the *Artic Ice* series. Designed for Thermo King Corporation, this work graces the world headquarters in Minneapolis, MN.

Internationally exhibited and published, Bergér has a history of outstanding collaborations with clients, galleries and design professionals.

Experienced and professional, worldwide service, timely delivery.

Also see these GUILD sourcebooks:
THE GUILD: 1, 2, 3, 4, 5
Designer's: 8, 11, 13, 14
Architect's: 6, 7, 8, 10, 11
Gallery: 1995
THE GUILD Hand Book: 1998

Arctic Ice I, 23"H x 12"W x 11"D, 55 lbs.

Arctic Ice II, 23"H x 10"W x 11"D, 55 lbs.

Photos by William A. Porter

Jeanine Briggs

PO Box 475441
San Francisco, CA 94123
TEL 415-567-4662
E-Mail: artlinks@pacbell.net

Jeanine Briggs creates wall-mounted reliefs and freestanding sculptures; some pieces also function as space dividers, screens, architectural curtains or light filters. Environmental concerns influence her constructive and finishing processes as well as her choice of materials — discarded wood, metal, ceramics, cardboard, paper, fiber, glass and plastics.

Commissions in any size welcome.

A *Dragon,* 2000, cardboard, acrylic, latex, 13" x 19.5" x 9.5"

B *Offering,* 2000, metals, 27.5" x 16" x 12.5"

C *Rainfall,* 1998, wood, metal, acrylic, 58.5" x 33" x 3"

A   Photo by Maximage

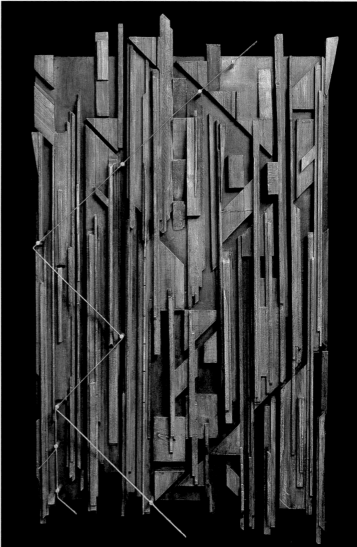

B   Photo by Maximage   C   Photo by Maximage

Lucile Driskell

RR 6 Box 78
Wellsboro, PA 16901
TEL 570-724-2804
E-Mail: **Drisk@epix.net**
Web: **www.sculpture.org**

Throughout her professional art career of over
30 years, Lucile Driskell has created sculpture
that emphasizes purity of form and response to
light. Her experience includes direct carving of
marble, wood and cast metals as well as fabrication with mixed media.

In addition to private collections, Driskell has
many corporate clients, such as Bell Atlantic,
Macy's, Hoffman-LaRoche, SAS Institute and
Subaru.

A *Sirocco*, bronze, 34" x 31" x 16"

B *Sirens' Song*, aluminum, 46" x 24" x 22"

C *Duet*, wood and porcelain, 39" x 16" x 9"

D *Vision*, stainless steel, 44" x 19" x 16"

A

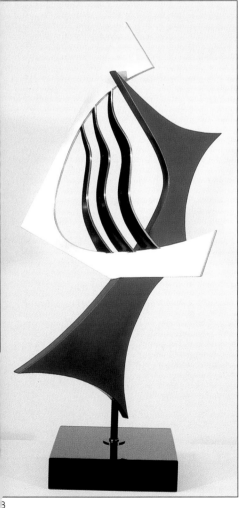

B

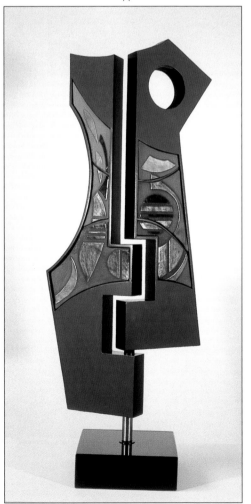

C

D

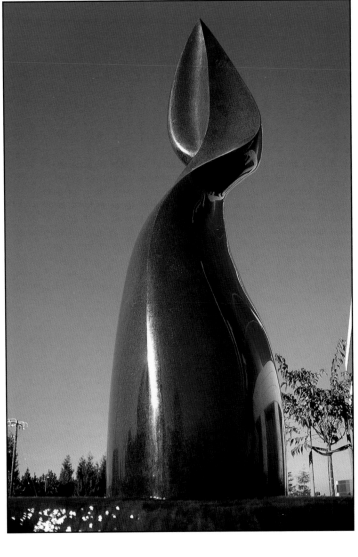

Gerald Siciliano

COMMISSIONING AGENT: Mozart Development Company

TITLE: *Balena*

DESCRIPTION: Black African granite sculpture, 10$\frac{1}{2}$'H, 8,000 pounds

SITE: Office complex in Mountainview, CA, alongside the new KPMG Peat Marwick offices

Developers John Mozart and Steve Dostart of the Mozart Companies in Palo Alto turned to *The Architect's Sourcebook 12* in their search for sculptors for their Middlefield-Ellis project in Mountainview, California.

Their original intent was to have three works commissioned: 3-, 6- and 9-foot sculptures by three artists for placement on the grounds of a new four-story office complex. After contacting a number of artists, galleries and consultants, the developers decided upon two sculptors to develop one work each within a relatively modest, but not insignificant, budget.

Steve Dostart and I discussed an enlarged version of the black marble work featured in the sourcebook. We explored the merits of bronze versus granite in a scale ranging from 6 to 10 to 12 to 15 feet. The theme moved from the more human biomorphic figurative abstraction to a similar biomorphic representation of a breaching whale.

To satisfy the myriad concerns of the developers, the city agencies involved and the artist, a comprehensive plan was enacted to produce a 10-foot black granite sculpture to be sited in a fountain base complete with pedestrian seating.

With the original sculpture as the starting point, I created a series of small maquettes for review by the developers. The developers selected their favorite, which was enlarged first to one-third scale and then to a full 10-foot model for "pointing" into black African granite at the Johnson Atelier of Sculpture in New Jersey. Under my careful supervision and that of the directors of the Atelier, the granite carving was completed in record time and truck-shipped to the site four months ahead of schedule.

The finished work, standing over 10 feet and weighing 8,000 pounds, is now permanently exhibited in its fountain base alongside a new KPMG Peat Marwick office on the corner of Middlefield and Ellis in Mountainview, California.

— **GS**

Ann L. Deluty

Randolph Associates Fine Arts
12 Randolph Street
Belmont, MA 02478
TEL 617-484-3136
FAX 617-484-0069
E-Mail: anndel@aol.com
Web: www.RandolphGallery.com

Ann Deluty strives to express the essence of natural objects in stone and wood. Her work ranges from abstract to extremely realistic. Her mastery of textures and carving techniques gives an air of realism to any object. A graduate of the School of the Museum of Fine Arts, she is also noted for portraits of people and pets in bronze, clay and cold-cast bronze.

Deluty has numerous works in private collections, and commissions are welcomed. Because of the variety of colors available in alabaster, she can carve to match any color scheme.

A *White Shell*, 17.5"H x 13"W x 7.5"D

B *Scarface Stallion*, 11"H x 17"W x 6"D

A

Photo by ARTSLIDES

B

Photo by ARTSLIDES

Jane Jaskevich

1110 Citadel Drive
Atlanta, GA 30324
TEL 404-320-9822
E-Mail: **jaskevich@mindspring.com**
Web: **www.jaskevich.com**

Jaskevich is a carver of dreams in stone. Her intriguing combinations of figures and animals create an ethereal quality. The permanence and beauty of the stone ehances the sculptural images.

Her larger sculptures offer serenity to a corporate boardroom or medical facility. Nationsbank Headquarters in Tampa has three Jaskevich sculptures. The smaller pieces add sophistication to a home when placed on a coffee table. She has two stone sculptures in the permanent collection of the Polk Museum of Art in Lakeland, FL, with one marble piece gracing the museum's sculpture garden. Her large-scale bronze sculptures are the focal point for the GTE Data Services Building in Tampa.

Prices start at $1000. Commissions are welcomed. Slide packets are available upon request.

Also see this GUILD sourcebook:
Designer's: 14

A *Magic,* Indiana limestone, 10" x 5" x 16"

B *Siren,* two alabaster stones, 22" x 14" x 15"

A

Photo by John Dale

B

Photo by John Dale

BJ Katz

Meltdown Glass Art & Design LLC
PO Box 2110
Tempe, AZ 85280-2110
TEL 800-845-6221
FAX 480-949-9809
E-Mail: MeltdownAZ@aol.com
Web: **www.meltdownglass.com**

BJ Katz has mastered a technique combining glass casting, draping and painting, creating "magic" with translucent light, color and texture. Triumphant in overcoming the inherent fragility of glass, she explores the literal and interpretive relationship of the figure to the painted surface. Katz communicates her ideas by utilizing the figure's skin as a conceptual membrane, exploring this physically and metaphorically, drawing attention to the glass surface as the protective border between interior and exterior worlds. Each torso celebrates the innate beauty of the human body.

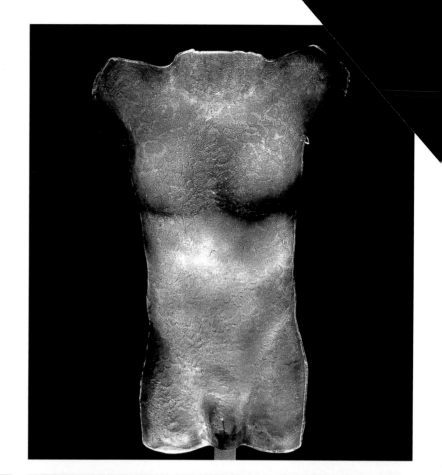

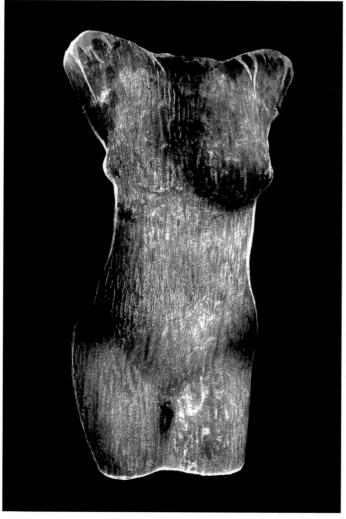

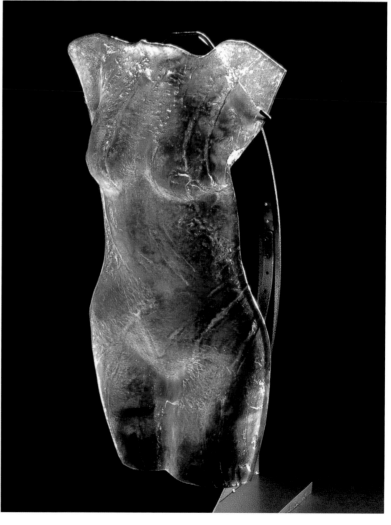

...... a painter and a sculptor. Her work includes both pedestal and monumental bronzes. Her sculptures are not sentimental. They embody integrity of material, grace of weight and simplicity of form. She doesn't force the dialog, but waits for the shapes to introduce themselves, then embraces and builds on what they suggest. The forms are complete in themselves without explanation or justification for being.

Her work lives in the homes and gardens of many private collectors.

Also see these GUILD sourcebooks:
Designer's: 14
Architect's: 13, 14, 15

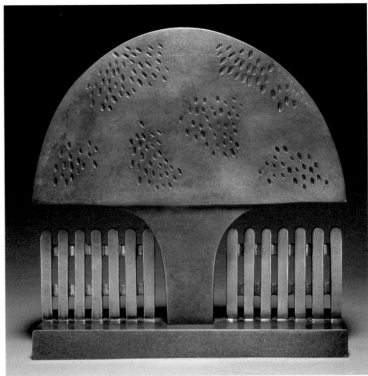

Between My House and Yours, 1999, bronze, 13"H x 12"W x 5"D   Photo by Bob Kohlbrener

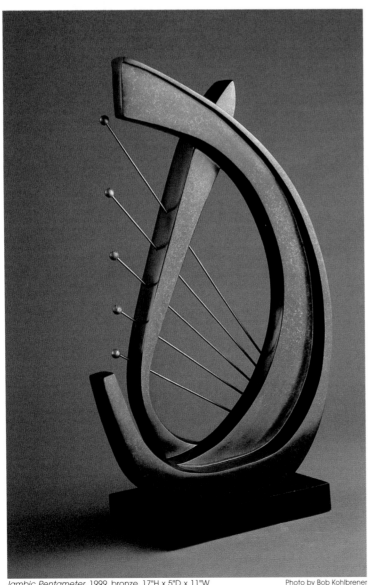

Iambic Pentameter, 1999, bronze, 17"H x 5"D x 11"W   Photo by Bob Kohlbrener

Connections, 1999, bronze, 18" x 5"D x 12"W   Photo by Bob Kohlbrener

Elizabeth MacQueen

Elizabeth MacQueen Sculpture and Fine Art
PO Box 12414
San Luis Obispo, CA 93406
TEL **805-543-1409**
FAX **805-543-8154**
E-Mail: **macqueen@c2on.net**
Web: **www.macqueenfineart.com**

Elizabeth MacQueen's passion as an artist is to translate the language of the body into a three-dimensional reality that symbolizes the real essence of movement, expression and human dignity. She sculpts in marble and bronze.

MacQueen takes public and private commissions and has numerous works in both the private and public sector.

Commissions include: *Honor the Past, Celebrate the Present, Hope for the Future,* Women's Basketball Hall of Fame, Knoxville, TN; *Sacagawea,* City of Antioch, CA; *Chinese Pioneers,* City of San Luis Obispo, CA; *Cowboy with Wagon and Bassett Hound,* Avila Bay Club, Avila, CA; torso of Puck, Biblioteca di Pietrasanta, Italy; bronze Puck, Carolyn Blount Shakespeare Theatre, Montgomery, AL; and life-size *Mudra,* Irvine Barclay Theatre, Irvine, CA.

A *Mudra,* bronze, marble base, 52.5"H x 42"L x 24"D

B & C *Sacagawea,* bronze, 19"H x 10"W x 18"D

A

B

C

James T. Russell

COMMISSIONING AGENT: Motorola Corporation in conjunction with Corporate Artworks

TITLE: *Spirit Song*

DESCRIPTION: Freestanding sculpture over a reflecting pool, 6'H

SITE: Motorola Corporation Headquarters, Beijing, China

In December 1997, Denise Rippinger of Corporate Artworks in Chicago contacted me to create a sculpture in Beijing, China. Motorola Corporation had seen my artwork in GUILD Sourcebooks and wanted me to propose a sculpture for the lobby of their new headquarters. I worked personally with their staff and architects to create *Spirit Song*.

Spirit Song is a 6-foot freestanding sculpture that rotates over a three-level reflecting pool. Drawing on elements of feng shui, the finished sculpture in its design and placement is symbolic and representative of energy, prosperity and harmony. According to feng shui, the flowing water of the reflecting pond invites prosperity to flow into the building, and therefore, into the company. Further, *Spirit Song* is designed to follow positive elements of feng shui, with its flowing curves and circular "infinite" shape. The single unbroken form of *Spirit Song* symbolizes the bond of Eastern and Western culture working together in eternal harmony.

The process involved three planning trips to Beijing and an artist-led installation. The whole production team went to China to personally install the artwork. We worked with wonderful and cooperative people employed by Motorola Corporation. In this fascinating foreign culture, our palates were tempted with snake bile, snake blood, pigeon and turtle, to name a few.

This was a very unique sculpture project for both my production team and me. Overcoming the constraints of distance, we worked across the country with Denise Rippinger of Corporate Artworks, and across the world with the staff of Motorola Corporation. This wonderful opportunity allowed me to explore another culture, learn principles of an ancient belief (feng shui), and to grow as an artist.

I appreciate the exposure and commissions I have received through advertising in GUILD Sourcebooks.

— JR

St. Elmo's, Inc.

Brad Jirka
Katherine Jones
2688 89th Court West
Northfield, MN 55057
TEL **612-652-6366**
FAX **612-652-2935**
E-Mail: **brad_jirka@mn.mcad.edu**

The artists of St. Elmo's have created masterfully crafted pieces for private collectors, designers, architects, corporate clients and public art spaces for 25 years.

The studio's works have ranged from scientific and nautically inspired objects to sophisticated patterning of objects in intarsia.

St. Elmo's uses a variety of materials, including hardwoods, metals, precious metals, plastics, light and motion.

Also see these GUILD sourcebooks:
Architect's: 7, 14, 15

A *Loci Newtonia, Instrument* series, illuminated base and "rocking" vessel, lacquered Honduras mahogany, machined brass, tektite (glass meteor), glass level vial, compass, plastic, electroluminescent panel, electric motor, 2'H x 1'W x 10"D

B *Voci Marconia, Instrument* series, listening device for Marconi's ghost with magnetic field disrupter, lacquered Honduras mahogany, machined brass, plastic, electric components, magnets, compass points, 2'W x 1'D, antenna height: up to 60'

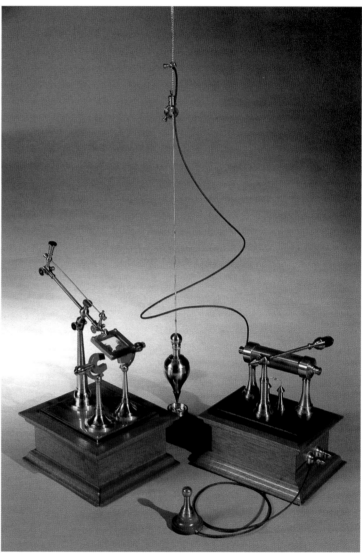

A

B

Edwina Sandys

565 Broadway #2
New York, NY 10012
TEL 212-343-7066
FAX 212-343-2979
E-Mail: edwinasandys@yahoo.com
Web: www.edwinasandys.com

Edwina Sandys is a sculptor and painter, the 1997 recipient of the United Nations' Society of Artists Award for Excellence.

The art of Edwina Sandys encompasses diverse subject matter ranging from lighthearted to profound. Her clearly recognizable style uses positive and negative forms to powerful effect. "If you have the image right, the piece will work regardless of scale or materials," she says.

Sandys' work is "people friendly" and she welcomes commissions for lively places both public and private. She would love to create art and murals for restaurants and hotels. In 1999, her 12-foot-high *Millennium Tulips* graced New York's Park Avenue.

A *Bird*, 1995, *Yin-Yang* series, paper collage

B *Tulip*, 1995, *Yin-Yang* series, paper collage

C *Pear*, 1995, *Yin-Yang* series, paper collage

D *Hands On*, 1990, marble sculpture with colored inlay, 39"H

A

B

C

D

Gerald Siciliano

Studio Design Associates
9 Garfield Place
Brooklyn, NY 11215-1903
TEL/FAX 718-636-4561
E-Mail: gsstudio@concentric.net
Web: www.concentric.net/~gsstudio

Working with figurative and non-representational themes, Gerald Siciliano creates classic sculpture and three-dimensional objects for discerning collectors, architects, designers and corporations worldwide.

Meticulously crafted sculptures created in durable materials — from the intimate to the monumental — are available from the studio or on a commission basis.

Current projects include the creation of two large-scale stainless steel relief panels using state-of-the-art water-jet technology as well as a realistic figure suite using traditional lost wax casting methods.

Your inquiries are invited.

Clients include:
American Airlines
American Axle & Manufacturing Company
Bristol-Myers Squibb Co.
The Brooklyn Museum
Canon USA
Dong Baek Art Center, Pusan, Korea
The John Templeton Foundation
The Mozart Companies
Olympic Park, Pusan, Korea
Sparks Exhibits & Environments Co.

Also see these GUILD sourcebooks:
Designer's: 14
Architect's: 12, 13, 14, 15

A *Three Point,* Massa marble, 20" x 21" x 18"

B *Back Study,* Carrara statuario marble, life-size

A

B

EVA ZERVOS

Art Advisor

As a corporate art advisor, Eva Zervos values creativity and artistic excellence highly. However, she is quick to point out that her first role in working with clients is to provide information and guidance to help them feel confident about their artistic choices.

"I've worked with both .public institutions and corporations in the Boston area for over 12 years," Zervos explains. "Most of my clients come from the Northeast, but the resources I use are nationwide. THE GUILD helps trigger my memory of what's available, and I often recommend GUILD artists for projects because they have the professionalism and experience that helps me do my job better."

Her firm is a full-service consulting business, which means she typically works through every stage of a project, from earliest contact with the artist to proposals, creation, installation and any services thereafter.

Zervos says that when a client selects or commissions original, site-specific art, they are often saying yes to something they haven't seen. "That requires a significant level of trust and comfort, and as a result, education is a large part of my job. The art has to be presented in a way that is both eloquent and accessible."

She cites her experience working with GUILD artist Robert Pfitzenmeier as a perfect example of the kind of professionalism that makes her job both easier and more rewarding. The project involved an atrium sculpture for a Boston health care center. "In the most successful projects, the client has a strong feeling of participation, and someone like Bob really helps keep the lines of communication open. His ideas were fascinating, his track record excellent and his presentation materials—from photographs to video to models of the sculpture—were superb. These are the tools that really help the client get excited.

"The completed sculpture is extraordinarily beautiful as you watch it move and the colors change. People absolutely love it."

Photo by Cecilia Hirsh

BOB PETERSON

Architect

A door can be just a door, or it can be a magical entry into another world created by the careful collaboration of architect, artist and client. Robert Peterson, the principal of Peterson Architects, a 12-person firm in Menlo Park, California, had the latter purpose in mind when he commissioned GUILD artist Al Garvey to create a doorway for a family room expansion.

Peterson's client was a wine connoisseur with a very substantial collection. Garvey gave substance to that interest by creating an imposing, 8-foot-high, 44-inch-wide, arch-topped doorway executed in bird's-eye maple. The antique-appearing doorway invites the visitor from the family living space into the wine cellar. "The earthy, slate floor and the very rich materials of the doorway beckon you into the new area and prepare you for a different experience from the rest of the house," Peterson explains. "This door provides excellent enrichment to the architectural design."

Since his teaching days at Stanford, and through decades of involvement with residential, commercial and civic design projects, Peterson has encouraged clients to use original art to enhance the architectural statement. He recalls one of his early projects from the 1960s, a psychiatrist's office that was done in bold, vibrant colors. For artwork, Peterson recommended a series of black-and-white photographs by Ansel Adams. Not only did the photography enrich the space and delight those who passed through, it's also proven to be the best investment the client ever made.

"People don't realize they can get something custom—something that's just for them—and it can be in their price range," Peterson says. "That's part of the pleasure of recommending original art."

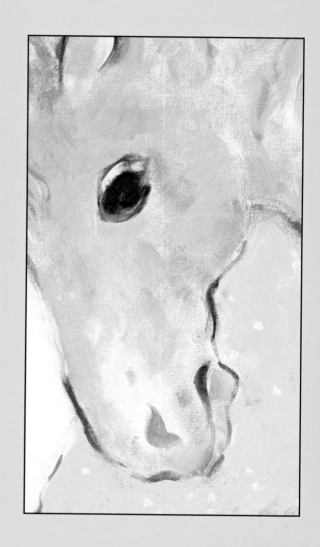

Todd Betts

Betts Art
231 Market Place, 357
San Ramon, CA 94583-4743
TEL **925-803-0463**
FAX **925-875-1026**
E-Mail: **TBettsArt@aol.com**

Working in a variety of mediums and techniques, Betts explores historical, traditional and whimsical themes as well as contemporary styles to create the perfect environment for your residential or commercial projects.

Betts brings a distinctive enchanting elegance to all of his creations. Over the past 10 years, his artwork has ranged from gallery fine art, classic frescos and sculpture to murals and decorative faux finishes. Betts is revered as a master of decorative faux finishes and trompe l'oeil murals.

In addition to his rare talents, architects, designers and discriminating private collectors are delighted with Betts' creative imagination, easygoing demeanor and professionalism.

Portfolio and references available upon request.

Also see this GUILD sourcebook:
Architect's: 15

Italian theme dining room, acrylic on standard wall (painted on site), 15' x 15' x 26'

Photo by Ken Perkes

A Day in Pompeii, acrylic on standard wall (painted on site), 20' x 9.5'

Photo by Ken Perkes

Fine Art Murals Inc.

Carl White / Darren Schweitzer
2305 5th Avenue NW
Calgary, AB T2N 0T1
Canada
TEL/FAX 403-244-8686
E-Mail: info@fineartmurals.com
Web: www.fineartmurals.com

Nicholas Jones
Glass Garage Fine Art Gallery
114 N. Robertson Boulevard
West Hollywood, CA 90048
TEL 310-659-5228
FAX 310-659-4558
E-Mail: murals@glassgaragegallery.com
Web: www.glassgaragegallery.com

The studio was founded in 1992 in response to professional demands for high-quality commercial and residential art services — to become a supplier of original, handpainted fine art murals.

Principal artists Darren Schweitzer and Carl White combine fine art degrees with ten years of practical mural painting experience.

The studio manager, Nicholas Jones, oversees U.S. operations with over 15 years of design and project management experience and a strong background in architecture.

The studio offers a full commitment to the highest professional standards in creating custom artwork for specific environments — sensitive and unique designs in the true spirit of fine art, based on historic reference or by original concept development.

List of commissions available upon request.

Debaji's Fresh Market, 1999, acrylic on board, pine and drywall, shopping center, 12'H x 80'W

After Russell – Salute to the Robe Trade, 2000, oil on drywall, 10'H x 17'W

Temple of Athena, 1999, acrylic on curved drywall, private residence, 12'H x 14'W

Photos: Roy White Photography

It was 123 degrees when we slipped out of the truck. My first thought was "this is going to be the mural installation from hell." No one was happy. In order to cope we worked at night (it dropped to a cool 100 degrees) and rested during the day. The trailer I brought was like a metal box of torture, so we stayed in air-conditioned hotel rooms to survive. The plan was to install the mural earlier that winter, when Palm Desert is comfortably warm. But due to construction delays of the shopping center, the only available time slot was summer.

We adapted. It started to cool a little and I began to enjoy the desert evenings. I met two local artists who wanted to help with the project. Both of them became friends and later joined the crew. What started out as "the worst of times" became one of my favorite commissions.

It began when Los Angeles architect Rod Chen contacted me the previous fall. Chen expressed interest in my work after seeing it in *The Architect's Sourcebook*. His firm was required by the city's Percent for the Arts program to provide site-specific public art for the shopping center they were building. Rod and I hit it off and I was soon developing a design concept for a 20' x 20' mural that was approved later by the Palm Desert Arts Commission. The mural, entitled *Crossroads*, was mostly completed in my studio on panels and then transported down south to the Desert Crossing Shopping Center. There we installed and painted the remaining 20 percent to insure its effective integration on site.

Based on the response from my clients as well as those who said hello to the illusionary woman, everyone is as pleased with the piece as I am.

— JP

John Pugh

COMMISSIONING AGENT: City of Palm Desert, Percent for the Arts program

COLLABORATING CLIENT: Rod Chen of Lowell Enterprises, Los Angeles, CA

TITLE: *Crossroads*

DESCRIPTION: Trompe l'oeil mural, acrylic paint on panels, 20' x 20'

SITE: Desert Crossing Shopping Center, Palm Desert, CA

Vicki Khuzami

Khuzami Studio
552 Broadway, Third Floor
New York, NY 10012
TEL/FAX   212-941-6054
E-Mail: khuzami@bway.net
Web: www.khuzamistudio.com

This year, Vicki Khuzami produced over 3,000 square feet of murals for Disneyland's Ikspiari Land in Tokyo, Japan, for Moo Studio. Other projects include historical murals for the Capitol in Washington, DC and a WPA-style mural for the Ironworkers Union in New York City.

Also see these GUILD sourcebooks:
Architect's: 11, 12 , 13

A Historical mural of New England Telephone for Evergreene Painting Studios (detail), 4' x 50'

B Mural for the VIP Room of Disney Ambassador Hotel, Tokyo, Japan, for Parker Blake Inc. (detail), 3' x 5.5'

C Ceiling mural for private residence (detail), New York, NY, 16' x 16'

A

B   Photo by Tom Baer

C   Photo by Maike Paul

PAINTINGS & PRINTS

I have shown my elegant screens and wall hangings in GUILD Sourcebooks for many years. Nancy Caslin Art & Design Inc. first noticed my work in *The Designer's Sourcebook 8* a little more than five years ago. The company was seeking an artist to commission for a retirement facility outside of Tokyo. They liked the works displayed in the sourcebooks, and were interested in commissioning an artist trained in the artistic techniques of Japan, ancient techniques passed down from generation to generation.

This project was a success and led to other commissions, the most recent being two wall-hanging screens for a hotel in Manila, the Philippines.

Samples of my work were included in the design firm's presentation to its clients. They proposed that I create a piece to be displayed in the entrance lobby of the hotel; this would be the first thing people see when they entered the building. I originally envisioned a small work. However, I worked with the designers to eventually create a wall-hanging screen measuring four square feet.

GUILD sourcebooks have helped me to connect with people who appreciate my work, allowing the world to see oriental serenity and beautiful simplicity.

— YH

Yoshi Hayashi

COMMISSIONING AGENT: Nancy Caslin Art & Design Inc.

TITLE: *Bamboo Forest*

DESCRIPTION: Wall-hanging screen

SITE: Hotel lobby, Manila, Philippines

Fred Bendheim

160 Underhill Avenue
Brooklyn, NY 11238
TEL/FAX **718-638-0219**
E-Mail: **Redbends@aol.com**
Web: **www.geocities.com/SoHo/Museum/9903**

Fred Bendheim is an accomplished painter of many genres and subjects. His work — beautifully crafted paintings in oil, acrylic or watercolor — depicts many aspects of his nature.

Bendheim has had numerous one-person and group shows. His work is in public and private collections worldwide. Commissions are welcomed; slides and prints are available upon request.

A *Third Level*, 1997, watercolor on paper, 30" x 22"

B *Approach*, 1993, acrylic on canvas, 72" x 54"

A

B

Dana Lynne Andersen, M.A.

TEL **877-463-7443 (Toll free)**
TEL **530-470-9626**
E-Mail: **dana@awakeningarts.com**
Web: **www.guild.com**
Web: **www.AwakeningArts.com**

Dana Andersen creates original works of great beauty, vision and refinement. Charged with a numinous quality, her work conveys a sense of penetrating intelligence. Collectors appreciate the depth disclosed over time, assuring long-term satisfaction.

Her exhibitions often include installation and live multi-media performances, as well as lectures and publications on the role of art in society.

Dana's large-scale, museum-quality paintings are an uplifting choice for corporate and public settings as well as for private and liturgical commissions. Dana is a fun and inventive collaborator — request a brochure for your upcoming project.

A *Whirling Earth in Churning Sea of Space*, acrylic on canvas, 96" x 96"

B *Emissary* (detail)

C *Emissary*, acrylic on canvas, 84" x 54"

A

B

C

Bruce R. Bleach

146 Coleman Road
Goshen, NY 10924
TEL 845-294-8945
FAX 845-294-9617
E-Mail: **brbleach@frontiernet.net**

For the past 25 years, Bruce R. Bleach has been creating unique and exciting works for the wall. Most recently he has been painting large acrylics on canvas and global wall sculptures in etched and painted aluminum and bronze.

These dramatic works are clear coated, maintenance free and appropriate for corporate and residential installations.

Listed in *Who's Who in American Art,* Bleach is recognized internationally for his etchings, monoprints, paintings and metal wall sculpture.

The artist is noted for his rich textural surfaces, dynamic colors and subtle blending. He enjoys working with designers, consultants and architects and will complete high-quality projects on schedule.

Selected collections include: Motorola; Lucent Technologies; SmithKline Beecham; America Online, Inc.; Trump Hotels & Casino Resorts, Inc.; Xerox; Intel; Pfizer; and Price-Waterhouse.

Drawings, photos and color maquettes available upon request.

Also see these GUILD sourcebooks:
Designer's: 8, 12

Painting on aluminum, painted wood frame, 22" x 22"

Global wall sculpture, etched and painted aluminum, Johnson & Johnson, approximately 5' x 6'

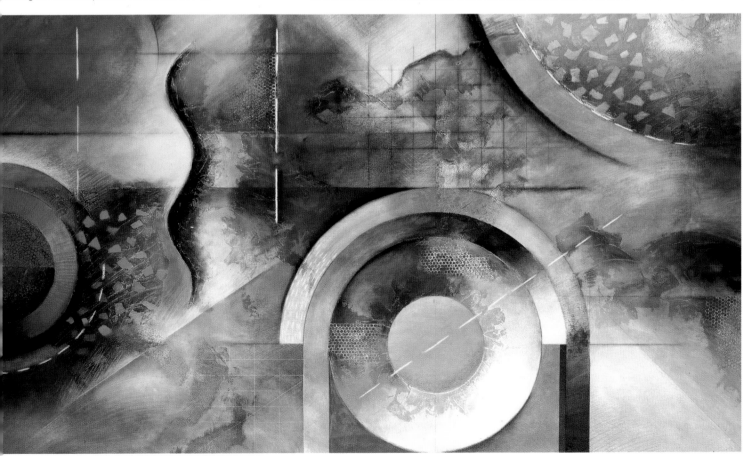

Japonica #23, acrylic on canvas, approximately 40" x 60"

Bob Brown

Bob Brown Studio
2725 Terry Lake Road
Fort Collins, CO 80524
TEL/FAX **970-224-5473**
E-Mail: **BobBrown-Artist@worldnet.att.net**
Web: **www.ktcassoc.com/artists/bob_brown**

Bob Brown's paintings focus attention and highlight an area by bringing the bright outdoors inside. The thick texture created with durable acrylic paint and a painting knife provides an interesting surface. Subjects are representational and mostly landscapes.

Brown's paintings have been exhibited in galleries and public spaces in the United States, Monaco and France.

Unframed paintings range from 16" x 20" to 30" x 36" and retail from $800 to $2500. Commissions considered.

A free color brochure is available upon request.

Also see this GUILD sourcebook:
Designer's: 14

A *"#16" Olive Shadow*, 1998, 24" x 30"

B *"#25" T.L. Path 2 N*, 1998, 24" x 30"

A

B

Fran Bull

PO Box 707
Closter, NJ 07624
TEL   201-767-3726
FAX   201-750-1368
E-Mail: **franbull@juno.com**
Web: **www.guild.com**

Fran Bull's art invites viewers into worlds of vivid color, biomorphic form and provocative narrative. Rich hues are combined with free-ranging shapes and maverick linearities to suggest a myriad of scenarios ranging from the vicissitudes of daily life to the grandeur of cosmic drama.

Exquisite handmade papers are among the materials Bull uses, as are paints which lend an opulence to surface qualities.

Bull has exhibited her work worldwide for more than 20 years, and is represented in numerous private, museum and corporate collections. Commissions are welcomed; slides and pricing available upon request.

Collections include:
Yale University, New Haven, CT
Baltimore Museum of Art, Baltimore, MD
Museum of Modern Art, New York, NY

A   *High and Low,* 1992, acrylic on paper,
    60"H x 40"W

B   *13 Moons of the Magdalene: God's Wife,*
    1995, acrylic on canvas, 90"H x 65"W

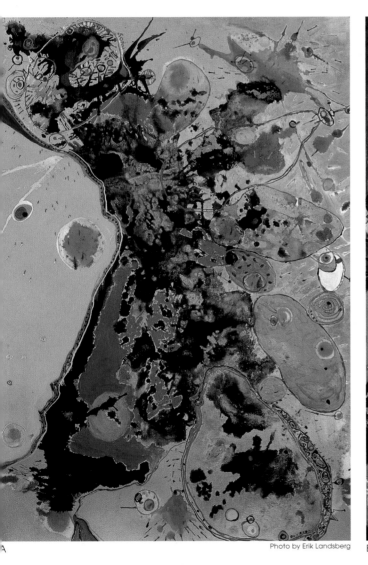

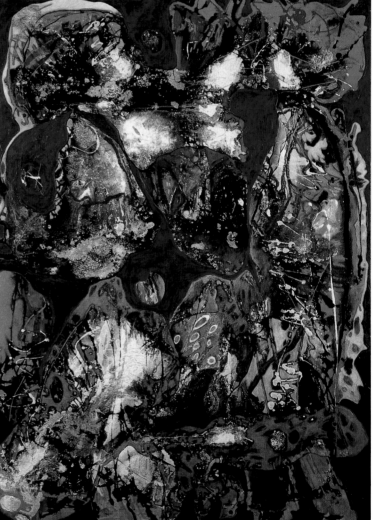

A   Photo by Erik Landsberg   B   Photo by Erik Landsberg

Karen Brussat Butler

169 West Norwalk Road
Norwalk, CT 06850
TEL 203-853-7757
FAX 203-853-3260
E-Mail: mail@waterstreetstudio.com
Web: www.waterstreetstudio.com

Butler has created her own distinctive style that combines vibrant color, faultless line, an innate sense of design and considerable humor. She is very much a storyteller. Her large paintings and prints are about people encountering life, reacting to one another in myriad situations that our existence brings everyday. She stops to see the humor all around us and hopes we will see it, too.

A *Very Mild, Chili Pepper* series

B *Chinese New Year*

C *Rub-A-Dub Dub...*

D *Starlight Boat Ride*

A

B

C

D

Karen Brussat Butler

169 West Norwalk Road
Norwalk, CT 06850
TEL 203-853-7757
FAX 203-853-3260
E-Mail: mail@waterstreetstudio.com
Web: www.waterstreetstudio.com

Many of Butler's paintings involve the common experience of people dining and drinking together — revealing interesting situations. Her work has been purchased for leading restaurants and food-related businesses from San Francisco, Chicago, New York, and as far away as Ireland and Italy. She enjoys doing special commissions, collaborating with the client to make the paintings unique to the project. Where budget is a challenge, she also has numerous limited-edition prints available.

A *See, The Six Stages of Wine Tasting* series

B *Evening to Remember*

C *Swirl, The Six Stages of Wine Tasting* series

D *Smell, The Six Stages of Wine Tasting* series

E *American Hot*

A

B

C

D

E

Karen Brussat Butler

169 West Norwalk Road
Norwalk, CT 06850
TEL 203-853-7757
FAX 203-853-3260
E-Mail: mail@waterstreetstudio.com
Web: www.waterstreetstudio.com

Butler's paintings have received numerous honors and awards from national arts organizations including the National Academy of Design, the American Watercolor Society and the National Watercolor Society. She won the gold medal in the first International Artist in Watercolor Competition held in London, England. Her paintings have been purchased for several public and private collections, including the Henry Ward Ranger Foundation of the National Academy, General Electric Corporation and Hearst Publications.

A *Autumn Retreat*

B *Crossroads*

C *Harvest Dance*

D *Traveling Route 80*

E *Intermission*

A

B

C

D

E

Karen Brussat Butler

169 West Norwalk Road
Norwalk, CT 06850
TEL **203-853-7757**
FAX **203-853-3260**
E-Mail: **mail@waterstreetstudio.com**
Web: **www.waterstreetstudio.com**

Psychic Portraits of Imagined People is a series of large watercolors and prints. Here the artist asks the question: Is it possible for a person to leave an imprint on an object that can be "read" by a psychic? Butler had a collection of old china cups read by an inspired psychic, and used these "readings" to create her imagined portraits of discovered people.

A *Reading Tea Leaves*

B *Catch a Falling Star*

C *Grew Old with Verve*

D *In the State of Flux*

E *Her Feet Were Flexible But Her Mind Was Not*

F *Unabashed by Nature*

G *Pomp & Circumstance*

H *Leaving Namesakes All-Over*

I *Searched the World Over to Find Everything in Her Heart*

B

C

D

A

E

H

F

G

I

Ione Turner Citrin

2222 Avenue of the Stars, Suite 2302
Los Angeles, CA 90067
TEL 310-556-4382
FAX 310-556-1664
E-Mail: icitrin@aol.com
Web: www.jolaf.com/ione/

"When I paint, I dip my brush in my soul. Being an artist is a life force, not a career choice. I present the world artistically as I see it, as I wish to see it, and occasionally as I once saw it. You see, it is my identity. Without this expression of self, I am nothing. Through my art I give love."

Ione Turner Citrin

Please contact the artist for prices. Slides and photographs are available upon request.

Also see these GUILD sourcebooks:
Designer's: 12, 13, 14

Willow Weep for Me, oil on canvas, 18"W x 24"H

Bridal Bouquet, oil on canvas, 30"H x 24"W

Beaucoup Bouquet, oil on canvas, 44"H x 32"W

Edward Spaulding DeVoe

219 Main Street South
Bridgewater, CT 06752
TEL 860-354-5072
FAX 860-354-9594
E-Mail: **esdevoe@aol.com**
Web: **www.artinmyhome.com**

Edward Spaulding DeVoe uses techniques of the Old Masters to render tranquil landscapes, still lifes and contemporary portraits. With a specially formulated medium, derived from his study of Renaissance manuscripts, he combines the brilliant glow of Flemish oils with the versatility of modern synthetics.

The paintings of this award-winning artist have been exhibited in museums and galleries and are in numerous private, public and corporate collections throughout the world. Prices on request. Commissions accepted.

Moon Bear, 32" x 44"

Melange, 34" x 54"

Claus Eben

A. Jain Marunouchi Gallery
24 West 57th Street
New York, NY 10019
TEL **212-969-9660**
FAX **212-969-9715**
E-Mail: **jainmar@aol.com**
Web: **www.jainmargallery.com**

Modern art is an adventure in orientation, and Eben is an important marker in our quest for bearings. The coordination of abstract devices of light, color and space is key for an art more unambiguously abstract. In Eben's paintings, images with a touch of the exotic flicker within kaleidoscopic fields of intense color.

Catalog available.

Commissions accepted.

A *Rolling Hills*, 59" x 79.5"

B *Bulldog*, mixed media, 80" x 54"

A

B

Kazuo Nishimura

A. Jain Marunouchi Gallery
24 West 57th Street
New York, NY 10019
TEL 212-969-9660
FAX 212-969-9715
E-Mail: Jainmar@aol.com
Web: www.jainmargallery.com

The works of Kazuo Nishimura reveal the resting person. The nature-inspired paintings and installations are visual poems about daily life.

Nishimura has exhibited thoroughut the world. Collections include major corporations, hotels and museums.

A *Moonlight,* silkscreen, 22.4" x 16.4"

B *Couple-4,* plank

C *Sitting Women,* oil on canvas, 21.2" x 29"

A

B

C

W. Logan Fry

2835 Southern Road
Richfield, OH 44286
TEL   **330-659-3104**
E-Mail: **Wloganfry@aol.com**

W. Logan Fry creates wonderful paintings, weavings and sculptural objects. His work has been exhibited extensively across the United States and Eastern Europe, and is included in major collections.

The painting illustrated here visually explores the beauty of our world. Painted on a wood panel, the work was color coordinated to complement the site for which it was commissioned.

Prices range from $1500 to $2000 plus shipping.

Commissions include:
Akron Children's Hospital Medical Center,
   Akron, OH
MetroHealth Medical Center, Cleveland, OH
Rainbow Babies & Children's Hospital,
   Cleveland, OH

Museum collections include:
The Renwick Gallery, National Museum of
   American Art, Washington, DC
The Cleveland Museum of Art, Cleveland, OH

Also see these GUILD sourcebooks:
Designer's: 6, 7

SHOWN: *Lovely, Blue-Green Planet,* 40"H x 48"W

Photo by Bruce Gate

Trena McNabb

McNabb Studio
PO Box 327
Bethania, NC 27010
TEL **336-924-6053**
FAX **336-924-4854**
E-Mail: **trena@tmcnabb.com**
Web: **www.tmcnabb.com**

The art of Trena McNabb is an elegant synthesis of realism and imagination. Her paintings of allegorical, brightly lit, realistically rendered, thematically related scenes are in her own harmonious technique. Clients throughout the U.S., Europe and Asia have seen their stories successfully rendered. McNabb's unique style of transparent overlapping images and montages of brilliant color inspires her collectors.

McNabb's prior work ranges from 20-foot long multi-canvas, site-specific corporate or public art commissions to small, elegant pieces for private residences. Because of this wide experience, she is especially skilled at tailoring size and price to fit the scope of a specific project without ever sacrificing artistic content or integrity.

Selected commissions include: Banner Pharmacaps, Fannie Mae Mortgage, Kaiser Permanente Hospital, KinderCare, Knight Foundation, Kuralt Centre, Lopez Nursing Home, Mecklenburg County Park & Recreation, Sara Lee Corporation and Truliant Federal Credit Union.

Also see these GUILD sourcebooks:
Designer's: 8, 14
Architect's: 6, 7, 8, 9, 10, 11, 12, 13, 14

SHOWN: *Feeding the World,* Greensboro, NC, five 36" square canvas panels, total size: 48" x 192" x 2"

Yoshi Hayashi

255 Kansas Street
San Francisco, CA 94103
TEL/FAX 415-552-0755
E-Mail: yoshihayashi@worldnet.att.net

Yoshi Hayashi's designs range from very traditional 17th-century Japanese lacquer art themes that are delicate with intricate detail to those that are boldly geometric and contemporary. By skillfully applying metallic leaf and bronzing powders, he adds illumination and contrast to the network of color, pattern and texture. His original designs include screens, wall panels, furniture and decorative objects.

Hayashi's pieces have been commissioned for private collections, hotels, restaurants and offices in the United States and Japan. Prices upon request.

Also see these GUILD sourcebooks:
THE GUILD: 3, 4, 5
Designer's: 6, 7, 8, 9, 10, 11, 12, 13, 14

A *Full Moon with Wisteria,* two panels, total size: 42" x 40"

B *Rising Moon,* three panels, total size: 46" x 72"

A

Photo by Ira D. Schrank

B

Photo by Ira D. Schrank

Steve Heimann

196 Stefanic Avenue
Elmwood Park, NJ 07407
TEL **201-797-5434**
E-Mail: **Heimann1@idt.net**
Web: **www.SteveHeimann.com**

The images in Steve Heimann's paintings are those he has worked with for the past several years. Like icons in their simplicity, his works employ few elements. He creates images which seek to engage the viewer into a feeling of resonance, much the way religious icons seek to elicit that response in believers.

Heimann's distinctive style is extended to an international audience through numerous commissions for postage stamps. Countries that have commissioned stamps include the British Virgin Islands, Grenada, Tanzania, Sierra Leone and Dominica, as well as the Antigua/Barbuda Postal Services. In 1999, seven paintings were featured in "Extreme Homes," a production of the Home & Garden Network. His work is also featured in the corporate collections of Ciba-Geigy Corporation and SmithKline Beecham.

A catalog is available upon request.

Keeper of the Code, 2000, oil on canvas, 12" x 16"

Contemplating the Intrinsic Value of a Stick, 1998, gouache on board, 10" x 8"

resents fine art

ejo Street #301
ancisco, CA 94123
415-567-5744
AX 415-563-2660
E-Mail: **info@jrepresents.com**
Web: **www.ericzener.com**

Eric Zener's figurative oil paintings reflect the meditative, introspective side of people.

Whether it is a woman diving in the water, laborers engaged in their work or a couple relaxing on a hillside, Zener paints the human form at its most vulnerable moments of joy, contemplation, serenity and determination.

Zener has exhibited his work nationally and internationally in Spain, Australia and Japan.

Selected collections and exhibitions include: Palm Springs Museum; Alfabia Museum, Japan; L'Escala, Spain; Walt Disney; Gap; Wellington Management; and Wyndham Hotels.

Commissioned paintings and limited-edition lithographs are also available.

Deep Spin, 1999, oil on canvas, 48" x 38"

Lovers on a Hill, 1999, oil on canvas, 52" x 54"

represents fine art

750 Vallejo Street #301
San Francisco, CA 94123
TEL 415-567-5744
FAX 415-563-2660
E-Mail: **info@jrepresents.com**
Web: **www.jrepresents.com**

Jrepresents is a private art dealer that promotes a diverse portfolio of contemporary fine artwork to individuals, designers and corporations.

Johannes Zacherl applies brilliant colors by creating palettes from his own pigments. Whether he paints an animal or a figure, the essence of the object can be found within the layers of his brush stroke.

James Leonard's contemporary abstract works are his expressions of self-fulfillment. Within layers of paint, forms appear between the shadows of light and dark.

Byron Spicer's stack paintings amass hundreds of individual paintings that are stacked and mounted onto one panel to create three-dimensional layers.

Eric Zener's contemporary figurative oils capture the most intimate moments of time. With the use of challenging compositions, highly characterized figures and rich color palettes, the soulfulness within his paintings emerges.

Bistrot, 1999, acrylic on canvas, 40" x 49", artist: Johannes Zacherl

The Prophet, 1999, acrylic on canvas, 60" x 60", artist: James Leonard

Squishy 439, 1998, acrylic on paper/wood, 48" x 60", artist: Byron Spicer

Night Diver, 1999, oil on canvas, 48" x 48", artist: Eric Zener

Michael L. Kungl

Michael L. Kungl Design
1656 Orange Avenue, Unit 3
Costa Mesa, CA 92627
TEL **949-631-2800**
FAX **949-631-9104**
E-Mail: **mike@mkungl.com**
Web: **www.mkungl.com**

"The beauty of great art is that it never tries too hard — that's the art of it."

Mike Kungl has been creating digital art since the birth of the Macintosh in 1984. His unique style and vivid palettes can be applied to a variety of modern and vintage themes for corporate, business and residential projects. Concepting and commissions are welcomed. Please visit his web site for additional samples and pricing, or contact him directly.

A *Cafe Nitro*, iris giclée, 22.5"W x 36"H

B *Fat City Cigar Lounge,* iris giclée, 24"W x 33"H

C *Lemon Drop Martini Bar*, iris giclée, 22.5"W x 36"H

A

B

C

Marie V. Mason

Works in Progress
1656 Madison
Kansas City, MO 64108
TEL 888-524-0258
TEL 816-842-5002
FAX 816-842-3771
E-Mail: bellamason@earthlink.net
Web: www.dogscatsart.com

Marie Mason was born in Ross, CA, and spent most of her formative years in the West. Since earning a bachelor's degree in fine art, Mason's work has been shown extensively on the West Coast and in the Kansas City area. Mason considers herself an expressionist painter, working primarily in acrylics on large canvases.

Mason's color palette is often vibrant, and much of her work incorporates the figure. She often seeks subjects to express the realm of her innermost personal experience. "People often tell me that my paintings visually express thoughts and feelings they have never found expression for before. I am heartened and grateful when people who admire my work recognize their own personal experiences reflected there, too."

Mason's art is available as traditional originals and also as limited-edition digital reproductions starting at $500. Commissions will be considered. Slides and additional information about the artist are available upon request.

A *Woman in Spring*, 1999, acrylic on canvas, 48" x 58"

B *Women's Circus Band*, acrylic on canvas, 48" x 58"

C *Red Dog*, 1999, acrylic on canvas, 58" x 48"

A

Photo by Charles Kay, Regency Photo

Photo by Scott Chapin

C

Photo by Scott Chapin

Marlene Lenker

Lenker Fine Arts
28 Northview Terrace
Cedar Grove, NJ 07009
TEL 973-239-8671
FAX 973-239-8671 *51

13 Crosstrees Hill Road
Essex, CT 06426
TEL 860-767-2098 (Studio)
E-Mail: lenkerart@prodigy.net
Web: www.guild.com

Marlene Lenker is an internationally recognized artist. Her landscapes have been collected worldwide by corporate and private clients. She paints in transparent and opaque layers, as well as mixed media. Her strokes and marks are a unique iconographic expression of subtle energy and bold spirit. She is listed in *Who's Who of American Artists, International Art, American Women* and *World Women*. Lenker is experienced in working with clients on special commissions both large and small. She welcomes inquiries.

Her work is represented in the following corporate collections: Arthur Young, PepsiCo, Vista Hotels, Kidder Peabody, Lever Bros., Hewlett-Packard, Ortho, Union Carbide, Prime Inc., Warner Lambert, Johnson & Johnson, Chubb Inc., Hoffman Laroche, Nasdaq, Pfizer and Swiss Aire.

Also see these GUILD sourcebooks:
Designer's: 10, 12, 13

Taos Spring, © 1999, 20" x 20"

Shoreside, © 1999, 30" x 48"

Barry Masteller

Claypoole-Freese Gallery
216 Grand Avenue
Pacific Grove, CA 93950
TEL 831-373-7179
FAX 831-373-1505

Barry Masteller's work has a living quality that touches the spirit. In the studio, he combines 35 years of experience with inspiration he finds as a witness to life's cycle of beginnings, endings and renewal. With a landscape as a reference, Masteller paints multiple layers and achieves a potent luminosity.

Masteller's work has been featured in extensive museum and gallery exhibitions and is owned by numerous museum, private and corporate collections around the world. He can be found in *Who's Who in American Art* and *New American Paintings, Volume 6.*

Color catalog $20. Additional information and visuals upon request.

A. *Time and Place 27*, 1997, oil on canvas, 18" x 18"

B. *Earth and Sky 99*, 1997, oil on canvas, 30" x 36"

A

B

Caroline Jasper

Caroline Jasper Studio
1113 Andreas Drive
Bel Air, MD 21015
TEL **410-838-4111**
FAX **410-838-4445**
E-Mail: **jasperinc@mindspring.com**
Web: **www.carolinejasper.com**

Caroline Jasper is a noted colorist whose original oil paintings are recognized for their halting use of light and shadow. Her evocative painterly scenes, whether landscape, water or architectural, are each prompted by an attraction to sunlight's luminous qualities.

Critically acclaimed in international juried competitions, Jasper also has had numerous solo exhibitions. Her works are in public and private collections across the country.

Commissions are welcome.

Slides and pricing information are available upon request.

A *Waken,* © 1999, oil, 18" x 24"

B *Sunbaked Shadows,* © 1999, oil, 24" x 18"

C *Pine Lines,* © 1999, oil, 30" x 40"

A
Photo by Daniel Whipps, Baltimore

B
Photo by Daniel Whipps, Baltimore

C
Photo by Daniel Whipps, Baltimore

Anne Marchand

Marchand Studio
1413 17th Street NW
Washington, DC 20036-6402
TEL 202-265-5882
FAX 202-265-0232
E-Mail: foster99@ix.netcom.com
Web: www.annemarchand.com

Anne Marchand's *Cityscapes* are lively representations of urban environments. Her use of vibrant color infuses her work with musical rhythms and energy.

Marchand's exhibitions include invitational, solo and juried shows.

Collections include: Allfirst, Baltimore, MD; IBM; Columbia Cellular; Centerstage Productions, VA; Alabama Power Co.; HealthSouth, AL; The Kennedy Center; Media One; US Trust, Washington, DC; and private collections.

Commissions, murals and completed works available. Inquiries are welcome.

Also see these GUILD sourcebooks:
Designer's: 13, 14

California Street NW, © 1999, oil on canvas, 38" x 50"

Photo by Greg Staley

Washington Spring, © 1999, oil on canvas, 36" x 48"

Photo by Greg Staley

Benjamin McCready

727 Center Street
Whitewater, WI 53190
TEL 888-473-7878
FAX 262-473-1977
E-Mail: mccready@idcnet.com
Web: www.benmccready.com

Benjamin McCready is one of the world's leading portrait painters. He has earned international acclaim for his stunning portraits of distinguished statesmen, corporate leaders and renowned educators. Four United States presidents have selected him for their portraits. He has more than 500 clients in 40 states and 17 countries. His paintings are featured in many of America's most renowned museums, government buildings and universities. The exceptional quality of his work, his impressive list of clients and an unsurpassed record of highly successful commissions puts him at the top of his profession.

Having a portrait painted by McCready is an exciting and rewarding experience, a special event you will cherish forever. Please call for a color brochure and complete information.

Patricia A. Reed

Patricia A. Reed Art
287 Laurel Avenue
Pacific Grove, CA 93950
TEL **831-372-2432**

Patricia Reed's oils on canvas bring an excitement to subjects that are often taken for granted.

A focus on a "farmers' market" theme has found an audience in many corporate and restaurant dining rooms. Additionally, Reed is creating a tandem body of work depicting — and painted for — hotel, restaurant and home interiors.

Slides, photos and price lists are available.

Corporate collections include:
Intel
Hewlett Packard
Union Bank
PGE
Nortel
GTE
Am-Gen Pharmaceuticals
Lockheed Martin

A *Room Service*, 60" x 36"

B *Farmers' Market*, 48" x 60"

A

B

James C. Nagle

James C. Nagle Fine Art
1136 E. Commonwealth Place
Chandler, AZ 85225
TEL **480-963-8195**
FAX **480-857-3188**
E-Mail: **extraice@msn.com**
Web: **www.jcnaglefineart.com**

For more than 25 years, James Nagle has worked as an artist, creating paintings and sculpture in a variety of mediums that are part of private, corporate and university collections worldwide. His work ranges from figurative to abstract, large to small.

In recent years, he has focused on dramatic stone sculpture and bold acrylic paintings, creating emotional imagery that explores the paradoxes of human strength and frailty.

Commissions and inquiries are welcomed.

Slides, brochures and prices are available upon request.

Also see this GUILD sourcebook:
Architect's: 15

Family Values, 1998, acrylic on canvas, 42" x 84"

Photo by Craig Smith

A Quiet Prelude, 1998, acrylic on canvas, 48" x 96"

Photo by Craig Smith

James C. Nagle

James C. Nagle Fine Art
1136 E. Commonwealth Place
Chandler, AZ 85225
TEL 480-963-8195
FAX 480-857-3188
E-Mail: extraice@msn.com
Web: www.jcnaglefineart.com

For Shame, acrylic on canvas, 66" x 54"   Photo by Craig Smith

Damsel of Dolor, acrylic on canvas, 60" x 48"   Photo by Craig Smith

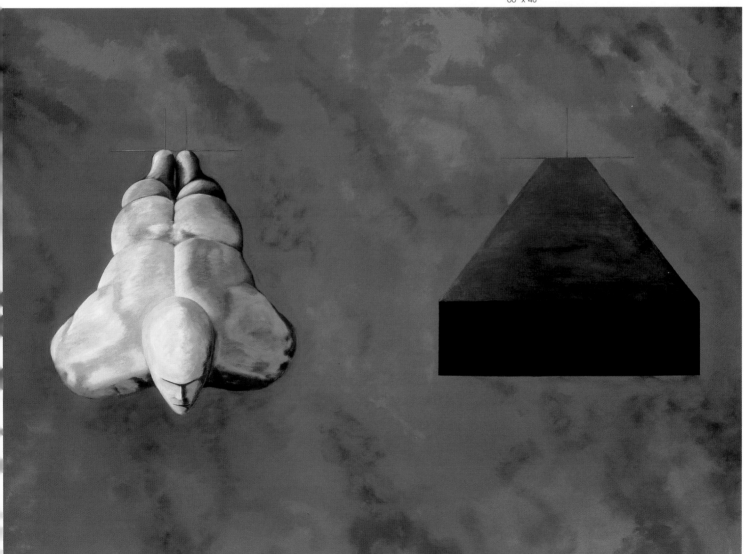

Finale, acrylic on canvas, 68" x 96"   Photo by Craig Smith

Marlies Merk Najaka

241 Central Park West
New York, NY 10024
TEL 212-580-0058
E-Mail: najaka@att.net
Web: www.watercolorart.com

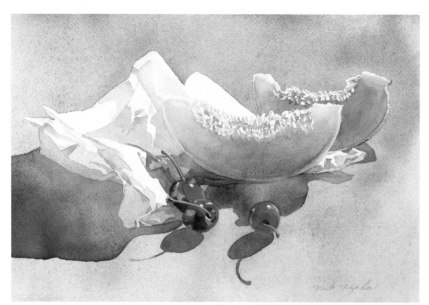

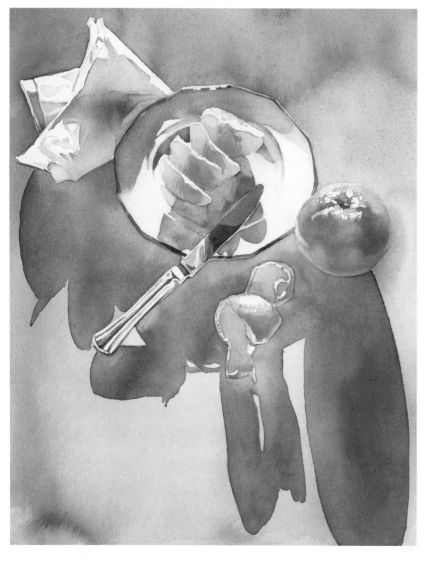

Marlies Merk Najaka

241 Central Park West
New York, NY 10024
TEL 212-580-0058
E-Mail: najaka@att.net
Web: www.watercolorart.com

"Marlies Merk Najaka explores the effects of light to create paintings that glow from within."

Her paintings are reproduced as limited-edition giclée prints on the same watercolor paper as the original painting. Each print is signed and numbered and has a certificate of authenticity.

Custom sizes and commissions are welcome.

Her work has been nationally exhibited and is included in corporate and private collections.

To view additional paintings and biographical information, please visit the artist's web site.

Brochure and price list are available upon request.

Also see this GUILD sourcebook:
Designer's: 14

Diane Petersen

Avatar, Inc.
225 Brush Road
Niles, MI 49120-9705
TEL 616-663-8710
FAX 616-663-3144
E-Mail: Diane@midwestcollection.com
Web: www.midwestcollection.com

"My art is about the significance of place; I seem to have been born with a need to record my life in this place."

Diane Petersen

Diane Petersen paints the beauty found in everyday objects and midwestern landscapes. Using impressionistic techniques, she paints evocative scenes about the significance of place. Light is brilliantly rendered in her work.

Petersen's critically recognized, award-winning artworks may be found in corporate and private collections throughout the world.

The artist welcomes commissioned work. Slides, pricing and scheduling upon request.

Also see this GUILD sourcebook:
Designer's: 14

Dayton Street: A Place, © 1999, transparent watercolor, 40" x 50"

Photo by Lighthouse Imaging, Mishawa, IN

Oxbow Summer, © 1999, transparent watercolor, 36" x 46"

Photo by Lighthouse Imaging, Mishawa, IN

Nancy Egol Nikkal

2 Dogwood Lane
enafly, NJ 07670
EL 201-568-0159
AX 201-568-0873
-Mail: nikkal@bellatlantic.net
Web: www.nikkal.com

ancy Egol Nikkal creates collages, paintings
nd prints with textured, layered surfaces and a
ophisticated color palette that includes muted
arthtone greens, beiges and smokey mauve
reys, as well as subtle to vibrant reds, blues,
ellows, rusts and browns.

Collages are paintings with hand-painted
apers. Paintings often include collage. Prints,
cluding unique and limited-edition monotypes,
ollographs, and Iris digital images from original
ides, also incorporate collage.

he artist exhibits nationally and internationally.
ides, resumé and a color catalog are available
pon request. Prices range from $800 to $5000.
Commissions are accepted.

lso see this GUILD sourcebook:
Designer's: 13

Talk Talk, collage and acrylic, 22" x 30"

Silence, collage and acrylic, 26" x 22"

A   Photo by John Ferrentino

B   Photo by John Ferrentino

Bob Russo

6332 North Hampton Drive NE
Atlanta, GA 30328
TEL **404-252-6394**

With 30 years of professional experience at the highest level, Bob Russo creates paintings that specifically enhance the purpose of a business or site on a foundation of authenticity, excellent design and workmanship.

Sample commissions include:
Executive lobby, Cox Enterprises, Inc., headquarters, 16' portrayal of Cox's role in society
Exhibit Center, U.S. Army Corps of Engineers, historical scenes, figures and an aerial view of the site
Entry areas, Atlanta Apparel Mart, 14' paintings signifying the type of clothing sold per floor
Nature signs, Callaway Gardens Foundation, indigenous plants, animals and topography
Business lobby, MAX Federal Credit Union headquarters, important regional sites, 60-figure, 50' mural of customers
State exhibit, Atlanta History Center, depiction of Georgia's natural and historical sites

Please call or write to discuss your project.

Red Rohall

6242 North Park Avenue
Indianapolis, IN 46220
TEL **317-254-8621**
E-Mail: **red_rohall@vtechworld.com**

Red Rohall paints classic and timeless scenes from urban landscapes. His realistic oil paintings are a fresh mix of intense color, crisp light and images of the unique and special.

Available completed works include paintings of Art Deco diners, vintage motels and funky road-side attractions. Rohall also welcomes commissions for painted "portraits" of commercial and residential buildings, such as the painting shown at the right, featuring a client's childhood home and cars.

A *A Good Start*, oil, 12" x 16"

B *Wympee*, oil, 18" x 24"

A

B

Koryn Rolstad Studios

COMMISSIONING AGENT: Joan Blackbourn Concepts in Art, Ltd.

DESCRIPTION: Atrium sculpture, 45'H x 120'L

SITE: Meriter Hospital atrium, Madison, WI

INTERIOR DESIGNER: Sharon Devonish, Devonish & Associates

After seeing the advertisement placed in GUILD Sourcebooks by Koryn Rolstad Studios/Bannerworks Inc., Joan Blackbourn of Concepts in Art, Ltd. contacted Koryn's studio to create a site-specific installation for Meriter Hospital in Madison, Wisconsin. The hospital had built a new Cardiac Care Center and was looking for a way to fill the open space in their new atrium, as well as create a peaceful, calming effect for the patients.

Impressed with the work she had seen in GUILD Sourcebooks, Joan Blackbourn sent KRS/Bannerworks Inc. a drawing of the area in question and asked the studio to develop concepts that could be presented to the hospital, as well as the hospital's interior designer, Sharon Devonish of Devonish & Associates.

KRS/Bannerworks Inc. devised a light and airy sculpture designed to complement the high ceilings and accent the natural light of the space. Long, narrow, sheer panels made in iridescent golds, purples, pinks, and blues were layered to evoke the image of light rays mixed with rain, and positioned to allow clear views of the architecture from many angles. Bird forms fabricated of metal, acrylic and holographic film were created to soar through the space, imparting a feeling of tranquility. The overall effect was one of beauty and serenity, and the ambiance of a natural setting enhanced the existing design of the atrium.

The Meriter Hospital atrium was received so well that it became a milestone for KRS/Bannerworks Inc. Since the project was installed in 1998, numerous companies and hospitals wanting similar artwork have approached the studio. Currently, KRS/Bannerworks Inc. is working on an installation of fabric sculptures displaying inspirational messages created for the Hope and Healing Center of the Church Health Center in Memphis, Tennessee.

— KR

E.A. Regensburg

Ed Regensburg
37 Willoughby Path
East Northport, NY 11731
TEL 631-493-0933
E-Mail: **eareg@systec.com**

Ed Regensburg, noted artist and art psychotherapist, paints ethereal atmospheres with celestial references that evoke a meditative response from the viewer. His channeled images are rendered in acrylic on both unprimed canvas and Arches paper, moving the viewer from states of fragmentation, stress and fear to gentler, more integrated realms of peace and well being.

Regensburg has numerous works included in private and corporate collections. Utilizing color and form to positively transform the environment and its people, he accepts a limited number of site-specific commissions each year.

Commissions welcomed; select giclée prints available.

A *Walk Between the Worlds,* acrylic polymers on Arches paper, 22"H x 30"W

B *Conference,* acrylic polymers on canvas, 32"H x 32"W

C *Second Son,* acrylic polymers on canvas, 32"H x 32"W

A

B

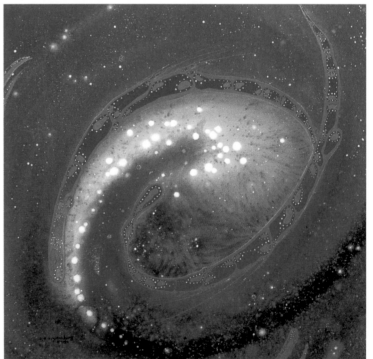
C

Kathy Stark

PO Box 905
Nantucket, MA 02554
TEL **508-228-7571**
TEL **508-228-6289**
FAX **508-325-6706**

Kathy Stark is a New York-born artist residing on Nantucket Island in Massachusetts. She has exhibited nationally and has been represented in New York, Boston and the Midwest. Her work is featured in numerous private and corporate collections throughout the United States.

Stark's personal and intuitive style combines an interplay and juxtaposition of color with a potent luminosity evoking rhythmic, modulating surfaces. Her paintings have been referred to as "color poems."

Commissions and site-specific projects are welcome.

A *Sitting Comfortably in the Now*, 41"H x 31"W

B *I Dreamed I Held Enchantment in the Palm of My Hand*, 44"H x 55"W

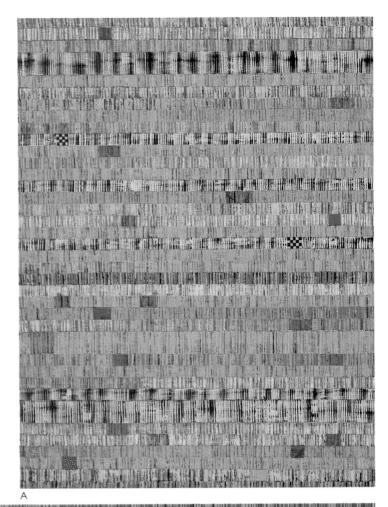

A

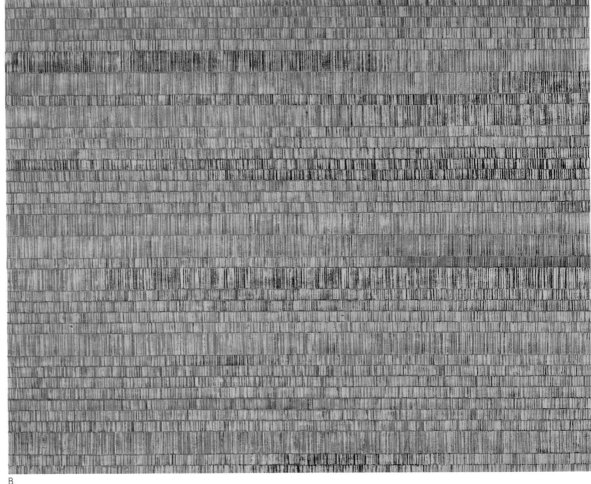

B

Susan Sculley

546 North Hermitage #2
Chicago, IL 60640
TEL 773-728-6109
FAX 773-728-9305
E-Mail: **sculley@ix.netcom.com**

Susan Sculley creates works that have the feel
of landscapes suffused with light. Stunning in
both contemporary and traditional settings, her
compositions of color and elusive form capture
the essence of the peace and beauty that one
experiences when communing with nature.

Sculley works in both oil sticks and pastels. She
has pieces in numerous private and corporate
collections, including those of Amoco Corporation
and Dean-Witter.

Commissions welcome; slides and prices
available upon request.

A *Pink Punch*, oil stick on canvas, 18" x 25"

B *October*, oil stick on canvas, 40" x 60"

A

Photo by Cynthia Howe

B

Photo by Cynthia Howe

Jane Sterrett

Jane Sterrett Studio
160 Fifth Avenue
New York, NY 10010
TEL **212-929-2566**
FAX **212-929-0924**
E-Mail: **sterjak@ix.netcom.com**
Web: **www.janesterrett.com**

Jane Sterrett's art is available as traditional originals and also as digital reproductions printed with archival inks on paper or canvas. Digital reproductions range from original size to large mural scale. These images are constructed as collages using her own photographs enhanced with paint and a variety of materials, including paper, cloth and bits of actual plant life. Commissions are accepted.

Her widely admired technique combines photographic imagery with mixed media and painterly effects to produce a unique and vibrant personal style that is strong in color and tactile values. Her art is versatile and adaptable to a variety of subject matters. It has been commissioned by both corporate and private clients and has been exhibited internationally. She has received numerous awards.

Jane Sterrett

Jane Sterrett Studio
160 Fifth Avenue
New York, NY 10010
TEL 212-929-2566
FAX 212-929-0924
E-Mail: sterjak@ix.netcom.com
Web: www.janesterrett.com

Jane Sterrett's art is available as traditional originals and also as digital reproductions printed with archival inks on paper or canvas. Digital reproductions range from original size to large mural scale. These images are constructed as collages using her own photographs enhanced with paint and a variety of materials, including paper, cloth and bits of actual plant life. Commissions are accepted.

Her widely admired technique combines photographic imagery with mixed media and painterly effects to produce a unique and vibrant personal style that is strong in color and tactile values. Her art is versatile and adaptable to a variety of subject matters. It has been commissioned by both corporate and private clients and has been exhibited internationally. She has received numerous awards.

Brian Stewart

5321 Xerxes Avenue South
Minneapolis, MN 55410
TEL 612-920-4653
E-Mail: trawetsb@aol.com
Web: www.stew-art.com

Brian Stewart paints scenes from industry in a traditional, representational, 19th-century style in oil on canvas for corporate and institutional environments. All paintings are executed from studies done on location *en plein aire* by the artist. Stewart is a signature member of the very exclusive Plein Air Painters of America and has works in private and corporate collections throughout the United States.

A *The North Shore,* oil on linen, Diversified Pharmaceutical, Minneapolis, MN, 66" x 96"

B *The Locks at Alma,* oil on canvas, 24" x 36"

C *The Dredger,* oil on canvas, 30" x 40"

A

B

C

Theresa Wanta

6 Dayton Avenue, Suite 003
Paul, MN 55102
TEL/FAX 651-298-9636

Theresa Wanta's oil paintings on canvas present figures, florals and fruit in a quiet, contemplative manner. They are classic compositions enlivened by painterly brushstrokes and warm color.

Wanta obtained her master's degree from The New York Academy of Art: Graduate School of Figurative Art. She also studied at the Art Student League of New York and received her bachelor of fine arts degree at University of Wisconsin-Stevens Point. She works with interior designers, gallery directors and art consultants.

Her work has been juried into exhibitions and is in private collections in the United States, including collections in New York, Sanibel Island, Boca Raton, New Orleans, Chicago, San Diego, Solana Beach and the Midwest. Her work is also collected abroad in London, Germany and Kuala Lumpur.

Slides are available upon request

Also see these GUILD sourcebooks:
Designer's: 13, 14

Peonies III, 14" x 18"

Candlelight, 72" x 48"

A

Photo by Jerry Mathiason Photography

B

Photo by Jerry Mathiason Photography

Barbara Zinkel

Barbara Zinkel Editions
333 Pilgrim
Birmingham, MI 48009
TEL **248-642-9789**
FAX **248-642-8374**

Barbara Zinkel, a longtime Michigan artist known for her dramatic use of color, creates limited-edition silkscreen prints for residential and corporate interiors. These silkscreen prints with saturated hues and graphic elements are complex in design, yet have a certain freedom and flow of movement. There is a balance of bright, clear colors and muted tones to create a harmony of color and a strong sense of dimension. Each print is hand pulled onto 100% acid-free two-ply rag paper in an edition limited to 250.

A *Sunrise,* silkscreen print, 30" x 30"

B *Midday,* silkscreen print, 30" x 30"

C *Sunset,* silkscreen print, 30" x 30"

D *New York at Noon,* silkscreen print, 60" x 40"

E *A San Francisco Night,* silkscreen print, 60" x 40"

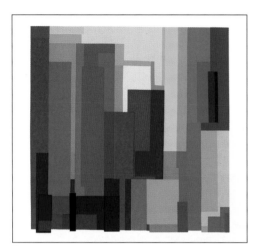

A

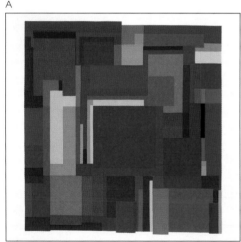

B

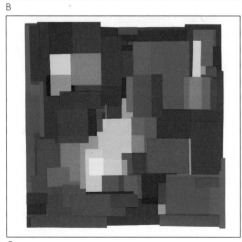

C

D

E

Barbara Zinkel

Barbara Zinkel Editions
333 Pilgrim
Birmingham, MI 48009
TEL 248-642-9789
FAX 248-642-8374

Selected collections include: Ford Motor
Company; DaimlerChrysler Corporation; CBS,
Inc.; Proctor and Gamble; Firestone Corporation;
Hilton Towers Hotel; Murdock Magazines; New
England Bell Telephone/AT&T; Texas Instruments;
and Vialle Autogas Systems, Son, The Netherlands.

A   *Wildwood*, silkscreen print, 32" x 38", edition of 250

B   *Wildwood*, silkscreen print (detail)

C   *Interlude*, silkscreen print, 39" x 44", edition of 250

A

B

C

JAN THOMPSON
Interior Designer

Houston interior designer Jan Thompson often works together with the architect, builder, client and artist from the very beginning of a project. This approach not only wins awards for the high-end residential projects that are her specialty, but also creates a close rapport between Jan and her clients. With this ideal in mind, Thompson, who is currently secretary of the Texas Association for Interior Design, has logged many miles traveling to galleries and showrooms with her clients to get a feel for what appeals to them.

"I have to say that the great advantage of THE GUILD for me is that it's such a great time saver. I can show clients an exceptional assortment of extremely high-quality work and ask what speaks to them. Furthermore, it's a real inspiration for me as a designer. It suggests creative ideas and combinations of materials I may not have seen before, or thought to use."

"GUILD artists are serious, professional, and in general just great to work with," she explains. "You don't need to worry about working over distance, because they're so

capable of handling details from beginning to end."

One of Thompson's favorite recent projects included the work of GUILD artist Elizabeth MacDonald of Bridgewater, Connecticut,

whose sophisticated, haunting tile murals suggest nature's erosion, the patinas of age and use, or the shifting patterns of clouds or smoke.

"We were working with one of my long-term clients, creating a study

in textures in her dining room. She wanted something for the walls with subtle, but vibrant, earth tones, something different from the oil paintings she had chosen for adjoining rooms."

Thompson sent MacDonald photographs of the space, along with dimensions and fabric samples.

"Elizabeth sent sample tiles and color renditions. It all went very smoothly. Within just a few weeks we had a design, and soon after, the tiles were shipped and installed. Her management of all the business details was just excellent. And most important, the work is beautiful, the client is very happy and I look forward to working with the artist again."

Photo by Gittings

"If an art consultant can't make recommendations for work that stands out, he or she is doing a disservice to the client."

DENISE RIPPINGER

Corporate Art Consultant

Chicago-area art consultant Denise Rippinger has built an enormously successful corporate practice in the last ten years. Her secret? Rippinger combines the sales and marketing savvy she learned while working in the highly competitive insurance business with her arts background and enduring contacts with many artists.

"I began with a handful of artist friends, the business contacts I had developed in my sales work, and a very aggressive, business-like attitude. Before I knew it, I'd outgrown my home office and had more business than I could handle," she explains. Today Rippinger juggles accounts from all over the world, employs 16 people, and works with dozens of artists, including many found through THE GUILD.

"I think THE GUILD is an incredible idea," Rippinger says. "Today, companies need to project a distinctive image that defines their corporate

identity; it helps them both do business, and attract business. Art, when it's distinctive and appropriate, is an important part of that environment. If an art consultant can't make recommendations for work that stands out, he or she is doing a disservice to the client. THE GUILD is a great resource for finding art that accommodates the needs of the client."

Recently, Rippinger's company purchased the corporate-art department of Chicago's Merrill Chase galleries, including a vast library of slides and other materials representing, literally, thousands of artists. "Even with this resource, we rely on THE GUILD," Rippinger maintains. "It's the easiest one-stop source for a huge variety of very capable artists."

Rippinger has commissioned work from a list of GUILD artists that reads like a *Who's Who* of fine North American craft: sculptor Joyce Lopez, ceramic muralist Tom Lollar, paper artist Karen Adachi, muralist Trina McNabb, and atrium sculptor Robert Pfitzenmeier, to name just a few.

"The artists I've worked with deserve all the credit in the world for their ability, creativity and patience," she says. "GUILD artists have the experience and the knowledge to help us avoid surprises and keep a project going smoothly. This is the key to their success."

Photo by Rich Malec

PHOTOGRAPHY

Rob Badger

33 Braun Court
Sausalito, CA 94965
TEL **415-339-1330**
Web: **www.robbadger.com**

For more than 30 years, Rob Badger has created images for a wide variety of clients and art buyers. His extensive collection of nature photographs (geographically and seasonally diverse) and abstracts range from dramatic, complex and colorful to soft and subtle.

Images (from 8" x 10" to murals) can be printed on a wide selection of surfaces, including iris prints on watercolor paper, vinyl wall coverings and banners, carpets and floor covering, and transparencies on Plexiglas for backlit light boxes and window adhesives.

Selected commissions/clients include: AT&T, Chevron, The Center for Russian Nature Conservation, DuPont, GM and Mercedes Benz.

Collections include: Kaiser Permanente, Santa Rosa, CA; Fawcett Corporate Art Collection, Tulsa, OK; Fireman's Fund Insurance, Novato, CA (22 prints); Mercy Retirement Center, Oakland, CA; Synopsis Corporation, Mountain View, CA; and Sierra Club Legal Defense Fund, San Francisco, CA.

Commissions welcomed.

Also see this GUILD sourcebook:
Designer's: 14

Rob Badger

33 Braun Court
Sausalito, CA 94965
TEL 415-339-1330
Web: www.robbadger.com

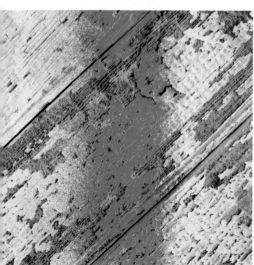

rtelstone

exico Fine Arts Gallery
Boulevard NW #162
M 87108
· ୨୦୦85
E-Mail: jan@photojan.com
Web: www.photojan.com

Museum-quality archival silver prints in limited editions. Large, detailed, luminous images for private or public areas. Original approaches to landscapes, surreal portraits and cultural statements.

Since 1984, Jan Bartelstone has owned an exclusive corporate fine art gallery, defining his art form to this venue.

Accurate laser reproduction tearsheets are available. Many unique images are available, and commissions are welcome as well.

A *The Worker*, 20" x 24"

B *First Wind*, 20" x 24"

C *The Dancer*, 18" x 36"

A

B

C

Paul Cary Goldberg

7R Hale Street
Rockport, MA 01966
TEL 978-546-7270

Using familiar objects and relating color, texture, form and space through light and the absence of light, Paul Cary Goldberg creates visual images with emotional depth and beauty.

Boston Globe art critic Cate McQuaid writes, "Paul Cary Goldberg is a standout."

Finished work is produced as iris prints. Dimensions can be modified on a per-print basis to meet specific needs, up to 44". Each image is limited to an edition of 30.

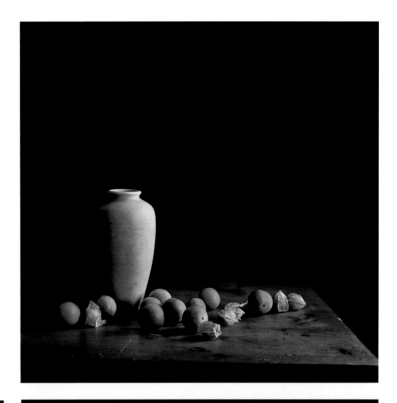

Allan Baillie

Studio 873, Inc.
40 Waterside Plaza, 29G
New York, NY 10010
TEL 212-685-9858
Web: **www.guild.com**

Allan Baillie photographs from nature and shows the details of our world close up. His work is graphic, and can be printed with a rich sepia tone.

Prints are in limited editions and signed on the verso. They can be made any size and combined in sequence for large spaces.

More samples and price information are available.

Work has been shown at the Fine Art and Photography Shows, New York, NY; The Katonah Museum of Art; The Baltimore Museum; and The Corcoran Gallery.

SHOWN: *Calla Lilly,* 1999, sepia-toned silver gelatin print on fiber paper, 11" x 14", limited edition of 25

Beyond Light
The Art of X-Rayography

Albert C. Koetsier
31721 St. Pierre Lane
Lake Elsinore, CA 92530
TEL 909-674-0207
FAX 909-674-0599
E-Mail: **ackoetsier@aol.com**

Albert Koetsier uses x-rays to make original images of nature's mysterious beauty. His images have been shown at exhibitions world-wide and numerous works are in private and corporate collections.

The images can be made in any size from 8" x 10" to approximately 40" x 50". Original images are in black and white and can be hand colored by the artist.

Scott M. Goldman

Scott M. Goldman Photography
3294 Glendon Avenue
Los Angeles, CA 90034
TEL   **310-441-9836**
FAX **310-474-5282**
E-Mail: **scottsyst@hotmail.com**

For 23 years, Scott Goldman has created abstract views that originate from elements and facades of existing structures. His subjects are often distanced from their original context so that they may inspire discoveries relating to form, line, shape and light.

Using films and archival papers that complement color and saturation, Goldman obtains a rich tonal depth and a keenly focused level of detail.

Constantly inspired by pattern and sculptural forms, his images leave the viewer to develop what the images only suggest.

Collected privately, his work is appropriate for any environment or space.

Ilfochrome and Fujiflex prints available in limited editions, measuring 11" x 14" and up. Samples and price information are available.

A *Old #7*

B *Americana #12*

C *Corpulence*

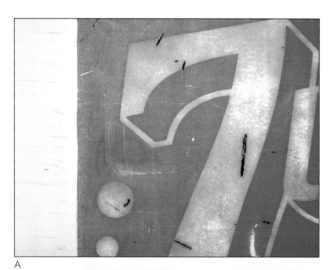

A

B

C

William Lesch

William Lesch Photography
26 South Otero Avenue
Tucson, AZ 85701
TEL 520-622-6693
FAX 520-622-0701
E-Mail: **coolie@theriver.com**
Web: **www.leschphotography.com**

For over two decades, William Lesch has been creating dramatic large-format color prints using his signature light-painting techniques. Working at night, he literally paints a scene with light, layering as many as 20 exposures into a single image.

Lesch typically works in extended series, including architectural and botanical studies, landscapes and cityscapes. He is particularly interested in commissions involving regional themes.

His work resides in over 200 corporate, museum and private collections worldwide.

Collections and commissions include: The Center for Creative Photography, Los Angeles County Museum of Art, Eli Lilly & Co., Dial Corporation, Coca-Cola of Japan and First National Bank of Denver.

Images can be printed in various sizes from 16" x 20" to 12 feet. All prints are limited edition; prices start at $500.

COMMISSION STORIES

15 years of GUILD commissions

Mark J. Levy

COMMISSIONING AGENT: Winterthur Museum

TITLE: *As the Path Narrows*

DESCRIPTION: Three-story front entryway, 10' x 34'

SITE: Winterthur Museum, Winterthur, DE

Our commission that resulted directly from GUILD Sourcebooks began with a phone call from the Winterthur Museum in Winterthur, Delaware. Their interior designer, Lucie Frederick, had seen our work and had some ideas for a client's home on the Atlantic Ocean in Avalon, New Jersey. Frederick flew out to California to visit our installations.

We were asked for five different schemes for the three-story front entryway, which encompasses 14 panels, rises 34 feet and is 10 feet wide. We based our concepts on the architects' design parti. One-of-a-kind, hand-ground ¾-inch thick optical prisms were integrated into the design. Each of the 19 prisms was different, and was based on the progression of the adjacent interior staircase. We made the decision to use only two textures of clear leaded glass so the ambient light would be enhanced, and not altered.

One unique aspect about this commission was the selection of a West Coast artist to do an East Coast project. If it hadn't been for the national reputation of the artists in GUILD Sourcebooks, we would not have been considered for this commission. The logistics and details involved with the successful crating and shipping of 14 panels of glass weighing 1,800 pounds from one coast to the other are monumental. As a result of this commission, it is safe to say that when it comes to the selection of art, distance has no bearing. GUILD Sourcebooks put us right where we needed to be.

The project took eight months, and came in under budget. We were retained for on-site installation supervision, which took five days. It was not until our last day that we met our clients. They were very pleased, and commissioned us for another piece for their home.

— ML

George Thomas Mendel

PO Box 13605
Pittsburgh, PA 15243
TEL 412-563-7918
Web: www.photo-now.com

George Thomas Mendel, a location/freelance and fine art photographer, has been working with the medium for more than 20 years. In this time, he has produced a verity of project portfolios which include architecture, waterscapes, still life and the human form.

Primarily working in black and white as an art form, limited-edition prints are produced by way of traditional fiber-based gelatin silver (cold or warm tone per request) or platinum/palladium processes.

His creative use of light and composition is matched by his master craftsmanship in the darkroom, producing the highest level of quality and archival stability. Project portfolios are available for view on his web site gallery, and commissioned project and documentation services are available by request.

Tulip Nevermore

Toronto Arches

San Francisco Museum of Modern Art

Jennifer Meranto

English Harbor
Antigua, West Indies
TEL/FAX **268-463-8035**
E-Mail: **merantoj@candw.ag**
Web: **www.yellowboat.com**

Jennifer Meranto is a fine art photographer based in the West Indies. Her archives hold spontaneous images of the natural Caribbean environment in black and white and color. Much of her rendered work is a fusion of old and new techniques, incorporating hand coloring and digital darkroom. Images are available as originals and high-quality prints on a wide range of paper choices and sizes. Her work hangs in many private homes and public places.

Call for a client list, catalog and pricing.

Talli Rosner-Kozuch

Pho-tal, Inc.
15 North Summit Street
Tenafly, NJ 07670
TEL 201-569-3199
FAX 201-569-3392
E-Mail: Talli@photal.com
Web: www.photal.com

Talli Rosner-Kozuch works in black and white, sepia tones, color, platinum prints, lithographs and etchings. Her areas of expertise include large-format photography. The images range in size, and vary in style from architectural portraiture and documentary through landscape to still life. Using signature techniques, she achieves a unique blend of minimalism and sensuality in her work.

Rosner-Kozuch has lived and exhibited in the United States, Europe and Asia. She is represented in several galleries and design centers, has been published worldwide and is also in the Polaroid collection. Her works are appropriate for any atmosphere or space.

Photographs are available in the following sizes: 8" x 10", 11" x 14", 16" x 20", 20" x 24", 24" x 30", 30" x 40", 40" x 50".

Also see these GUILD sourcebooks:
Designer's: 14

A *Male Sunflower,* 1997, color print from a unique Polaroid film

B *Tulips at Night,* 1998, photographed at night with candlelight, 20" x 24"

C *Female Sunflower,* 1997, color print from a unique Polaroid film

A

B

C

Joan Z. Rough

Fox Hollow Studios
560 Milford Road
Earlysville, VA 22936
TEL **804-973-9621**
FAX **804-973-6630**
E-Mail: **foxholo@aol.com**

Rich in intimate detail, Rough's photographs are meditations on the natural world, reminding us of our tiny place on a continuum ranging from microscopic organisms in a drop of water to the ocean of stars above our heads.

"... Rough displays a deep and happy knack for meaningfully exploring the distinction between the real and the imagined, the natural and the visionary... (She) wonderfully reimagines nature above and beyond itself even as she faithfully captures it in verdant stasis."

Gerrit Henry, contributing editor, *Art News*

Also see this GUILD sourcebook:
Designer's: 14

Ireland 1994: Landscape #4

Ecuador 1992: Cotopoxi #2

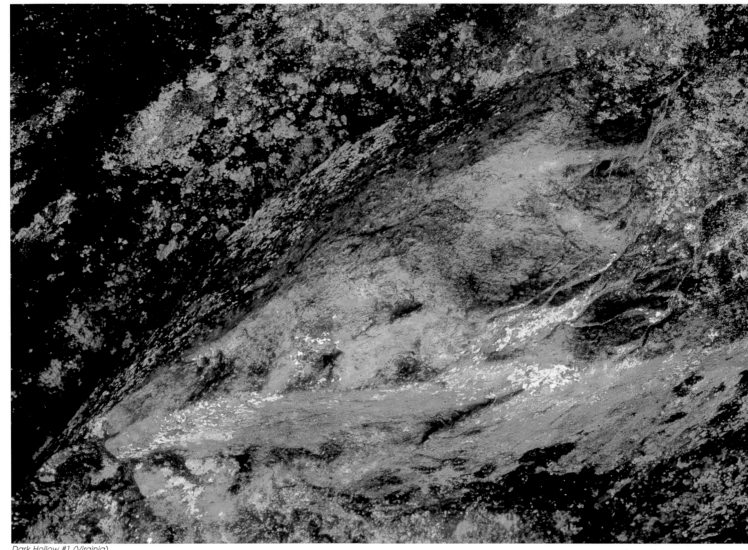
Dark Hollow #1 (Virginia)

Joan Z. Rough

ox Hollow Studios
60 Milford Road
arlysville, VA 22936
EL   804-973-9621
AX   804-973-6630
-Mail: **foxholo@aol.com**

igned Ilfochrome prints are limited to editions of
5, 11" x 14" and up.

Peony #11

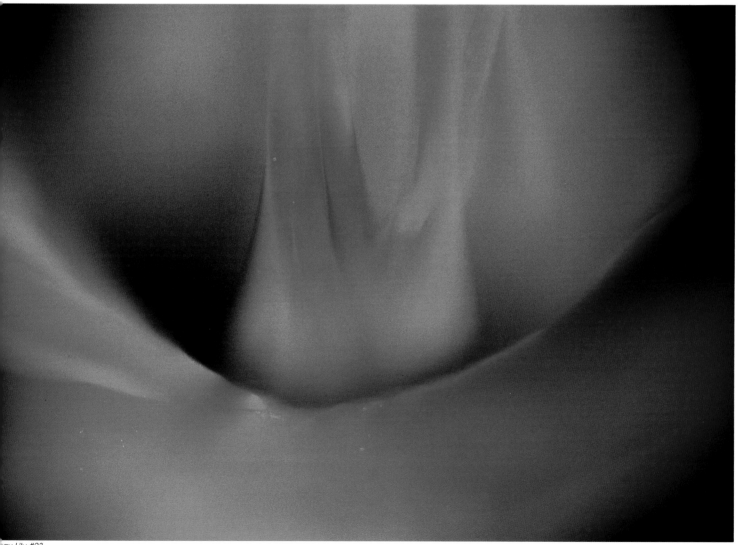

ay Lily #23

Thea Schrack

Thea Schrack Photography
80 Montcalm
San Francisco, CA 94110
TEL **415-647-1174**
FAX **415-647-1182**
E-Mail: **theaschrack@jps.net**

Thea Schrack is a photographer with a penchant for the past. Her photographic forays have taken her to English country estates and Czech castles in search of places with a sense of beauty and mystery. She is known internationally for her use of the panoramic format, subtle hand coloring and romantic vision. Her collection is now available as limited-edition Iris prints.

Series include: *Enchanted Gardens & Castles, Flowers, San Francisco, Wine Country and Pacific Coast.*

Catalog available upon request.

Michael A. Smith

Smith/Chamlee Photography
PO Box 400
Ottsville, PA 18942
TEL 610-847-2005
FAX 610-847-2373
E-Mail: michael@michaelasmith.com
Web: www.michaelasmith.com

For over 30 years, Michael A. Smith's distinctive vision has resulted in international recognition, including three books, one of which was awarded the prestigious *Le Grand Prix du Livre* at the International Festival of Photography in Arles, France, as well as numerous other awards and grants.

Smith's work is included in over 100 museum collections in the United States, Europe and Asia, including MOMA and the Metropolitan Museum of Art in New York; Art Institute of Chicago; Bibliothèque Nationale, Paris; Stedelijk Museum, Amsterdam; Victoria and Albert Museum, England; and the National

Museum of Modern Art, Kyoto, Japan. He has had over 200 exhibitions as well as four major commissions to photograph American cities.

He works with large view cameras: 8" x 10", 8" x 20" and 18" x 22". Thousands of exquisite black-and-white prints, many of which can be seen in books, are available as contact prints or as enlargements up to six feet long. Selected commissions accepted.

A *Canyon Del Muerto, Arizona*

B *Prague, Czech Republic*

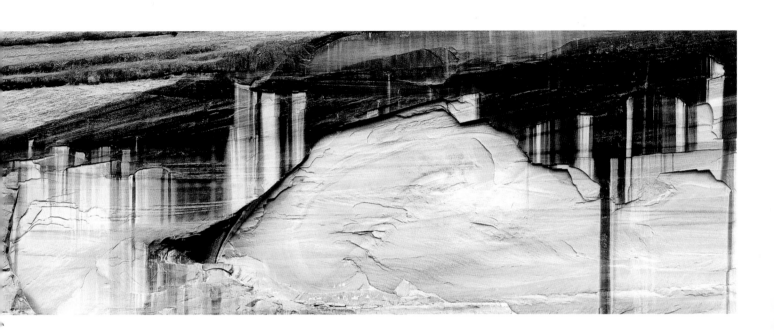

Dar Spain

PO Box 880
Arcata, CA 95518
TEL 707-839-1997
E-Mail: **agate@humboldt1.com**

For over 15 years, Dar Spain has worked in the hybrid medium of hand-colored photography to explore color, feeling and imagery. Starting with her own black-and-white photographs as a canvas, she uses photo oil colors, oil paint and colored pencil to create still lifes, studio compositions, architectural details and landscapes.

In addition to her extensive exhibition credits, her photographs are included in numerous private and corporate collections across the country.

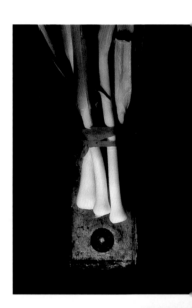

Julie Betts Testwuide

82 Underhill Avenue
Yorktown Heights, NY 10598
TEL 914-962-5096
FAX 914-962-9655
E-Mail: jbt@juliearts.com
Web: www.juliearts.com

Julie Betts Testwuide is known both for her evocative color images that are a mixture of photography and painting as well as for her black-and-white fine art photographic prints.

Her black-and-white work includes landscapes, portraiture and her latest passion, porches, represented in the series *American Porch Life*.

Her color images are captured on film and printed on watercolor paper. She then uses a unique method with pastels, pencils and paints to transform them into what she refers to as "painterly photographs." Testwuide creates works of art that are delicately detailed and saturated with the light and mood reminiscent of an impressionist painting. Whether the scene has been captured in the United States or Europe, her images are timeless and focus on simple beauty.

Testwuide has won numerous awards. Her work has been widely published, exhibited in galleries and appears in many private collections.

A selection of her artwork can be viewed and purchased on her web site at www.juliearts.com.

Also see this GUILD sourcebook:
Designer's: 14

Yvonne Viner

y's eye
3568 Wesley Street
Culver City, CA 90232
TEL   **310-299-6048**
FAX   **310-841-0688**
E-Mail: **yseye1@earthlink.net**

The kaleidoscopic images found within Yvonne Viner's extreme close-ups of quartz crystals are demonstrative of the artist's love of vibrant color and light refraction, as well as her joy in discovering the worlds which exist within tiny shards of Earth's most common mineral.

Prints are available in sizes from 5" x 7" and up, and are on Ilfochrome (Cibachrome) archival material in signed limited editions. Backlit installations also are available. Please contact the artist for pricing and other information.

Also see this GUILD sourcebook:
Designer's: 14

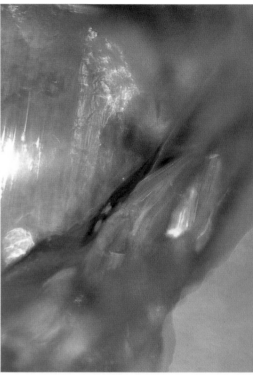

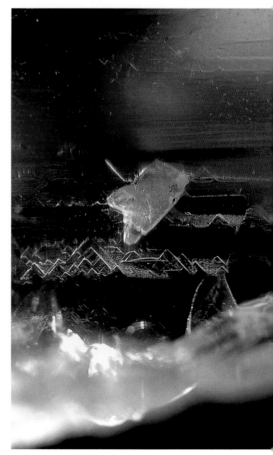

Shevaun Williams

Shevaun Williams & Associates Commercial
  Photography, Inc.
21 East Main Street
Norman, OK 73069
TEL 405-329-6455
E-Mail: shevaun@telepath.com
Web: www.shevaunwilliams.com

After over 20 years of experience in commercial and fine art photography, Shevaun Williams has developed a signature style. Her investigations of abstract forms yield timeless images from unique points of view. She takes familiar objects and structures and gives them dramatic new life through innovative compositions, interesting textures and light.

Work is available in a variety of sizes and subject matter, featuring locations throughout the United States and abroad. The artist accepts special assignments and commissions.

Other examples of Williams' black-and-white infrared images as well as color selections are available by contacting the artist.

A *Ushiku Daibutsa, Japan*

B *Blenheim Palace, Great Britain*

C *Atlanta, Georgia*

B

A

C

Nita Winter

Nita Winter Photography
33 Braun Court
Sausalito, CA 94965
TEL 415-339-1310
Web: www.nitawinter.com

For more than 20 years, Nita Winter has been creating photographs for hundreds of clients and art buyers. Her unique images have helped art consultants and interior designers create the desired mood for a new environment, or enhanced and beautified existing interior and exterior spaces.

Her extensive collection of photographs clearly and emotionally portrays the spirit and diversity of America's adults, teens and children.

Commissions include:
Marin Arts Council Community Art Project, CA
Children's Defense Fund, Washington, DC
Utah Arts Council, Children's Special Needs Clinic
Kaiser Permanente, CA and TX
Bronson Hospital, Kalamazoo, MI
Mercy Retirement Center, Oakland, CA
WestEd, San Francisco and Los Angeles

Images are available in black and white, color and hand colored. Photographs can be printed on a variety of surfaces, including iris prints on watercolor paper (up to 30" x 40"), vinyl wall coverings or banners, ceramic tiles, floor and window adhesives and Plexiglas for backlit boxes or cutouts. Images are available in 8" x 10" to mural size. New commissions and assignments are welcomed; additional samples available upon request.

Also see this GUILD sourcebook:
Designer's: 14

Nita Winter

Nita Winter Photography
33 Braun Court
Sausalito, CA 94965
TEL 415-339-1310
Web: www.nitawinter.com

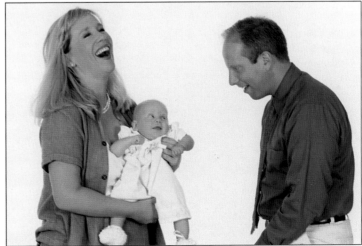

I was contacted by Sarah Hall at Soho Myriad Gallery in Atlanta, Georgia, when she saw my ad in *The Designer's Sourcebook 14*. The image that caught her eye was a scene of a girl on the beach on the Riviera. Sarah was working with the design firm Hirsch Bender & Associates, which was selecting and commissioning artwork for a new Marriott Hotel in Tampa, Florida. After reviewing additional images of my work, they commissioned four pieces.

I start my process by capturing images on film, manipulating the images, and printing them on watercolor paper. I then use pastels and pencils to transform them into "painterly photographs." I create pieces that are delicately detailed and saturated with the light and mood of an impressionist painting.

The four pieces that were chosen include a 20" x 20" print of an antique automobile surrounded by palm trees (for the men's lounge); a 30" x 30" print of a pink rose and floral diary (for the spa); and two 8" x 8" prints (both for the women's lounge) — one of a child in a colorful sundress on the French Riviera and one of a flower-lined street and vineyards.

This commission is important to me since this is exactly the market I had hoped to reach through my ad in GUILD Sourcebooks. It is the first time I have advertised in a sourcebook, and I am getting calls from private collectors, art buyers and galleries that are leading to sales and wider exposure of my work.

The installation was completed in February 2000. The Marriott plans to publish a book about the artists and artworks exhibited at the hotel.

— JBT

Julie Betts Testwuide

COMMISSIONING AGENT: Soho Myriad Gallery and Hirsch Bender & Associates

DESCRIPTION: Four iris prints: *South Beach Miami* (shown); *LeGrande, Paris*; *Mandelieu, France*; and *Bordeaux, France*

SITE: Marriott Hotel, Tampa, FL

Allan Bruce Zee

Allan Bruce Zee Fine Art Photography
240 Southeast 24th Avenue
Portland, OR 97214
TEL 503-234-3211
FAX 503-236-2973
E-Mail: zeebliss@spiritone.com
Web: www.allanbrucezee.com

For 30 years, his unique vision, painterly approach, impeccable printing technique and extraordinary range of imagery have contributed to the enthusiastic response nationally and abroad to the photography of Allan Bruce Zee. Prominent private and corporate collections include IBM, AT&T, Merrill Lynch, Sloan Kettering Hospitals and World Bank.

Examples of imagery include interpretive landscape; abstract textures and "rustscapes"; international travel; and oriental, impressionistic and architectural motifs.

Print sizes range from 10" x 14" up to 40" x 60".

Slide or color copy portfolio available on request.

Also see this GUILD sourcebook:
Designer's: 14

The Yellow Roses of Burano, Burano, Italy

Eucalyptus Tree Bark, Maui, Hawaii

The Road Less Travelled, rusting Datsun pick-up, Bandon, Oregon

Old Town, Lisboa, Portugal

"When art is carefully integrated into a project, it can serve as a highly visible and very effective selling point."

JIM CARLEY
Developer

Art in public spaces too often becomes a lightening rod for criticism and controversy. But when art is carefully integrated into a project, it can serve as a highly visible and very effective selling point. Such was the experience of Jim Carley, chair of the commission created to build an expanded exposition center for Dane County, Wisconsin. The space incorporates two works on a grand scale by artists found through THE GUILD.

For the large lobby and mezzanine area, artist Michele Oka Doner has created a terrazzo floor incorporating more than 1,000 bronze castings, each reflecting some aspect of the county's history. Cork Marcheschi's 600-linear-foot neon sculpture brings the center's lobby to life with an ever-changing sequence of moving lights.

Carley describes the process of working with both artists as "a wonderful experience. They are professionals in their art and our architects were thoroughly impressed." So, too, were prospective users of the meeting facility. One exhibitor was so excited by the work-in-progress that he actually made a significant contribution toward funding the art work. Another brought his stockholders together in the unfinished space for their annual meeting.

Naturally, this kind of enthusiasm and support is extremely satisfying to Carley, a strong supporter of the arts, both private and public.

For the Dane County project, a selection committee sifted through a list of more than 200 artists. Nine finalists were asked to submit site-specific proposals, for which they were paid. Carley believes that having a knowledgeable selection committee and a rigorous selection process greatly aided public support for the work. Despite the scale and the highly visible nature of the art, there has been only enthusiastic support from county officials, exhibitors and the public.

Carley's advice to other developers is to build broad support for art early on and to choose work that fits the project. "If appropriate art is chosen," he says, "it can't help but sell the building."

Artwork by Jerome Ferretti

"I really believe the decision to use original art in a design can make or break a project."

CARY FERNANDEZ

Interior Designer

Designer Cary Fernandez believes the right original artwork can be the element that lifts a design from 'attractive' to truly exceptional. "I really believe the decision to use original art in a design can make or break a project," she says.

A designer with the Diane Joyce Design Group in Miami, Florida, she and 15 other architects and interior designers plan space for both corporate clients and individuals. "We do a great deal of design for the hospitality industry—hotels, resorts and restaurants, as well as high-end residential work," she explains. Her firm, she adds, is always seeking particularly unique and exciting design solutions for customers that include Disney and the Sandals Resorts located throughout the Caribbean.

A recent project that was especially successful used architectural glass designed by Kenneth vonRoenn of Architectural Glass Art, Inc. (AGA). Trained as an architect himself, and with a wealth of experience in creating and installing very significant architectural elements in major projects, vonRoenn has precisely the skills and creative sensibilities Fernandez was seeking when she began the design for a Japanese restaurant at the Sandals Resort in Antigua. "I couldn't find what I wanted from artists in our local area," she recalls, "so I turned to THE GUILD, and was immediately struck by Ken vonRoenn's work. I called him up and discussed what we had in mind via phone and FAX. The presentation we got from AGA was fantastic—and incredibly professional. The glass samples were unbelievably beautiful and exciting, and the photographs of his completed projects were thoroughly impressive.

"Ken created wood-framed glass screens for our space and they are very, very important elements in the architectural design. He was wonderful to work with from day one, and a real source of inspiration for our team. The restaurant is fabulous, the client is ecstatic and, needless to say, we're thrilled."

Photo by Elizabeth Cerejido

ART FOR THE WALL: CERAMICS

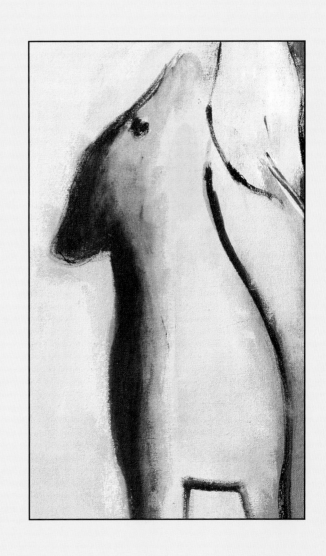

Mary Lou Alberetti

Alberetti Studios
16 Possum Drive
New Fairfield, CT 06812
TEL **203-746-1321**
E-Mail: **MLALB@aol.com**
Web: **www.southernct.edu/~alberett/**

Textural clay layers are hand carved into Italian-inspired architectural reliefs, evoking an aura of timelessness and antiquity. Completed units, 15" to 25", single or combined, are wired for easy installation. Commissions are welcomed.

Alberetti works with art consultants and galleries. She is represented in private, corporate and civic collections, including the City of New Haven, CT; HBO World Headquarters, New York City; and GE World Headquarters, CT.

Also see this GUILD sourcebook:
Designer's: 14

A *Modena,* 22"H x 16"W x 2"D

B *Parma,* 22"H x 16"W x 2"D

C *Petra II,* 17"H x 24"W x 2"D

A   Photo by Leo Philippe

B   Photo by Leo Philippe

C   Photo by Leo Philippe

Architectural Ceramics

Elle Terry Leonard
1958 Adams Lane
Sarasota, FL 34236
TEL 941-952-0463
FAX 941-954-1721
E-Mail: elle@archceramics.com
Web: www.archceramics.com

Architectural Ceramics specializes in site-specific commissions in clay, marble and glass for corporate and residential clients. Studio specialties include murals, mosaics and furnishings as well as a line of handmade tile.

Complete studio services range from concept and consultation to production, shipping and installation. Installations are suitable for both interior and exterior spaces.

Samples, portfolio and prices available upon request.

Clients include:
Tampa International Airport
Arvida Corporation
Chamber of Commerce, Sarasota, FL
City of Venice, FL
Barnett Bank NA
Polo Grill, Palm Beach Gardens
Worldgate Marriott Hotels
Kaiser Permanente
Johns Hopkins Hospital

Also see these GUILD sourcebooks:
THE GUILD: 1, 2, 3, 4, 5
Designer's: 6, 13, 14
Architect's: 8, 9, 10, 11, 12, 13, 14

SHOWN: Ceramic mirror and table, mirror: 28"W x 36"H, table: 36"H x 15"W x 42"L

Joan Rothchild Hardin

Joan Rothchild Hardin Ceramics
393 West Broadway #4
New York, NY 10012
TEL **212-966-9433**
TEL/FAX **212-431-9196 (Studio)**
E-Mail: **joan@hardintiles.com**
Web: **www.hardintiles.com**

Drawing on 30 years of experience as a ceramic artist, Joan Rothchild Hardin creates witty and sophisticated custom art tiles. Designs can be developed for almost any location where beauty and durability are desired — installations such as murals, friezes and back splashes or framed tiles hung as paintings. These art tiles are hand painted on commercial blanks, facilitating installation by ensuring standard sizes. Hardin enjoys collaborating with clients to design work meeting their aesthetic and budgetary needs.

Recent awards, clients and collections include:
Architecture Award, fourth annual Silverhawk
    Fine Craft Competition
Battery Park Veterinary Hospital, New York, NY
American Art Clay Company, Indianapolis, IN
al benessere aromatherapy products,
    New York, NY
Private residences, New York and California

Also see this GUILD sourcebook:
Designer's: 14

Tiles for a New York City veterinary clinic installation

Photo by Erik S. Lieber

Woman Dressing, terra cotta tile, 11.75" x 7.88"

Photo by Erik S. Lieber

Nancy Heller

Design Originals
101 Melvin Drive
Highland Park, IL 60035
TEL 847-432-8644
TEL 847-226-5062
E-Mail: nheller@aol.com

Award-winning artist Nancy Heller combines extraordinary talent with a master's degree in ceramic chemistry. Her work is expressive yet realistic and ranges from wall murals in relief to large and small woven vessels.

She has more than 30 years of experience and her work currently appears in corporate offices and galleries throughout the country. Her pieces are actively sought by interior designers and private collectors.

Heller is open to commissions of all sizes, and she works closely with clients to accommodate specific needs.

Also see this GUILD sourcebook:
Designer's: 6

A. *The Kiss,* adaptation into clay of Gustav Klimt's *The Kiss,* private collection, ceramic tile, 43" x 42" x 2"

B. *Flowers of the Sun,* ceramic mural in relief, 22" x 22" x 2"

C. *Spring Bouquet,* ceramic mural in relief, 24" x 24" x 2"

A

B

C

Claudia Hollister

PMB 158
333 South State Street, Suite V
Lake Oswego, OR 97034-3691
TEL 503-636-6684
FAX 503-226-0429

Utilizing hand-built colored porcelain, Claudia Hollister creates site-specific architectural wall pieces for public, corporate and residential environments. Highly textured and richly colored, Hollister sets her work apart by combining the intricate techniques of inlaying, embossing and hand carving three-dimensional elements on tiles.

Recent commissions include:
Air Pax, Indianapolis, IN
Beth-El Zedeck Synagogue, Indianapolis, IN
Longmont United Hospital, Longmont, CO
Marriott Hotel, Denver, CO
Upper Chesapeake Medical Center, Belair, MD

Also see these GUILD sourcebooks:
Designer's: 8, 11, 13, 14

A General Instrument cafe, Horsham, PA, center section, 3' x 6'

B Kelsey Seybold Medical Center cafe (detail), Houston, TX, 9" sq.

C Kelsey Seybold Medical Center cafe, Houston, TX, detail of installation on 25' curved wall

A

Photo by Jerome Lukowi

B

Photo by Joe Aker

C

Photo by Joe Ake

Margie Hughto

0 Henderson Road
nesville, NY 13078
315-469-8775

Margie Hughto is nationally recognized for her ceramic paintings, collages and tiles. These elegant wall reliefs and tiles are made of stoneware clays, slips and glazes, and are constructed of beautifully colored and textured elements. The works range in size from small intimate pieces up to installations of architectural scale suitable for public, corporate and residential environments. Commissions are welcome. Prices, slides and further information are furnished upon request.

Works are represented in numerous museum, corporate and private collections including the Museum of Fine Arts, Boston, MA; Everson Museum, Syracuse, NY; IBM; Kodak; Mayo Clinic; Summerlin Casino, Las Vegas, NV; and the Cortland Street and 81st Street MTA subway stations, New York, NY.

A Ceramic wall relief installation, private residence, Arizona

B Ceramic wall relief, 32"H x 50"W

C *Golden Threads,* three large wall tiles, private collection, each: 41"H x 19"W

B

Elizabeth MacDonald

PO Box 186
Bridgewater, CT 06752
TEL 860-354-0594
FAX 860-350-4052
E-Mail: **epmacd@aol.com**

Elizabeth MacDonald describes her work in clay as "part architecture, part sculpture and part painting." Her mosaic-like creations, comprised of dozens of hand-formed, textured tiles that evoke images of land, sea and sky, have been aptly termed "ceramic canvases" by one reviewer.

MacDonald's works have been exhibited extensively throughout the United States and internationally, and are held in dozens of private, corporate and museum collections. Her stoneware creations grace the walls of hotels in Tokyo and Hong Kong, a hospital in Denver, an arts center in Arizona, and corporate offices from New York to California. In Connecticut, her work can be seen at the Hartford Courant, Pitney Bowes, Aetna Life Insurance, US Trust, and Norelco, among other locations.

Also see these GUILD sourcebooks:
THE GUILD: 1, 2, 3, 4, 5
Designer's: 6, 7, 8, 9, 10, 11, 12, 13, 14
Architect's: 6, 7, 8, 9, 10, 11, 12, 13, 14, 15

A Earthenware with slip in relief, 1999, 32.5" x 32.5"

B Earthenware with slip in relief (detail)

C Earthenware with stain (detail)

D Earthenware with stain, 1999, 39" x 78"

A
Photo by Bob Rush

B
Photo by Bob Rush

C
Photo by Bob Rush

D
Photo by Bob Rush

E. Joseph McCarthy

Custom Tile Studio
76 Hope Street, Suite B2
Greenfield, MA 01301-3515
TEL **413-772-8816**
FAX **413-772-8811**
E-Mail: **cts@crocker.com**
Web: **www.crocker.com/~cts**

E. Joseph McCarthy and his staff have been designing and executing fine ceramic tile environments for over 20 years.

Specializing in large-scale murals, they custom design each piece to fit into the decor and configurations of a specific location.

From representational to abstract, McCarthy's work encompasses a variety of styles and imagery.

Commissions include:
Tampa International Airport, FL
Merck and Company, NJ
Edsel B. Ford Center, MI
Valley Children's Hospital, CA
Kahalan Madarin Orient Hotel, HI
Celebrity Cruise Line, FL

Also see these GUILD sourcebooks:
THE GUILD: 5
Designer's: 7, 11, 13, 14
Architect's: 9, 10, 12, 13, 15

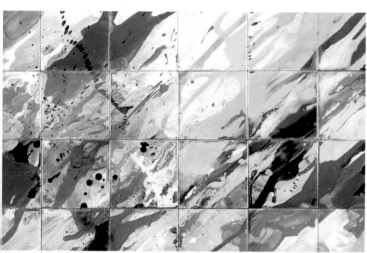

Abstract Blue, 22" x 32" Photo by André Banville

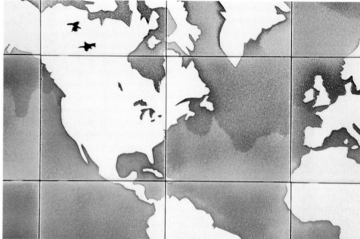

Etched World, 12" x 16" Photo by André Banville

Abstract terra cotta tiles, 18" x 25" Photo by André Banville

Carolyn Payne

Payne Creations Tile
4829 North Antioch
Kansas City, MO 64119
TEL **800-880-8660**
TEL **816-452-8660**
FAX **816-452-0070**
E-Mail: **golftile@swbell.net**
Web: **www.paynecreations.com**

Since 1984, Carolyn Payne, M.A., owner of Payne Creations Tile, has been known for using manufactured tile as her canvas. Designers respect her creativity and ability to customize her work specifically for their projects. Her work is easily incorporated into residential, commercial and public works.

Payne has a unique style of applying layers of ceramic glaze to achieve richly-textured art.

Her expansive repertoire, designed for interior and exterior applications, includes ceramic murals, signage, fountains, historic landmarks and donor recognition walls. Her tiles can be installed permanently or on removable panels.

SHOWN: Murals created for Harrah's, East Chicago, IN

A Restaurant entrace mural (detail), 6" tile

B Fresh Market International Cafe entrance mural,
    4' x 5'

A

Photo by Ken Sco

B

Photo by Ken Sco

Carolyn Payne

Payne Creations Tile
4629 North Antioch
Kansas City, MO 64119
TEL 800-880-8660
TEL 816-452-8660
FAX 816-452-0070
E-Mail: golftile@swbell.net
Web: www.paynecreations.com

Commissions include:
Harrah's Casino, East Chicago, IN
Park University, Parkville, MO
University of Kansas, Lawrence, KS
Lehigh University, Bethlehem, PA
J.C. Nichols Co., Country Club Plaza,
 Kansas City, MO
Wesleyan College, La Quinta Preservation
 Foundation, Bartlesville, OK

Also see these GUILD sourcebooks:
Designer's: 11, 12, 14

A Chicago market (detail), 6" tile

   Buffet area, Chicago market theme, 6' x 3.5'

Photo by Ken Scott

Photo by Ken Scott

Laura Shprentz

Spiral Studios
168 Irving Avenue #400E
Port Chester, NY 10573
TEL/FAX 914-939-6639
E-Mail: lshprentz@erols.com
Web: www.erols.com/lshprentz

Laura Shprentz's tile work blends ancient methods with a contemporary view of historic themes. The artist's tiles have carved surfaces and high relief combined with opalescent glazes. Glazes vary with every firing, making each tile unique. Mosaic elements are incorporated into some pieces, further enhancing their special character.

The artist has had extensive experience working with clients and enjoys collaborative projects. Her commission work explores the "art of the tile" while balancing the pragmatic needs of client and job. A portfolio is available upon request.

Also see this GUILD sourcebook:
Designer's: 12

Small Portal #3, handmade tile, mirror mosaic, altered frame, 9"W x 10"H x 2"D   Photo by D. James Dee

Celtic Flatfish, framed tile panel, 24"W x 18"H x .5"D   Photo by D. James Dee

Castle Arch, framed tile panel, 16"W x 8"H x .5"D   Photo by D. James Dee

Nicho, tiled niche, Santa Fe, NM, 29"W x 34.5"H x 4.5"D   Photo by Kevin Murphy

Maria Simon

5831 SE Belmont Avenue
Portland, OR 97215
TEL **503-235-9403**

Maria Simon uses elements of light and shadow, texture, color, gesture and movement in natural landscapes to evoke a sense of place and to resonate with the inner human "landscape."

Her unique process with carved terra cotta imparts both sculptural and painterly qualities. Each ceramic bas-relief is recessed into a painted wooden field and framed in light wood. Limited-edition bronzes, currently in progress, invite the possibility of larger-scale works.

In corporate and residential settings, Simon's pieces create a tone that is at once inviting and thought provoking. Her work is included in private and corporate collections throughout the country.

Commissions are welcomed; scale is negotiable. Slide portfolio and pricing available upon request.

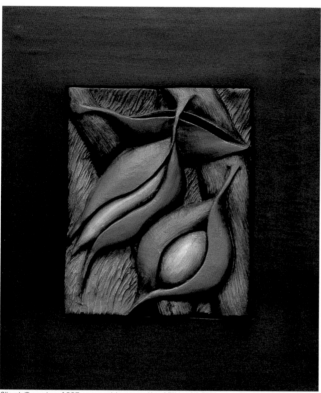

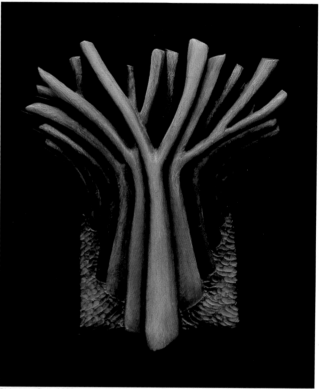

Silent Opening, 1997, carved terra cotta, 17"H x 14.5"W x 1.5"D   Photo by Bill Bachhuber

Rising as One, 1998, carved terra cotta, 28"H x 19"W x 1.75"D   Photo by Bill Bachhuber

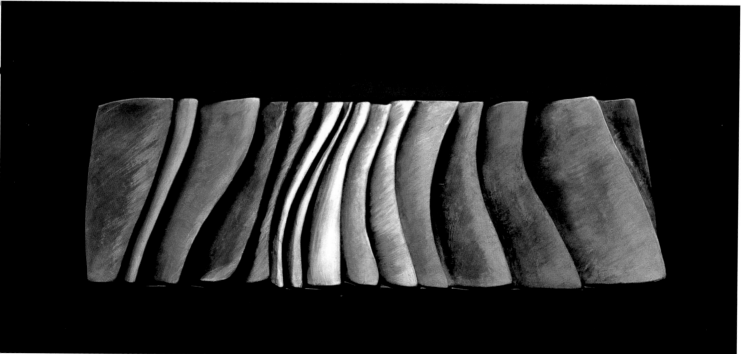

Breathing: Lesson I, 1999, carved terra cotta, 17"H x 38"W x 1.75"D   Photo by Bill Bachhuber

"It's like having an exhibit in our office!"

JUDITH LEPOW
ELAINE GALMAN

Corporate Art Advisors

With almost 20 years of experience as corporate-art advisers based in the Philadelphia area, Judith Lepow and Elaine Galman have had the pleasure of seeing many of the collections they helped build grow in value and stature with the passing years.

Galman Lepow Associates (GLA) provides a complete art service for its clients, with a great many contacts among both established and emerging artists. "THE GUILD is a wonderful resource for us," says Judith Lepow. "It's like having an exhibit in our office! It gives us a very successful way to find fine new artists throughout the country and the world."

Fiber artist Janet Kuemmerlein, who helped GLA solve an especially complex design challenge, is a case in point. When Dupont built a new world headquarters for its Textile Fibers Division, Galman Lepow Associates managed the project, including one highly unusual commission. For the focal area of an atrium space, the client wanted to use a work of art that would incorporate over 50 types of fiber, all created by Dupont.

"We found Janet through THE GUILD, and were intrigued with her bundling and stitching

technique worked on the surface of the fabric," says Judith Lepow. "She flew into Philadelphia from Kansas, met with everyone and contacted all of the divisions she needed to work with to obtain fibers for the project. The finished work exceeded expectations and she was there for the installation, which went extremely well. Janet was someone we would never have found without THE GUILD."

GLA has worked successfully with other GUILD artists as well. Bruce Bleach, for one, brought terrific drama and dynamic energy to a recent GLA lobby-design project with his innovative, sculptural metal relief paintings.

Lepow and Galman note that they have found three distinct ways to use GUILD sourcebooks. Elaine Galman explains: "We often use THE GUILD to stimulate the client's imagination; it offers such a range of visual imagery and this is very helpful. We also use it, of course, to find artists. But we put it to work in a third way, too. When we travel to other parts of the country, we sometimes need to get in touch with people in our field. Then we turn to the informational listings in the back of the book. Over the years, we've developed some very good relationships through this network."

Photo of Elaine Galman (left) and Judith Lepow by Norman Levinson

*"She helped make sure there were no
unanswered questions, which is, of course,
crucial for everyone's comfort level on a
large-budget project."*

ANN AYRES

Corporate Art Advisor

Ann Ayres, a Chicago corporate-art adviser and partner in Ayres-Steinmetz Ltd., has built her business with a careful mix of aggressive marketing, clear thoughtful communication, and an intuitive creativity that helps her understand, define and obtain the kind of work her clients require. Many of her clients are financial institutions or large healthcare providers, and they expect a very systematic approach, she explains. This is certainly true when they are contemplating the purchase or commissioning of highly creative art.

"I think the key to building a successful partnership with my clients, as well as with the artists we use, is an emphasis on clear communication," she says. For this reason, she has found working with GUILD artists particularly satisfying. "I recently had the opportunity to commission a wonderful sculptural wall-piece — a large triptych — from paper and mixed-media artist Martha Chatelain. Martha presented the client with a well-organized approach to the project, and helped to provide a clear, step-by-step explanation of how the commission process moves from preliminary sketches to finished product. She helped make sure there were no unanswered questions, which is, of course, crucial for everyone's comfort level on a large-budget project."

After Chatelain was chosen for the project, she and Ayres worked closely — not just with each other, but with the client as well — to insure that what began as a series of abstract ideas for the space would become a tangible reality that met all expectations.

"We talked early on with the client about the feel of the piece: 'like a billowing drape,' and about the color: 'like the sky at twilight.' Then I provided Martha with some very specific details, things like room light, dimensions, and how close people would be to the artwork when they look at it," Ayres explains.

Working with that information, Chatelain responded with simple, elegant sketches, plus samples of colors and materials she proposed using for the richly textured wall sculpture. The client was delighted as the piece began to take shape through these tangible items, knowing that the artist understood what was wanted.

The finished piece has been well-received, and the client feels very much a part of its success.

ART FOR THE WALL: GLASS

Dawn Adams
Dale Steffey

Salt Creek Glass Company
315 South Arbutus Drive
Bloomington, IN 47401
TEL 812-333-2903
E-Mail: **dsteffey@compuserve.com**

Currently celebrating 20 years of working with glass, Dawn Adams and Dale Steffey create unique glass "paintings." The works feature intricate surface textures and depth, intense color, and Adams' virtuosity in design.

Works can be commissioned in almost any size, with prices starting at $1000. Resumé, current photos or slides, and prices available upon request.

Commissions include:
Riley Children's Hospital, Indianapolis, IN
Indiana University Medical Center Cancer
   Pavillion, Indianapolis, IN

Also see these GUILD sourcebooks:
Designer's: 7, 14

A *A Moment of Peace,* © 1999, fused glass and
   painted found frame, 29" x 44", $3000

B *Passage to Perception,* © 1999, fused glass and
   painted found frame, 34" x 53", $4000

A

B

Shawn Athari

Shawn Athari's, Inc.
14332 Mulholland Drive
Los Angeles, CA 90077
TEL 310-476-0066
FAX 310-476-9ART
E-Mail: shawn@shawnathari.com
Web: www.shawnathari.com

Shawn Athari has been working with glass since 1975. Her focus has been to recreate historical artifacts, usually limited to view in museums and books, bringing them to life in a contemporary form. Through her glass expertise and visions of history, she has done commissions which run the gamut from creating the Disney figures for Walt Disney Corp. to demonstrating the parting of the Red Sea in a 220 sq. ft. synagogue window. The techniques Athari uses make her work unique within her field.

Also see these GUILD sourcebooks:
Designer's: 6, 7, 8, 9, 10, 11, 12, 13, 14

A *Arrowheads*, origin: Pacific Northwest

B *Kifwebe Mask*, origin: Africa

C *Fish*, origin: contemporary

A
Photo by Robert Bawmbach

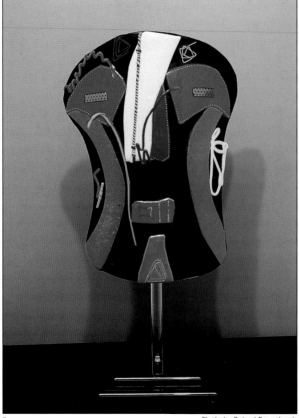

B
Photo by Robert Bawmbach

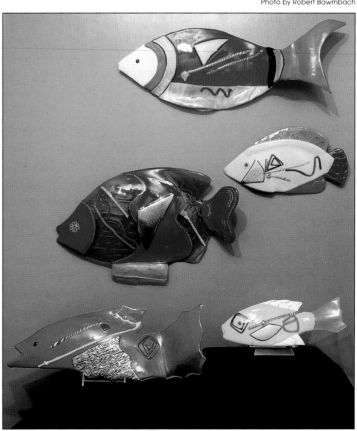

C
Photo by Robert Bawmbach

Peter Mangan

COMMISSIONING AGENT: Design Development Company and Bob Puccini

DESCRIPTION: Five chandeliers measuring 5' x 5' x 5' each, and one measuring 2.5' x 2.5' x 2.5'

SITE: Sazerac Restaurant in Hotel Monaco (a Kimpton Hotel), Seattle, WA

The Sazerac Restaurant project started with phone call out of the blue asking if I was th "artist who made lights." Someone had see my work in one of the GUILD sourcebooks, an wanted to include it in a restaurant proposal.

I drew sketches for large chandeliers and was asked i they could be made even larger. I revised the design i a way that enabled me to make the largest chandelier I'd ever created (5' x 5' x 5'). Time went by and I fig ured I'd probably not been chosen for the project. I some ways, that was OK. Six months earlier, I'd gon on a trip around the world with my girlfriend to cele brate turning 40 years old. At the pyramids in Egyp my horse stumbled and threw me off. My left wris was fractured and required a cast. After getting ove that, my right wrist developed a medical problen requiring an operation and another cast. The day returned home from the hospital, I got a call saying had the Sazerac job.

I said I could do it, knowing it would be a test of m abilities. Thanks to careful planning and a hardwork ing and talented group of people who assisted me, th chandeliers turned out great. There are five large chan deliers in the restaurant and one smaller chandelier i the entrance. I was invited to the opening and it wa gratifying to see an idea turned into reality. If you ar in Seattle, check it out — the food's delicious, too.

— PN

"When art is integrated into an architectural design from the beginning, it plays a crucial and irreplaceable role in animating the space."

JERRY MACNEIL

Architect

Jerry MacNeil, president of Jerry MacNeil Architects Ltd. in Halifax, Nova Scotia, and a Fellow of the Royal Architectural Institute of Canada, is a passionate advocate for including art in architectural projects. "When art is integrated into an architectural design from the beginning, it plays a crucial and irreplaceable role in animating the space. It often makes a client more excited about a project and encourages people to experience the space in a more active, intelligent and engaged way."

MacNeil specializes in designing institutional buildings, especially churches, and says he'd encourage a client to leave a portion of a building unfinished rather than save money by cutting the art out of the budget. He reasons that, "They'll always eventually raise the money to finish construction, but they might not raise the money to pay for the art, and that would be a terrible loss."

MacNeil uses artists from all over North America on his projects. "Sometimes it's better to use an outside artist rather than someone local," he says. "An outsider brings a different vision that can be exciting and surprising."

According to MacNeil, distance is not a problem as long as the architect and artist share a vision and a professional attitude. To facilitate that trust and understanding, MacNeil sent one of his architects to the States to work for over three weeks with GUILD glass artist Steve Melahn. The result of that international collaboration has been four architectural glass projects—including one in MacNeil's home.

"Working with Steve is a great pleasure," says MacNeil. "We know how he and his staff work, and what we need to provide in terms of schedules and guidelines. And he is well aware of the flexibility an artist must have when working with buildings. It's an excellent situation for all of us."

ART FOR THE WALL: METAL

r

in Wire Mesh

12

...er@sover.net

...b. **www.boyermesh.com**

Eric Boyer creates original sculptures in woven wire mesh. The work juxtaposes classical nudes with an exciting industrial material. Formed by hand, these lightweight and resilient figures have been exhibited nationally and collected internationally since 1989.

Works are created for wall hanging from a single point or for free standing with a wood or masonry base. Sculptures are black, rusted or patinated, and are powder-coated for an extremely durable finish. Work may be commissioned in a wide range of sizes and scales with prices starting at around $1000.

A *Recommended Summer Reading*, 1998, steel wire mesh and copper pigment

B *Twisting Male*

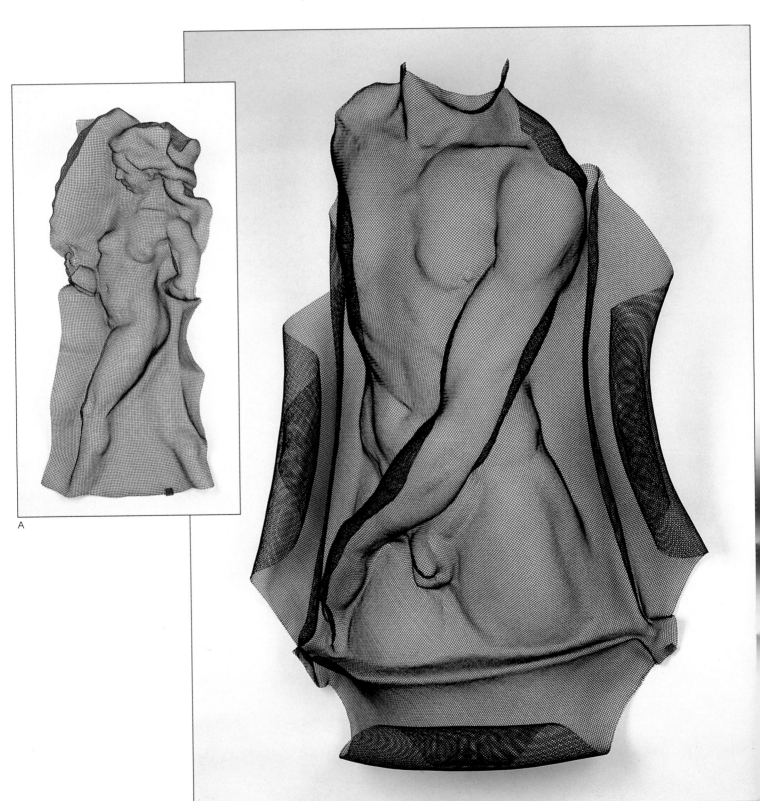

A

B

Lois Key Giffen

1600 79th Street Ocean
Marathon, FL 33050
TEL/FAX   305-743-3546
E-Mail: **bobgiffen@aol.com**

Lois Giffen has lived and worked on five continents, and her paintings and sculptures are collected worldwide. For the last ten years she has lived in the Florida Keys, and draws inspiration from the beauty of her surroundings.

Always seeking to express the spiritual in art, she creates an atmosphere of serenity and peace. She works in clay, stone, bronze, copper and steel as well as painting in oils and acrylics. She also enjoys printmaking, particularly monotypes, as she prefers "one of a kind" to mass production.

Commissions for specific spaces are welcome.

Giffen's work is collected in Australia, Austria, Cyprus, Great Britain, East and West Malaysia, Malta, Sweden and the United States.

Also see these GUILD sourcebooks:
Designer's: 13
Architect's: 12, 14

A *Mermaid's Mirror*, 1997, steel, 25"Dia

B *On the Reef*, 1997, steel, 30" x 26" x 4"

A

Photo by Bill Keogh

B

Photo by Bill Keogh

Studios

...uol.com

Internationally acclaimed, Joan Giordano has created a highly personal technique, employing such disparate elements as handmade paper, copper, aluminum and acrylic. Giordano's unique use of tactile surfaces and the dramatic contrasting of metals and fibers amplify the interplay of light and shadow in her one-of-a-kind wall sculptures. Her sculptures can be adapted and adjusted to accommodate an unlimited number of design and architectural challenges.

Giordano's works are the focal point of many collections, such as PepsiCo, Inc.; CBS; Merrill Lynch; and the United States Embassy in Cyprus.

Commissions and site-specific projects are welcome. Contact the artist for more information.

Time and the River, shown here, can be configured in a variety of ways. It can spread out into the room or stay on the wall and change size. It can hang from the ceiling as well.

A *Time and The River*, aluminum, paper, steel, wire mesh, 60"H x 60"W x 12"D

B *Putting on a New Skin*, 1999, wire, steel, Japanese rice paper, bark paper, wax, 96"H x 72"W x 24"D

Photo by D. James Dee

A

Photo by Maja Kihlstedt

B

Giordano Studios

Joan Giordano
36 Grand Street
New York, NY 10013
TEL 212-431-6244
FAX 212-481-3128
E-Mail: **JAGGIOR@aol.com**

A *Beneath the Skin*, paper, steel mesh, wax, copper, copper cable, 72"H x 32"W x 10"D

B *From out of the Earth*, Tig-welded and painted aluminum, 72"H x 48"W x 36"D

C *Red Swamp*, 1999, pigmented paper, copper cable, steel mesh, wax, paint, 26"H x 52"W x 6"D

A

B

C

Photo by D. James Dee

Linda Leviton

Linda Leviton Sculpture
1011 Colony Way
Columbus, OH 43235
TEL 614-433-7486
FAX 614-433-0806

Linda Leviton's one-of-a-kind copper sculptures are known for their natural forms and use of color. Drawing on the inherent beauty of burnished copper, Leviton enhances her work with techniques from jewelry, sheet metal, blacksmithing and textile disciplines.

Flat pieces are oil on copper, varnished and riveted together. They can be made in complementary units and can be customized for color and size.

Three-dimensional forms of copper wire frame and varnished woven copper wire can be hung and lit to appear either translucent or solid.

Contact the artist for more information about completed works and commissions.

A *Eve's Gown,* varnished copper wire, 40"H x 30"W x 30"D

B *Over and Under,* copper, oil, varnish, patina 36"H 72"W x 2"D

C *Autumn Improv,* copper, oil, varnish, 30"H x 72"W 2"D

A

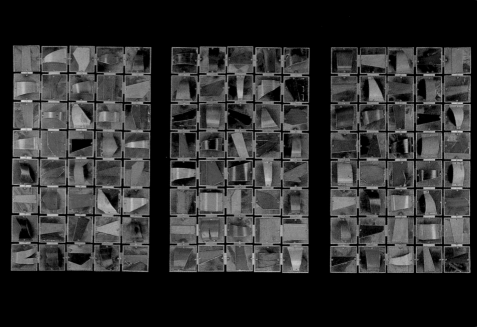

B

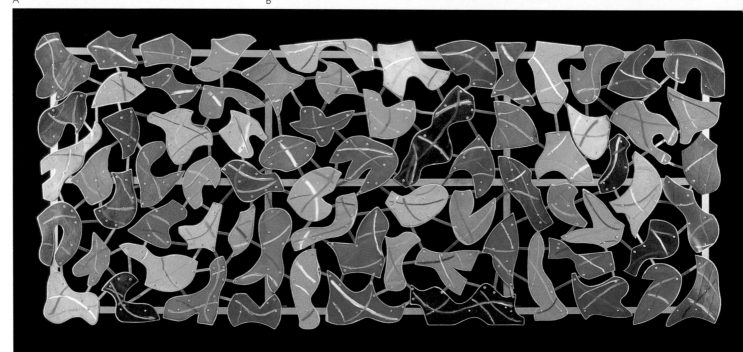

C

Susan McGehee

Metallic Strands
540 23rd Street
Manhattan Beach, CA 90266
TEL 310-545-4112
FAX 310-546-7152
E-Mail: **MetlStrnds@aol.com**

Susan McGehee weaves wires and metals into striking forms. Applying standard weaving techniques to nontraditional materials, she uses her loom to create contemporary hangings that seem to float on the wall. These lightweight, easily installed pieces complement both residential and commercial settings.

Commissions invited. Additional information available upon request.

Also see these GUILD sourcebooks:
Designer's: 12, 13, 14

A *Moon Shadows Banner*, woven anodized aluminum wire, 18"W x 33"H

B *Revelry Triptych*, woven anodized aluminum wire, 52"W x 34"H

A

Photo by Andrew Neuhart

B

Photo by Andrew Neuhart

Martin Sturman

Martin Sturman Sculptures
416 Cricketfield Court
Westlake Village, CA 91361
TEL **805-381-0032**
FAX **805-381-1116**
E-Mail: **mlsturman@aol.com**
Web: **www.steelsculptures.com**

Martin Sturman conceives and creates original decorative, architectural and functional steel sculptures suitable for placement either in indoor or outdoor locations. All sculptures are fabricated from stainless steel finished with a burnished surface or carbon steel painted with acrylic or enamel. Site-specific collaborative commissions are encouraged to achieve complete client satisfaction.

Also see these GUILD sourcebooks:
Designer's: 7, 8, 9, 10, 11, 12, 13, 14
Architect's: 12, 14, 15

A Table, 1999, burnished stainless steel, 20"H x 31"W x 23"D

B Floral wall hanging, 1998, burnished stainless steel, 42"H x 74"W x 2"D

Photo by Barry Michlin

A

Photo by Barry Michlin

B

Cathy Williams

PO Box 2225
Santa Fe, NM 87504
FAX 505-983-6737
E-Mail: **cathywilliams@cnsp.com**
Web: **www.cnsp.com/cathywilliams**

The plaques shown begin as soft fiber forms and are then transformed to bronze. In addition to the classic patina colors used on bronze, the artist has turned to a new palette of color possibilities for interior and exterior pieces.

Commissioned pieces may either be editions or one of a kind. A commission from an Internet-related business, for example, could begin as a bronze plaque but also serve as a company logo.

The work is suitable for installation in foyers, entry-ways, waiting areas, landings, courtyards and on exterior walls.

Design collaboration, installation planning and site-specific commissions for both public and private art collections are welcome. Prices are based on size, installation requirements and shipping cost to the site.

Pinwheel, © 1997, bronze, 18" x 18"

Internet I (AP), © 1997, bronze, 23.5" x 25"

A

Photo by Leigh Photo

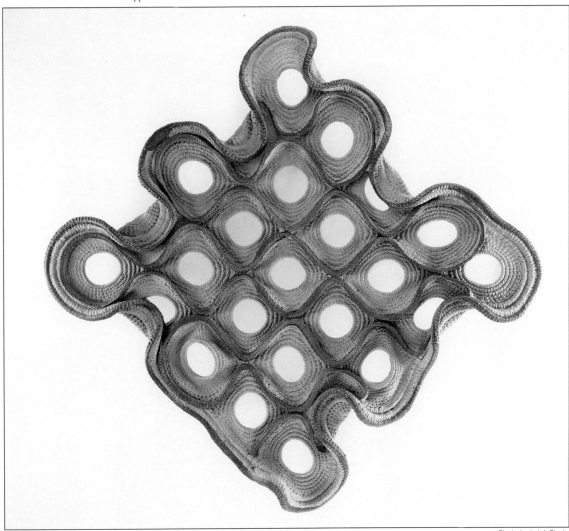

B

Photo by Leigh Photo

ART FOR THE WALL: MIXED MEDIA

April Berger

April Berger Works of Art
41 Lapidge Street
San Francisco, CA 94110
TEL **415-863-9543**
E-Mail: **april@aprilberger.com**
Web: **www.aprilberger.com**

April Berger's tapestries are created by layering fabrics, paper and paint on canvas. These pieces are then framed in fabrics that interact with the flavor of each piece. Her richly textured wall hangings add harmony, warmth and energy to sites of all sizes.

Berger has traveled and studied art in Europe and Africa, and exhibits and sells her work both internationally and domestically.

Works range from $500 to $10000. References and portfolio are available upon request.

Also see this GUILD sourcebook:
Designer's: 14

A *Meditation,* 2000, fabric, paper and paint on canvas, 55" x 31"

B *Cerberus,* 2000, fabric, paper and paint on canvas, 57" x 32"

C *Les Danseuses,* 1998, fabric, paper and paint on canvas, 56" x 35"

A

B

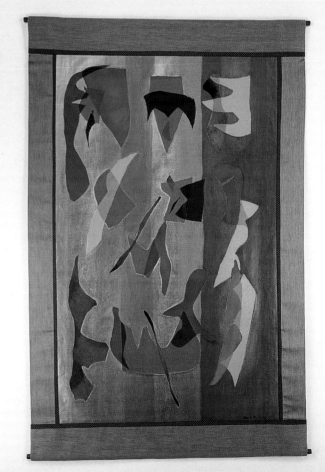

C

Nancy Loo Bjorge

Lotus
1321 Jana Drive
Lawrence, KS 66049-4424
TEL **785-842-6546**
TEL **785-766-2886 (Cell)**
FAX **785-843-4283**
E-Mail: **nbjorge@idir.net**

Nancy Loo Bjorge creates intriguing original compositions using folded paper and a wide variety of other materials. Her fascinating blending of geometric and organic lines, sublime sensitivity to color and finely detailed craftsmanship give her works a unique aesthetic quality.

Bjorge's art has won numerous awards, and during the past year she had two one-person shows. Her pieces come in any size and shape and add beauty to homes, offices and larger spaces.

Commissions are welcome; slides, a video and a price list are available upon request.

A *Flowers in Boxes*, 20"H x 23"W x 2"D

B *Purple Net*, 15"H x 20"W x 2.5"D

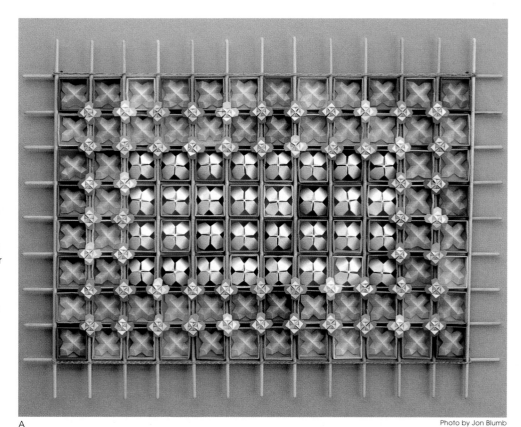

A

Photo by Jon Blumb

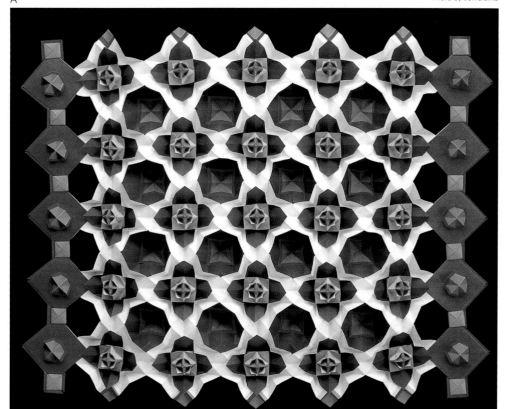

B

Photo by Jon Blumb

Bill Hopen

COMMISSIONING AGENT: The Adorers of the Blood of Christ

TITLE: *Woman of the New Covenant*

DESCRIPTION: 6' patinaed bronze figure atop a 14" sandstone slab

SITE: Chapel of the New Covenant, The Adorers Provincial Center, Wichita, KS

I have been in GUILD sourcebooks for six years. In 1998, I received over $100,000 of commissions in response to my page. Here's one of my favorite success stories: I received a phone call from 80-year-old Sister Bernadette Schmidt from Wichita, Kansas. She was looking at my page in *The Architect's Sourcebook 10*, which liturgical architect Robert Habiger had lent to her. Her order, The Adorers of the Blood of Christ, were designing a new chapel and were searching for a figurative sculptor to create a new image of Mary, "Woman of the New Covenant," Mary as co-redeemer.

While talking with Sister Bernadette, I felt the history of art, spirituality, and our own social evolution intersect. I wanted to sculpt the 2,000-year-old spiritual figure, Mary, for our time. Her history recorded in art echoed the evolving power of women in modern society. The sisters invited me to meet with their architect and liturgy committee. I stayed several days to listen, to understand, to intuit what this sculpture needed to say. I was commissioned to create a patinaed bronze figure over a red sandstone base. With the architect's help, I chose a 6,000-pound chunk of red sandstone from digital images on the Internet, then flew to Wichita to help position the stone "floating" into the worship space. I made a large mold to recreate the stone back at my studio. I wanted to sculpt Mary's bare feet pressing perfectly into the irregular rock.

After installation, I revisited the sculpture in the chapel. I saw the vision of Mary that I felt in the hearts of the sisters, and I was thankful to be an artist. I am currently sculpting another bronze figure for the sisters and have established a great connection with an important liturgical architect, Robert Habiger.

— **BH**

Shawn M. Agosta

The Soul and the Iris
313A First Avenue South
Seattle, WA 98104
TEL 206-262-0335
E-Mail: **thesoulandtheiris@juno.com**

Emerging artist Shawn Agosta brings new life to the field of sculpture.

Agosta creates sculpture that is large, yet light enough to get off of the floor and onto the wall. Layering various materials to create depth and texture, these pieces are powerful and dynamic. Demanding authority, they become the focus of any space.

Agosta enjoys experimenting with both size and style. His current work ranges from life size to smaller freestanding pieces, from the detailed figure to the abstract.

These sculptural pieces fit very well in a corporate, residential or health care setting. With an understanding of the client, the artist has the sensitivity to create a work that achieves the client's vision.

Commissions accepted.

Guardian, 1999, pulverized paper mixed with adhesives on wood, 5' x 7'

Photo by Ron Robin

...ONSHIP, pulverized paper mix with adhesives on wood, 5' x 5'

Photo by Ron Robin

Miani Carnevale

Gallery East
229 East 10th Street
Loveland, CO 80537
TEL **888-252-6520**
TEL **970-667-6520**
FAX **970-669-6518**
E-Mail: **info@galleryeast.com**
Web: **www.galleryeast.com**

Bold, vibrant and full spirited describe Miani Carnevale's three-dimensional mixed-media work.

A graduate of the Ringling School of Art in Sarasota, FL, she has also studied art in Oslo, Norway, and Florence, Italy. Carnevale has over 25 years of experience in her field, and is represented in public, corporate and private collections throughout the country.

Commissions are welcomed.

A *Merging With the Present,* 42" x 42"

B *The Way Shower,* 12" x 36"

C *Window of Opportunity,* 36" x 36"

A
Photo by Photo Craft La

B   Photo by Photo Craft Labs

C
Photo by Photo Craft La

Miani Carnevale

Gallery East
229 East 10th Street
Loveland, CO 80537
TEL 888-252-6520
TEL 970-667-6520
FAX 970-669-6518
E-Mail: **info@galleryeast.com**
Web: **www.galleryeast.com**

Miani Carnevale creates a visual dance upon a textured surface with oils, pastels, chalks, pencils and found three-dimensional materials. Her process is one of building, layering and sanding, which allows previously applied color and texture to be revealed. Making tactile as well as visual decisions, she works as a conductor might, orchestrating each piece to completion.

Her work delights the senses. You can almost hear the color as the texture of the piece pulls you beneath its surface. Her creations beg to be touched.

Collaborations with architects, designers and their clients are welcome.

Portfolios are available upon request.

A *Framing Things in a New Light,* diptych, 48" x 56"

B *Having a Random Thought,* triptych, 48" x 56"

A

Photo by Photo Craft Labs

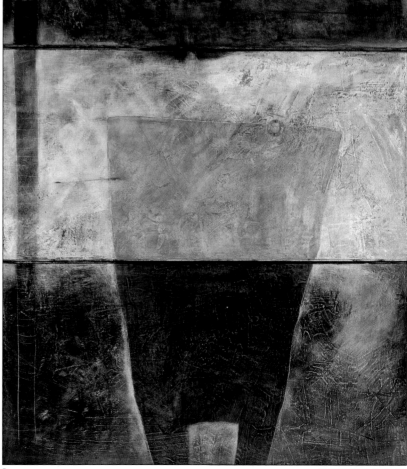

B

Photo by Photo Craft Labs

Carol Cole

PO Box 164
Bala Cynwyd, PA 19004
TEL **610-664-2825**
E-Mail: **cc@carolcole.com**

Carol Cole makes one-of-a-kind sculpture by encrusting familiar objects with handmade paper. Multiple layers of paint protect the work, enhance the textures and create an ancient-looking patinaed surface. The pieces are substantial and appear heavy, but weigh less than ten pounds and are easily hung on any wall.

A professional artist for 25 years, Cole's work is in many corporate and private collections. She specializes in commissioned sculptures which incorporate objects related to or provided by the client.

Recent clients include Children's Hospital of Philadelphia; Educational Testing Service, Washington, DC; and Imasco USA, New York, NY.

A *Shield*, mixed media with shredded currency, coins, tax forms, Isdaner & Co., Certified Public Accountants, 49"H x 31"W x 4"D

B *Computer Goddess*, mixed media with computer parts, 74"H x 17"W x 4"D

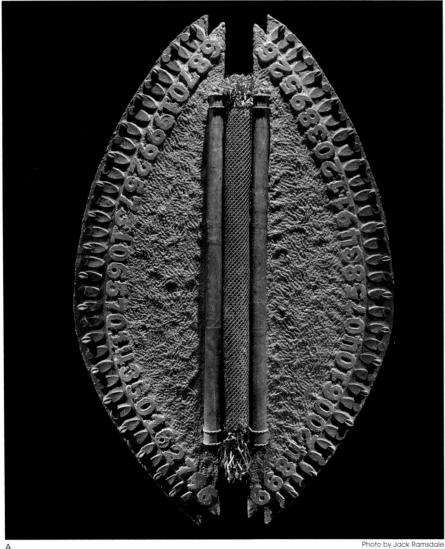

A

B

Photo by Jack Ramsdale

Photo by Jack Ramsdc

Alonzo Davis

2080 Peabody Avenue
Memphis, TN 38104
TEL 901-276-9070
FAX 901-276-0660
E-Mail: **artalonzo@aol.com**
Web: **www.globeart.com**

Alonzo Davis' *Power Poles* and *Bundles* are paintings in the round on bamboo that take on a sculptural form. He enhances them with color and a variety of other materials, including wax, copper, canvas with burned patterns, and leather. Varying in length from four to eight feet, the bamboo works can function individually or in a grouping, as a bundle or installation. They can be propped against a wall or suspended. The viewer will find manipulated symbols from ethnic and spiritual sources in these unique pole compositions.

A *Bamboo Bundle IV* (detail), mixed media on bamboo, 10"H x 48"W x 5"D

B *Palos de Azul,* mixed media on bamboo, neon, 10"H x 96"W x 6"D

A

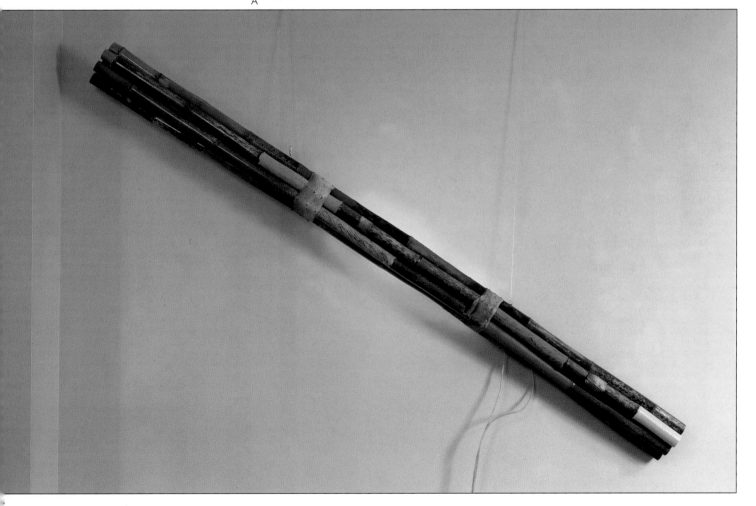

Gretchen Lee Coles

The Great Circle Press
PO Box 456
Glen Ellyn, IL 60138-0456

Gretchen Lee Coles is a cartographer and
sculptor with more than 20 years of professional
experience. Her bas- and haute-relief maps
range in design from geographic realism to
playful abstraction.

She constructs three-dimensional maps using
various appropriate materials to express the
physical and ephemeral spirit of a place.

Maps traditionally result from collaborations
between cartographers and map users. Coles
welcomes teamwork in designing unique maps
of real places. Cartographic design consultation
is available.

Her maps are included in numerous exhibitions
and collections in the United States and abroad.
Please contact The Great Circle Press for a map
list and prices.

Also see this GUILD sourcebook:
Designer's: 14

SHOWN: *Mapping a Sea of Grass* (details), 90"H x 126"W

Photo by Eugene Sladek, College of DuPage

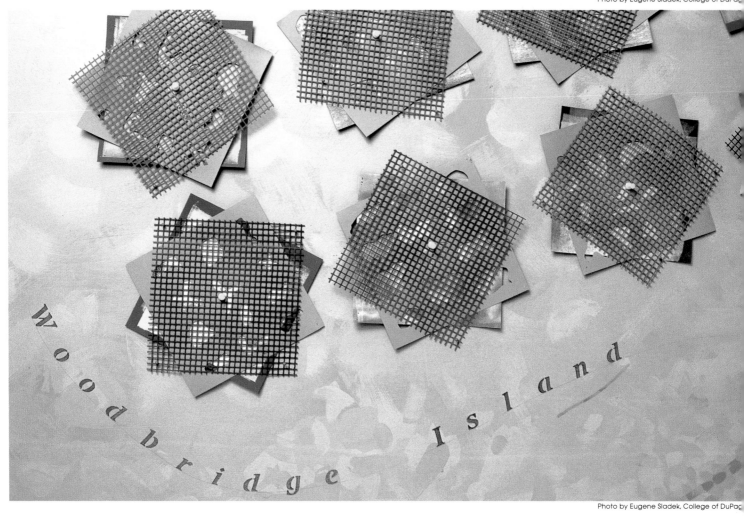

Photo by Eugene Sladek, College of DuPage

Stephanie Gassman

135 Central Parkway
Cincinnati, OH 45214
TEL 513-241-1557
FAX 513-984-3943 (Call first)
E-Mail: **stephanie_gassman@fuse.net**

Stephanie Gassman created this commissioned wall relief for a New York investment company lobby. The unusual format, using traditional materials, tells of the historic past and present of this corporation that has been in existence since 1864.

Stephanie's work can be found in public, corporate and residential environments around the United States.

Commission list, slides and pricing available upon request.

Also see these GUILD sourcebooks:
Designer's: 13, 14

SHOWN: Wall relief, 1999, oil on canvas, 80"H x 96"W x 9"D

Photo by OMS Photography

Photo by OMS Photography

Kam Ghaffari

Kam Ghaffari Design
225 South Woody Hill Road
Westerly, RI 02891
TEL **401-322-1885**

Kam Ghaffari creates imaginative sculpture and finely crafted sculptural furniture for private and corporate clients as well as for large-scale public art commissions. He is proficient with a wide variety of materials, including wood, stone, metals and plastic. Ghaffari's work has a narrative quality — telling a story, conveying a feeling. Materials and technologies are chosen, and often combined in innovative ways, to suit the nature of the particular project.

Ghaffari enjoys working with consultants, architects, interior designers, galleries and individuals to create a unique work of art for a client and a space. Wall art can include "murals" of relief-carved slate combined with colored glass or other materials, as well as mixed-media collages (for either indoor or outdoor installation).

Ghaffari's broad range also includes freestanding sculpture, mobiles, fountains and garden work.

A   *Stone Face Sconce*, carved slate and mixed-media wall light, 10" x 20" x 2"

B   *Glacier, Shoot, Tropic, Breeze (Seasons)*, two-sided mixed-media collage screen, client: Fidelity Investments, 74.5" x 110" x 1.25"

C   *Grand Canyon*, variegated red slate, Ultrasuede®, wood, 31" x 38" x 1.5"

D   *The Long Winter Through* (detail), relief-carved slate, polyester resin, 15.5" x 22"

E   *Screaming Into the Millennium*, Swiss pear wood, color-anodized aluminum, vinyl, 17" x 21" x 3"

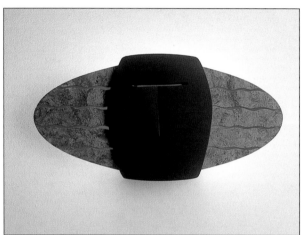

A

Photo by Ric Murray

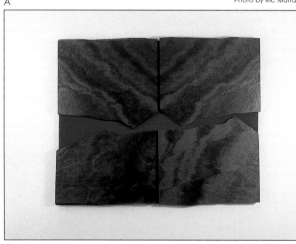

C

D

B

Photo by Dean Pow

E

Chris Griffin

230 West 105th Street #3D
New York, NY 10025
TEL/FAX 212-663-3056
E-Mail: **griffinch@aol.com**

Chris Griffin's career spans 20 years of national exhibitions, outdoor public sculpture, grants and commissions in public, private and corporate sectors. Her work is in prominent museums as well as corporate and private collections.

The artwork illustrated here shows Griffin's recent pieces using artificial flowers as a medium. From small room to lobby size, residential or commercial, this work has been very well received by the general viewing public, and integrates easily into many different contexts.

Prices, resumé and slides on request.

A *The Crown,* 24"H x 62"L

B *The Bird,* 46"H x 36"W

C *The Garden,* 96"H x 36"W

A

B

Photo by D. James Dee

C

John Charles Gordon Studios, Inc.

4-B Pine Street
Avondale, GA 30002-1001
TEL 404-294-8080
FAX 404-294-4442
E-Mail: jcgstudios@mindspring.com

John Charles Gordon Studios has produced art products for corporate clients since its beginning in Los Angeles 36 years ago.

The studio offers solutions to development, budget or mechanical issues and produces originals or multiples.

Studio capabilities are extensive, including metal wall sculptures, collage assemblies, shadowboxes, framed visuals, maps and globes, dimensional plaques, custom light fixtures, painted furniture and theatrical props.

A Forged aluminum organic wall forms, Deauville Resort Hotel, Miami Beach, FL, 5'H x 1'W x 6"D

B Pearl/satin-finished polyvinyl, steel armature, Intercontinental Hotel, Miami, FL, 6'H x 12' W x 3"D

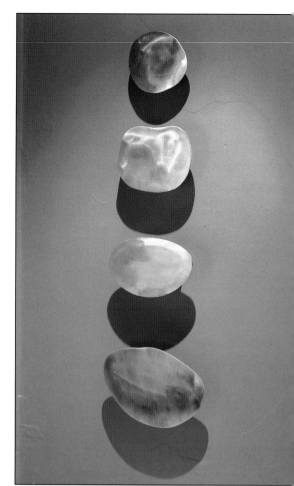

A

Photo by Departure Studio

B

Photo by Departure Studio

John Charles Gordon Studios, Inc.

-B Pine Street
vondale, GA 30002-1001
EL 404-294-8080
AX 404-294-4442
-Mail: jcgstudios@mindspring.com

ohn Charles Gordon Studios has produced art
products for corporate clients since its beginning
n Los Angeles 36 years ago.

he studio offers solutions to development, budget
r mechanical issues and produces originals or
multiples.

studio capabilities are extensive, including metal
wall sculptures, collage assemblies, shadowboxes,
ramed visuals, maps and globes, dimensional
plaques, custom light fixtures, painted furniture
and theatrical props.

Banana Leaf, Westin Resort Hotel lobby, St. John, U.S. Virgin Islands, hand-manipulated fiber-based sculpture, acrylic paint, gold leaf, 18" x 48"

Photo by Drew Stauss, Departure Studio

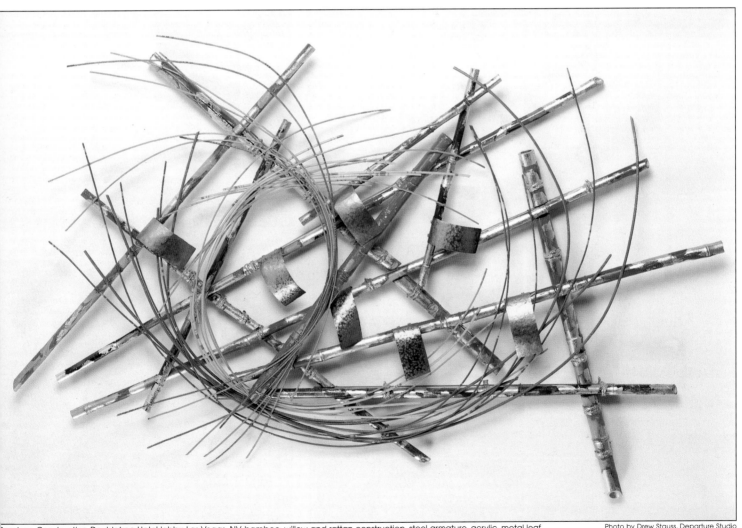

Bamboo Construction, Doubletree Hotel lobby, Las Vegas, NV, bamboo, willow and rattan construction, steel armature, acrylic, metal leaf, hammered brass elements

Photo by Drew Stauss, Departure Studio

Jacques Lieberman

Jacques Lieberman Editions
170 Mercer Street 3W
New York, NY 10012-3263
TEL **212-219-0939**
FAX **212-925-8545**
E-Mail: **jalie@mindspring.com**
Web: **www.jacqueslieberman.com**

Jacques Lieberman has a background in architecture, design, photography, lithography, serigraphy, acrylic painting and digital fine art. He creates original images published in limited editions and posters in sizes from 16" x 23" to 46" x 56". Some images are in brilliant color, while others are in striking black and white.

Images are also incorporated into cast acrylic tiles, specially treated for toughness and abrasion resistance. These ultra-modern creations enhance any architectural interior, public or private. Tiles measure 4" x 4" to 16" x 16"; installations are unlimited in size. They are also available for individual display on desktop acrylic easels.

Also see this GUILD sourcebook:
Designer's: 11

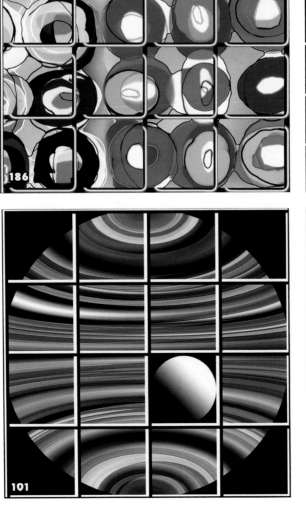

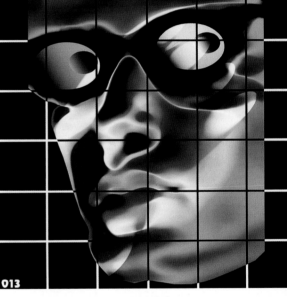

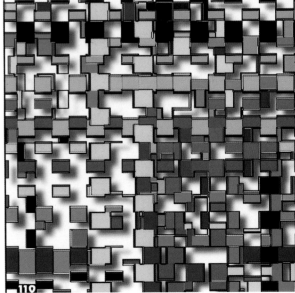

Susan Sandler

1693 San Vicente Boulevard, Box 268
Los Angeles, CA 90049
TEL   310-459-8305
FAX   310-459-5285
E-Mail: **susan@s.sandler.com**
Web: **www.ssandler.com**

Susan Sandler arrived at her unique style of mixed media after 20 years of painting. Her craftsmanship is immediately obvious. In a non-derivative realistic style, she combines the hard edge of found objects with the soft edge of painting — usually of nature. The effect is a striking three-dimensional painting grabbing the viewer's eye and sometimes jarring the senses with unusual juxtapositions.

She has shown in museums and galleries nation-wide and is in collections worldwide.

Commissions are welcome. Slides and additional information on request. The artist's full portfolio appears on her web site, www.ssandler.com.

SHOWN: *Torii Gate* series, each piece: 24"H

Susan Venable

Venable Studio
2323 Foothill Lane
Santa Barbara, CA 93105
TEL **805-884-4963**
FAX **805-884-4983**
E-Mail: **copperwyrd@aol.com**
Web: **www.venablestudio.com**

Susan Venable's work is non-objective — an exploration of structure and surface. The reliefs are constructed of twisted copper wire and steel grids. The paintings are encaustic and oil. In both, layers are stacked to create a rich and complex surface, maximizing the physicality of the materials.

Venable's wall reliefs have been installed in public spaces as well as homes and museums in the United States, Europe, Asia and Australia.

The materials are durable, low maintenance and suitable for installation in public areas.

Also see these GUILD sourcebooks:
Designer's: 6, 10, 14

A *Borderline*, 3' x 6'

B *Sol Siena*, 6' x 9'

A

Photo by William Nettle

B

Photo by William Nettle

Bill Wheeler

Studio 1617
1617 Silver Lake Boulevard
Los Angeles, CA 90026-1310
TEL/FAX 323-660-7991
E-Mail: info@studio1617.com
Web: www.studio1617.com

Bill Wheeler has been creating limited-edition original prints and paintings for public and private commissions since 1970. He also has more than 25 years of experience working in collaboration with art consultants, designers and architects to create site-specific installations. His wall constructions are made of MDO plywood panels and/or plastic materials. They are created to the client's color and size specifications. Commissioned works have ranged from 2' x 2' to 10' x 164'. All of his works are supported on concealed frames and can be security mounted to the wall.

Wheeler is a versatile artist whose lighthearted and joyous compositions enliven the space around them. He is able to accept and incorporate the client's and designer's suggestions and modifications into the finished works of art. Such teamwork results in an installation that becomes an integral part of the interior space.

Commissions include:
AMOCO Learning Center, Downer's Grove, IL
Princess Cruise Lines, The Grand Princess
Hewlett/Packard
Health South
Malcolm A. Love Library, San Diego
Kaiser/Permanente, Glendale, CA

His paintings and prints are also in numerous other private and corporate collections worldwide. Pricing is available upon request.

Also see these GUILD sourcebooks:
THE GUILD: 4
Designer's: 6, 7, 9, 11, 13

Photo by Deer Studio

Photo by Deer Studio

DEBRA RHODES

Art Consultant

As an art consultant and appraiser with 20 years experience in the corporate-art business, Debra Rhodes has clearly defined notions about her mission and what she needs to do to help her clients.

"I want to help my customers select work that will endure, work that has the kind of quality that never loses its effect. What I look for is something that goes beyond just decorating. At this level you look for something with a distinctive and unique kind of creativity, as well as a great deal of artistic integrity. I think that's what you find with artists whose work is represented in THE GUILD."

Trained as an artist herself, Rhodes finds that part of her role is to negotiate between her clients — primarily corporations and luxury hotels — and the artists who provide the kind of extraordinary, highly creative work she advocates. When Rhodes was asked to provide a recommendation for artwork for the American Airlines VIP lounge at Philadelphia International Airport, she suggested GUILD artist Karen Adachi of Santa Cruz, California.

"At the time we began working on this project, there was beginning to be a fair amount of interest in cast paper, and there were a certain number of people working within this medium. Karen's work, however, wasn't just cast paper; it incorporated other materials in a fascinating, multi-dimensional way which took it to another level. Work created at this level never becomes dated; it has an enduring kind of value."

Rhodes says she takes prides in seeing both sides of the equation, understanding both the artist's perspective and the client's needs. "I think this perspective helps me find some of the best work," she explains.

"THE GUILD is a wonderful inventory, and a great time saver, as well. Even though I often have a sixth sense about what the client wants, it's a real advantage to be able to use THE GUILD to show a range of quality work in a very accessible, very visual form."

Photo by Peter Wallburg Studio, Inc.

"Properly selected and properly made, art can pull an entire space into the next level."

SUSAN JAKOBER

Interior Designer—Allied Member A.S.I.D.

"Using original art sets me apart from other interior designers in my area," says Susan Jakober, president of Interior Arts, a small Midwestern design firm. "I enjoy working with artists, and I've found it's good for my business because clients are fascinated with both the artwork and the process."

A designer for 15 years, Jakober has been interested in THE GUILD since it was first published. "A friend of mine had a copy of the first GUILD. I made notes of people in our area and thought, 'wouldn't it be fun to work with these people!' " Over the succeeding years, Jakober has had a number of opportunities to do just that.

One of her most gratifying projects involved GUILD artist Robert Walsh of R. Walsh Forge and Foundry. "My clients had a wonderful project, a grand country house with beautiful dark wood and an Italian marble floor in the foyer. I contacted Bob to create a wrought iron staircase railing for the entry.

"I think the clients were a little anxious at first, until they saw his drawings and suggestions. His

design was beautiful, with a lattice and three-dimensional calla lilies. They loved it so much that they added two additional balconies.

"The finished work is spectacular, and gives a remarkable signature to the house. This guy really knows what he's doing!"

Jakober has discovered other artists through THE GUILD as well. "GUILD artists are real professionals and they can work well within a budget," she says. "It doesn't need to cost an arm and a leg. You just tell the artists what you're willing to spend and they tell you whether they can work within that range.

"I think what you get in value is so much more than the cost. Properly selected and properly made, art can pull an entire space into the next level."

Photo by Richard Long

ART FOR THE WALL: PAPER

Karen Adachi

702 Monarch Way
Santa Cruz, CA 95060
TEL **831-429-6192**
FAX **831-423-4431**
E-Mail: **Adachik99@yahoo.com**

Karen Adachi creates three-dimensional hand-made paper pieces by using layers of irregularly shaped vacuum-cast paper. Her work is shown nationally through major galleries and representatives.

The pieces are richly textured and embellished with dyes, acrylics and metallics. Painted bamboo and sticks are used to create a dramatic statement of pattern and line.

Collections include:
American Airlines
AT&T
Marriott Hotels
Stanford Hospital
Bally's Hotel
Bank of Reno
Saks Fifth Avenue
Bloomingdale's
International Paper

Custom work available in any size, shape and color. Call for slides and additional information.

Bella Bella Arts
By Lara Moore

Lara Moore
3910 South Old State Road 37
Bloomington, IN 47401
TEL **812-323-1637**
FAX **812-323-1638**
E-Mail: **webmaster@bellabella.com**
Web: **www.bellabella.com**

Lara Moore's work is defined by crisp design and sumptuous color. Using hand-cut paper with a sleek resin finish, she creates distinctive wall pieces, tables, mirrors and screens. The glossy surface is heat-, water- and alcohol-resistant for easy care and cleaning.

Stylized natural motifs dominate Moore's designs, but she's also inspired by iron trellis-work, mosaics, Italian ceramics and French fabrics. She likes the surprise of paper in this context. The deep, mottled colors intrigue viewers: Is it stone, velvet, metal?

To browse Moore's pattern archive, please visit www.bellabella.com, or call for more information.

A *Apples, Artichoke, Tomatoes,* 1999, paper, resin, wood, Cassady's restaurant, 36" x 36"

B *Bowser Collection,* 1999, paper, resin, wood, 16" x 48", 18" x 34", 18" x 12"

C *Red Vase,* 18" x 12"

A

Photo by Shawn-Paul W. Luchin

B

Photo by Shawn-Paul W. Luchin

C

Photo by Shawn-Paul W. Luchin

Martha Chatelain

Artfocus, Ltd.
PO Box 9855
San Diego, CA 92169-0855
TEL 858-581-6410
FAX 858-581-6536

Martha Chatelain creates richly textured three-dimensional handmade paper and mixed-media wall sculptures enhanced with fiber dyes and iridescent powders.

Call to discuss design specifications, client environment and/or site-specific commissions. Allow four to six weeks following design approval.

Prices, from $800 to $5000, depend on size and complexity.

Selected collections: American Airlines, Bank of America, Champion Paper, IBM, International Paper, Potlatch, Upjohn and Xerox Corporations, Hilton and Sheraton hotels, Nordstrom.

A *Finesse,* 45" x 53" x 6"

B *Waves Upon the Shore,* 48" x 70" x 5"

A

B

Ellen Mears Kennedy

210 Midwood Road
Ilver Spring, MD 20910
EL **301-587-4782**
AX **301-587-7223**
-Mail: **emearskenn@aol.com**
Veb: **www.guild.com**

Ellen Mears Kennedy's artwork is constructed of hundreds of double-sided papers, all hand-made in her studio from pigmented pulp. Each paper has a left and right side that displays a unique shade. When the paper is folded, one color shows on the left side and a second color shows on the right. As viewers walk past each construction, the colors subtly change as they see alternating sides of the design — the hues shift, growing darker or lighter, depending on the observers' positions. The design is always in motion. The geometry of intersecting color patterns is softened by the texture of each paper's deckled edge and made fluid by the viewers' movement.

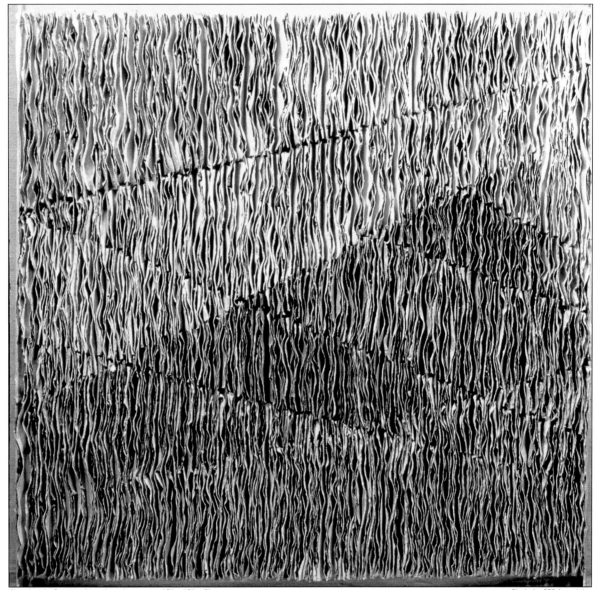

Shadow in Square, handmade paper, 60" x 60" x 5"   Photo by PRS Associates

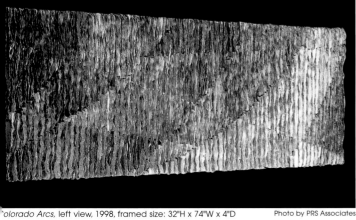

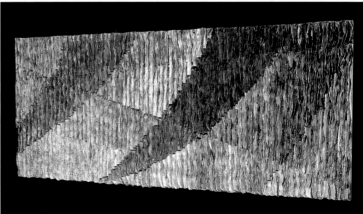

olorado Arcs, left view, 1998, framed size: 32"H x 74"W x 4"D   Photo by PRS Associates

Colorado Arcs, right view, 1998, framed size: 32"H x 74"W x 4"D   Photo by PRS Associates

Joan Kopchik

1335 Stephen Way
Southampton, PA 18966-4349
TEL 215-322-1862
FAX 215-322-5031
E-Mail: jkopchik@voicenet.com

Joan Kopchik casts freshly made sheets of handmade paper into plaster forms to create sculptural wall pieces. She adds earth elements, stone, wood and metal to create a rich, complex and personal iconography.

She has worked with consultants and design professionals for more than 20 years, and her work is included in corporate and private collections. Information packets are available upon request.

Also see these GUILD sourcebooks:
Designer's: 6, 7, 8, 11

SHOWN: *Messengers,* left: 15"H x 11"W x 3.5"D, center: 15"H x 8.5"W x 3.5"D, right: 15"H x 9.5"W x 3.5"D

Photo by John Wood

Photo by John Wood

Saaraliisa Ylitalo

961 Quebec Street NW
Washington, DC 20016
TEL 202-244-3205
E-Mail: **saaraliisa@bellnet.com.pe**

Saaraliisa Ylitalo's sculptures and wall pieces capture the translucent beauty inherent in her handmade paper. While living in Japan for five years, she mastered oriental paper-making techniques which she incorporates in her delicate work. For over 25 years, she has explored a variety of striking personal ideas in her quietly elegant pieces.

Saaraliisa Ylitalo's work has been exhibited nationally and internationally in public and private collections in the United States, Japan, Peru, Costa Rica, England, Australia, Norway, Hungary, China, Slovenia and Moldova. She is currently represented in the Art in the Embassies program.

Prices range from $400 to $4000.

A *Catalepsis*, mixed media, 36.5" x 12.5"

B *Archives*, mixed media, 36.5" x 12.5"

C *Angst*, mixed media, 29" x 18" x 13"

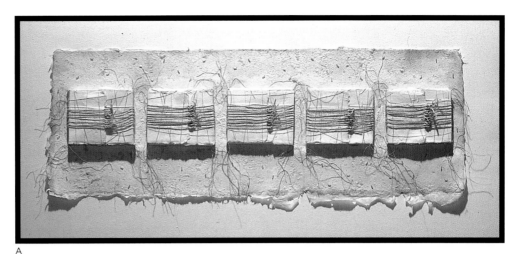

A

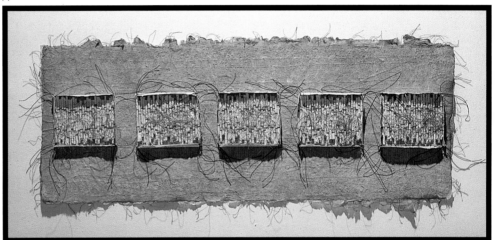

B

C

ART FOR THE WALL: ART QUILTS

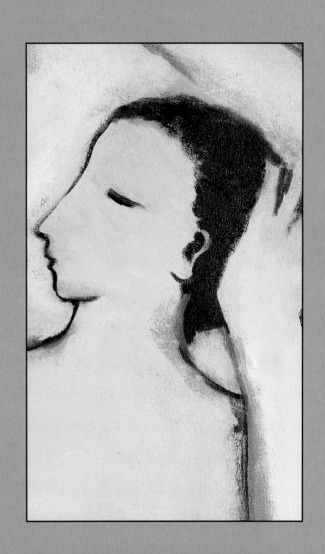

Priscilla Bianchi

Art Quilts Unique
7801 NW 37th Street, Section 2903-GUA
Miami, FL 33166-6559
TEL **011-502-369-3461**
FAX **011-502-331-4121**
E-Mail: **contesse@quetzal.net**
Web: **www.priscillabianchi.com**

Priscilla Bianchi, born, raised and living in Guatemala, Central America, represents a unique personality in today's art quilting world. In only two years, her career has been both prolific and successful.

Her distinctive style is characterized by a use of bold, bright colors that make a statement; a daring approach to choosing and combining fabrics and textures; a thirst for experimentation and risk-taking; and a definite ethnic appeal.

Her one-of-a-kind art quilts incorporate the richness of Guatemalan textiles, colors, patterns and symbolisms, giving life to a myriad of pieces that are fresh, vibrant and innovative. The magic, mystical Mayan culture sets them apart by imparting a delicious Latin American flavor.

Commissions are welcomed; photos and pricing available upon request.

A *Purple Dance* Kaleidoscope (detail), 41"H x 41"W

B 1,000 Rainbow Pyramids, 71"H x 42"W

C *Lightning by Day*, 47"H x 54"W

A

B

C

Lauren Camp

25 Theresa Lane
Santa Fe, NM 87505
TEL **505-474-7943**
FAX **505-474-8427**
E-Mail: **laurendavid@dsrt.com**

Lauren Camp creates original art quilts infused with the soul of jazz music and the joy of color. She works intuitively, effectively combining textures and colors to design larger-than-life portraits of musicians and vibrant abstract studies.

Exceptional handwork and machine skills, glorious hand-dyed fabric and dense machine quilting make these one-of-a-kind treasures.

Commissions accepted.

A *The Whole Damn Orchestra*, 1998, 52"H x 51"W

B *Quaternity #1: Verde Que Te Quiero*, 1999, 39"H x 72"W

Photo by Hawthorne Studio

A

B

Photo by Hawthorne Studio

Robin Cowley

2451 Potomac Street
Oakland, CA 94602-3032
TEL 510-530-1134
FAX 510-482-9465
E-Mail: robin@potomacwaterworks.com
Web: www.potomacwaterworks.com

A colorist with a sense of whimsy, Robin Cowley creates abstract fabric fantasies with an upbeat attitude. Constructed using several layers of fabric and thread, these easily hung works are suitable for a variety of settings.

Successfully working with clients to provide custom pieces, Cowley combines colors and textures with a sure hand and a keen understanding of the interaction between elements.

Cowley has numerous works in private and corporate collections. Commissions are welcomed; slides and pricing available upon request.

Also see these GUILD sourcebooks:
Designer's: 11, 12, 13, 14

A *Fortune Cookie: Red-Haired Stranger,* 18"W x 18"H

B *Line Dancing,* 64.5"W x 10.5"H

C *Talisman,* 120"W x 45"H

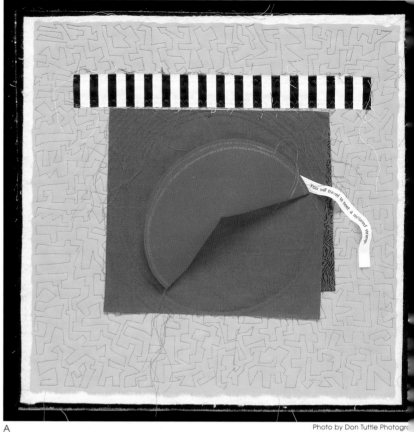

A

Photo by Don Tuttle Photogr

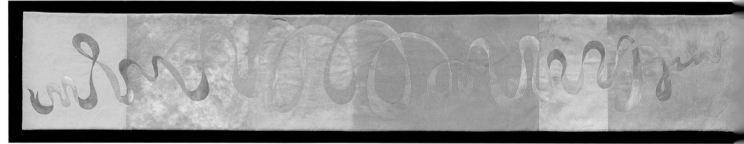

B

Photo by Don Tuttle Photogr

C

Photo by Don Tuttle Photograp

Marcia Hewitt Johnson

71 Llanfair Circle
Ardmore, PA 19003
TEL/FAX **610-649-7282**
E-Mail: **marhewjohn@home.com**
Web: **members.home.net/marhewjohn**

Marcia Johnson's art quilts for the wall and contemporary fiber constructions are influenced by her photography, allowing her to create abstractions of specific places and scenes.

She creates her own colors in graduated palettes, bringing vibrant visual drama to each piece. Quilts come with easy-to-install hardware or can be framed or put on stretchers, bringing color and texture to interiors.

Johnson's pieces are exhibited worldwide and are in residential and corporate collections including US Pharmacopeia, American Airlines and Loew's.

Please call for custom portfolio and price list.

Also see these GUILD sourcebooks:
Designer's: 11, 12, 14

A *Alsace,* 1999, silk on canvas, 33" x 30"

B *Red Road 2 Piedras Rojas,* 1999, 39" x 39"

C *Alpine Borders,* 1999, 43" x 73"

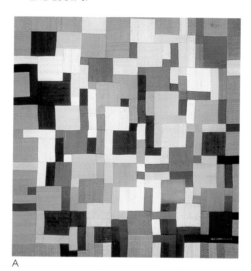

A

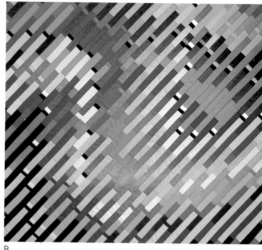

B

C

Sherri Young Dunbar

Sherri Dunbar Quilted Designs
105 Hewett Road
Wyncote, PA 19095
TEL **215-887-5633**
E-Mail: **Dunbar@worldnet.att.net**
Web: **www.dunbarquiltart.com**

Sherri Dunbar's tranquil landscapes of flora and fauna and her fantasy waterscapes reflect the colors and contemplative beauty of our natural environments.

Her finely detailed work combines machine quilting and contemporary surface design techniques to create colorful scenes which invite the viewer to come closer to the embroidered and quilted textures of the surface. Hand-painted fabrics, yarns, threads and beads are carefully selected to create visual impact.

Dunbar's work has been exhibited nationally and is found in collections in the United States and Europe. She specializes in site-specific commissions.

Also see this GUILD sourcebook:
Designer's: 14

A *Approaching Storm*, mixed media, 36" x 26.5", private collection

B *View from the Bottom*, mixed media, 35" x 31", private collection

A

Photo by John Carlano

B

Photo by John Carlano

Linda Filby-Fisher

Linda Filby-Fisher Quilt Artist
6401 West 67th Street
Overland Park, KS 66202
TEL 913-722-2608
Web: www.guild.com
Web: www.saqa.com/gallery.htm

Linda Filby-Fisher's quilts, with their color, texture and embellishments, are created through traditional and unique processes. They are works of detailed design and visual impact.

Each piece, often double sided, includes an embroidered legend, grounding the quilt in history and meaning.

The artist's work can be found nationally in exhibits, collections and publications.

Commissions are welcome. Slides and resumé available upon request.

A *ORIGIN, Celebration of Life* series, international fabrics, embroidered poetry, fetishes, 52"W x 74.5"L

B *BECOMING, Celebration of Life* series, silk and metallic threads, 79.5"W x 49.5"L

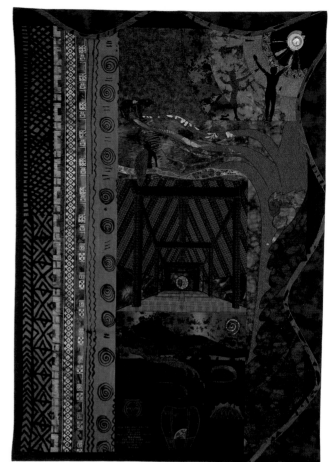

A

Photo by P-TN/Eric Berndt

B

Photo by P-TN/Eric Berndt

My richly textured and layered handmade paper wall sculptures have been installed at numerous corporate sites. Reiger Fine Arts, located in San Francisco, California, is a major influence in the arts in the area. *The Designer's Sourcebook* is an important reference for the company and their clients.

Private collectors commissioned the pieces shown here for their newly built, architecturally modern, five-level home next to Coit Tower in San Francisco. The shapes of the pieces emphasize the angular walls, skylights and ceilings of the home's interior.

The pieces are made of 100% cotton rag and abaca fiber with bamboo. They are formed on a vacuum table and airbrushed with pearlescent, metallic and acrylic paints and dyes.

Each wall sculpture measures 4' x 6' and enhances the atrium wall with a striking presence. Sunset colors of salmons, pinks and purples, offset by the palm leaf greens, bring a sense of the organic foliage from the outside landscape inside to soften the angular lines of the building. Architecture and art go hand in hand to create an environment of exciting lines, forms, color and textures.

— KA

Karen Adachi

COMMISSIONING AGENT: Private collectors through Reiger Fine Arts, San Francisco, CA

TITLE: *Horizons*

DESCRIPTION: Cotton rag and abaca fiber, vacuum-formed and painted, with painted bamboo

SITE: Private residence, San Francisco, CA

Ree Nancarrow

PO Box 29
Denali Park, AK 99755
TEL/FAX 907-683-2376
E-Mail: **reenan@mtaonline.net**

From her remote home in Alaska's interior, Ree Nancarrow is producing vibrant, energetic quilts in bold and unusual colors. She is an established national quilt artist, with acceptance in an impressive number of both juried and invitational shows. Her work is generally abstract, but full of fluid, organic movement. The fabrics she uses are her own hand-dyed or dye-painted fabrics, often contrasted with commercial fabrics.

Prices begin at $100 per square foot. Completed works are available, and commissions are welcome.

A *Ohio Star,* 53"H x 52"W

B *Purple Lights,* 46.5"H x 67.5"W

A

Photo by Ree Nancarrow

B

Photo by Ree Nancarrow

Peggy Printz

Coat of Many Colors
317 North Fourth Street
Shenandoah, VA 22849
TEL **540-652-3268**
E-Mail: **peggy-p@rica.net**

The artist's impressionist landscapes are pieced of hand-dyed and other fabrics, or are painted with permanent dyes on silk or cotton. They are quilted and further embellished with a variety of surface design and textural techniques to capture the essence of a special place or concept, drawing the viewer in. She has created many site-specific art quilts for private, professional and religious settings.

Additional information is available upon request.

A *Springtime in Virginia,* 24" x 22"

B & C *Soar,* 38" x 27"

A

B

C

Judy Speezak

Speezak Quilt Studio
425 5th Avenue
Brooklyn, NY 11215
TEL **718-369-3513**
FAX **718-369-7319**

Judy Speezak's talents for geometry, balanced compositions and use of color — aided by her "palette" of contemporary, vintage and antique textiles — reflect her reverence for early 20th-century paintings and 19th-century quilts.

Her private and corporate commissions have included wall quilts, bed quilts, throw pillows and *chuppahs* (wedding canopies). Slides and prices upon request.

A *Bowties Open,* 1994, wall quilt, cotton, 60" x 48"

B *String Squares #1,* 1998, bed quilt, cotton, 86" x 106"

A

Photo by Karen Bell

B

Photo by D. James Dee

Carolyn C. Wagner

Habitat Quilts
4943 Carole Drive NE
Olympia, WA 98516-9235
TEL **360-456-5666**
E-Mail: **olywagners@olywa.net**

Inspired by earth and sea, light and motion, Carolyn Wagner's quilts are exquisitely crafted. Her superb use of fabric brings warmth to any setting. A passion for detail ensures close-up interest; quilting and embellishments add to the interplay of color, light and texture.

Designing for a particular "habitat" has provided a joyful challenge since 1989. Carolyn's works reside in private collections nationwide.

Commissions and inquiries are welcomed.

A *Embraced by Light,* 1999, 56" x 26"

B *Flying Kimonos,* 1997, 80" x 36"

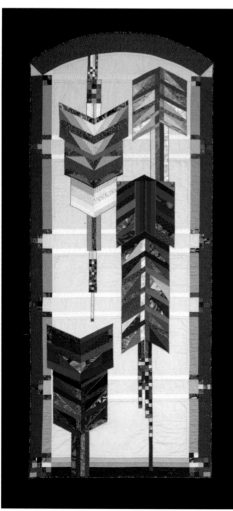

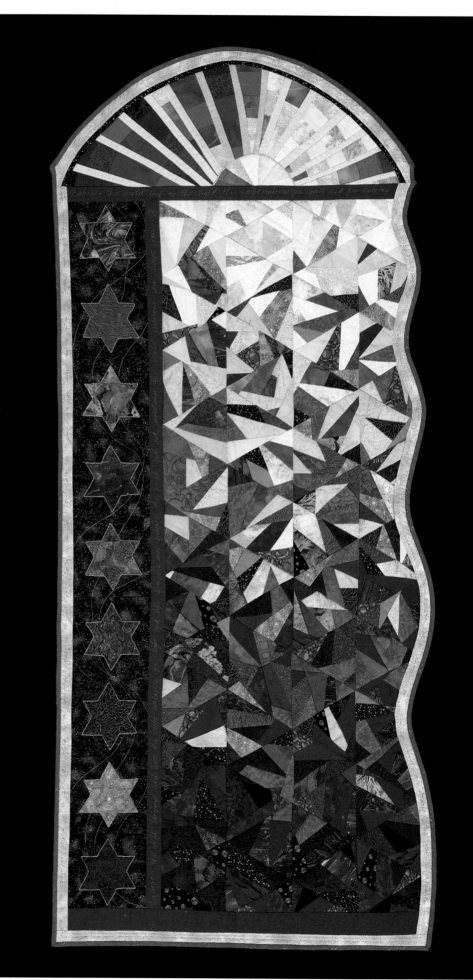

A   Photo by Roger Schreiber

B   Photo by Roger Schreibe

Meiny Vermaas-van der Heide

Meiny Vermaas-van der Heide:
Studio Art Quilts
1219 East La Jolla Drive
Tempe, AZ 85282-5574
TEL/FAX   480-838-5262
E-Mail: meiny@aol.com
Web: www.guild.com
Web: www.saqa.com/meiny.htm

Meiny Vermaas-van der Heide's quilts are known for their strong graphics, minimalist appeal and the "color magic" of visual illusions. They are contemporary classics with an heirloom appearance. Her work has been published and exhibited worldwide, and is in residential, corporate and public art collections.

She has been making art quilts since 1985, machine piecing and quilting her work using hand-dyed and commercial cotton fabrics. Washing and preshrinking the work is part of her construction process in order to create the desired wrinkled heirloom appearance.

Commissions, exhibition opportunities and studio visits are welcomed.

Resumé, slides and prices upon request.

Prices begin at $100 per square foot.

Completed works are available.

Also see these GUILD sourcebooks:
Designer's: 12, 13

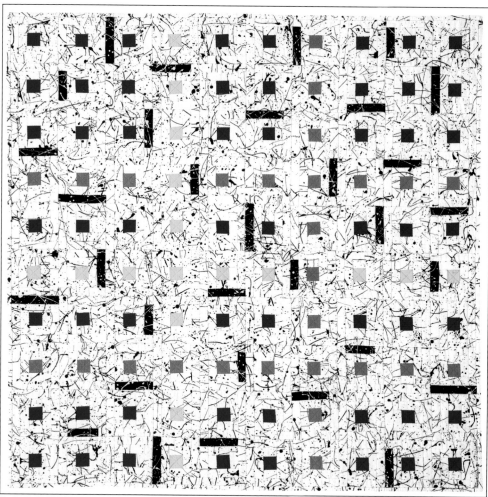

Earth Quilt #53: Homage to Mondriaan XXIV, studio art quilt, 1995, 47"H x 47"W

Photo by Sharon Risedorph Photography

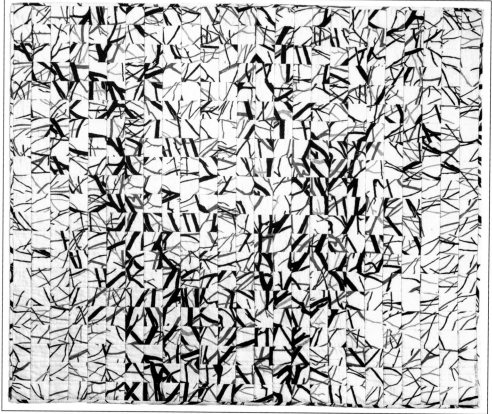

Earth Quilt #44: Lines V, studio art quilt, 1994, 48.5"H x 58"W

Photo by John Peele

SUZY LOCKE

Art Consultant

Suzy Locke has been a professional art consultant in the San Francisco area for 18 years, serving corporate, civic and private clients. But, despite her thorough knowledge of the field and the rich selection of artists of all kinds available in her part of the world, Locke often turns to THE GUILD to search out exactly the right artists for her demanding and sophisticated clients.

"We have a long and excellent craft tradition here in the Bay area, but I use THE GUILD to remind myself of the range of work available throughout the country," she says. "As I look at art for clients, I'm considering everything from tabletop sculpture to monumental works."

Recently, Locke found just the right bronze sculpture by GUILD artist James Barnhill of Greensboro, North Carolina, for a client with an extensive art collection. "They were looking for a full-size bronze of a standing nude female for a specific site, but fell in love with a smaller, bronze nymph James had made. They were completely satisfied with the work, and the nymph seems right at home on a rock ledge overlooking a gorgeous indoor swimming pool. I can't tell you how thoroughly thrilled my clients were.

"It was a delight to work with James. He was prompt about sending the slides and collateral material we asked for, and he was thoroughly professional in every way, from consulting about the patina on the piece, to the shipping arrangements. Commissioning art over the phone and through correspondence is not a problem when you're dealing with artists of this caliber and experience."

Locke also recommends using the glossy tear sheets THE GUILD makes available to its artists. She uses them as leave-behinds, a very professional, very persuasive marketing tool.

"When we live with arts and crafts, it's very much like living with silent friends ... This feeling should be protected, nurtured and appreciated."

MARK SIMON

Architect

"Architects need to include elements that give richness and meaning to people's lives," says Mark Simon, "and among the most important of these elements are fine arts and crafts. They mark an environment with finger and thumb prints, and show human care in a way that nothing else can."

Simon, one of five partners with Centerbrook Architects, is an enthusiastic advocate for using original art in the built environment. For years he's encouraged his clients to use artists as collaborators with the design team as a way to create spaces that win not only awards, but raves from those who live and work there.

He recalls working on a private lodge with special fondness. "We started with the flavor of an Adirondacks Great Camp, but from the beginning I wanted to integrate artwork as a way to enrich the texture and provide a signature." As a result, every room in the house is rich in exquisitely-executed arts and craft details, including works by two GUILD metal artists. Joel Schwartz created custom-designed door hardware and Ira DeKoven contributed an intricate, one-of-a-kind fireplace screen. "It was a wonderful, fascinating project," says Simon, "and best of all, the client absolutely loves the place."

Simon encourages other architects to use artists, and to interview them carefully. "You need to be clear about deadlines and contractual responsibilities. And listen to artists carefully, because they often have wonderful suggestions. Most of all, be ready to collaborate.

"We need to remember to design environments that invite habitation, places we want to be," he says. "When we live with arts and crafts, it's very much like living with silent friends. We feel accompanied—less alone. This feeling should be protected, nurtured and appreciated."

Photo by Jeannette Montgomery Barron

ART FOR THE WALL: FIBER

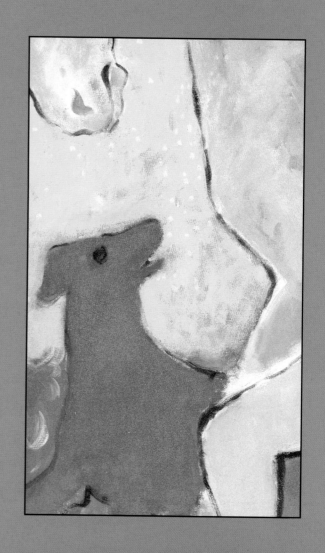

Heather Allen

Heather Allen Studio
PO Box 7646
Asheville, NC 28802
TEL 828-253-2693

Heather Allen is a surface designer who creates vibrant textiles that combine an artist's eye for color and space with a craftsman's attention to detail.

Each piece is made of cloth that has been dyed, painted and layered using numerous techniques to evoke emotion and convey visual depth. Working intuitively with color and pattern, she creates textiles that enliven environments.

Allen has work in private and corporate collections. Commissions are welcomed; slides and pricing available upon request.

98 Broadway, dye, textile ink, cotton, linen, silk, 91" x 49"   Photo by Tim Barnwell

38 Ponder, dye, textile ink, cotton, linen, silk, First Union Bank, 96" x 48"   Photo by Tim Barnwe

Journey, dye, textile ink, cotton, linen, silk, 18" x 81" x 3"   Photo by John Luc

Lynn Basa

2510 East Ward
Seattle, WA 98112
TEL **206-328-3269**
FAX **206-328-3004**
E-Mail: **lynnbasa@lynnbasa.com**
Web: **www.lynnbasa.com**

Lynn Basa creates site-specific installations for the wall and floor in collaboration with art collectors and design professionals. Densely hand-knotted in Nepal of wool and silk from the artist's drawings, each piece tells a story with symbols.

Shown here are two of five portraits in symbols from the *Five Citizens* series commissioned by the City of Seattle. The artist chose five Seattle residents, interviewed them with an identical set of questions and wove their answers into portraits as unique as the individuals themselves.

Denbernesh, top, is an Ethiopian shopkeeper who was born along the Blue Nile. Using the subject's favorite colors, the foreground consists of talismanic forms from traditional healing rituals, while the background spells "Ethiopia" in Amharic, one of the world's oldest alphabets.

LaMar, bottom, honors a venerable curator and supporter of crafts in Seattle. Chamber music, gardening, abstract art and animals are her passions. Her personal symbol is the crow.

Also see this GUILD sourcebook:
Designer's: 14

Photo by Russell Johnson

Photo by Russell Johnson

George-Ann Bowers

1199 Cornell Avenue
Berkeley, CA 94706
TEL 510-524-3611
FAX 510-526-8064
E-Mail: tmslbwrs@earthlink.net

George-Ann Bowers weaves in multiple layers to transform her perceptions of nature into warm, dynamic compositions for commercial and residential interiors. Richly colored and textured, Bowers' complex weavings draw the viewer into an intimate exploration of natural phenomena and invite personal response to her imagery.

Bowers has created commissions and exhibited her work nationally for more than 15 years. Commission inquiries are welcomed — visuals and pricing available upon request. Completed pieces are also available.

Also see these GUILD sourcebooks:
Designer's: 11, 13, 14

A *Lily of the Nile,* 2000, weaving, 23.5" x 22"

B *River of Change,* 1999, weaving, 30" x 72"

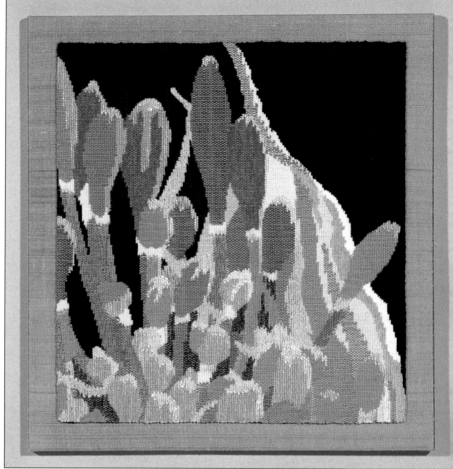

A

Photo by Dana Dav[...]

B

Photo by Dana Dav[...]

Laura Militzer Bryant

595 30th Avenue North
St. Petersburg, FL 33713
TEL 727-327-3100
FAX 727-321-1905
E-Mail: knitlb@ix.netcom.com

The colorful and evocative weavings of Laura Militzer Bryant enliven many corporate and public spaces as well as private homes. Pieces begin with white threads that are dyed with high-quality lightfast dyes, then are woven in a complex double-weave technique that merges several different color systems into one enigmatic whole.

Bryant has received multiple awards, including National Endowment for the Arts and Florida State Individual Artist grants. Her works hang in corporate and public collections such as Humana Hospital, Valparaiso University, Xerox Corporation and the City of St. Petersburg.

Also see these GUILD sourcebooks:
Designer's: 10, 11, 12, 13, 14

To The Light, weaving, 59" x 45.5"

Millenia, weaving on copper, 42" x 64"

A

Photo by Thomas Bruce

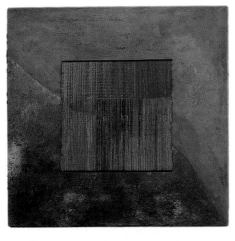

B

Photo by Thomas Bruce

Myra Burg

6180 W. Jefferson Boulevard, Suite Y
Los Angeles, CA 90016
TEL   310-399-5040
FAX 310-399-0623
Web: www.myraburg.com

Quiet Oboes and custom sculptural installations combine a fiber symphony of luxurious color with the crispness of burnished metals for solutions elegant in design and brilliant in color and engineering. Burg produces innovative site-specific art, enjoying unusual or complicated site parameters. Completed works and custom *Quiet Oboes* are also available. Sizes range from tabletop to airplane hangar for freestanding, wall-mounted and aerial constructions.

Architectural installations such as room dividers and specialty doors are also available.

Since 1976, Burg has produced installations for private collections and public spaces both domestically and abroad. An award winner in both careers, art and architecture, her work is considered of investment quality. Collaborations welcome.

Also see these GUILD sourcebooks:
Designer's: 9, 13, 14
Architect's: 13, 14, 15

Aladdinesque, 1998, aluminum, fiber, 6' x 3' x 4'   Photo by Ron Luxemburg

Quiet Oboes (detail)   Photo by Ron Luxemburg

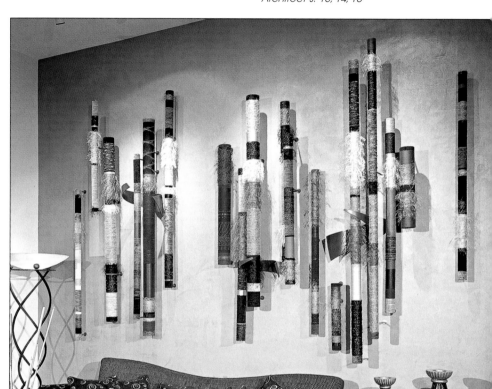

Quiet Oboes, 1998, fiber, bronzed aluminum, sizes vary   Photo by Ron Luxembu

Poppa's Music, 1998, aluminum, fiber, 6' x 5' x 4"   Photo by Ron Luxemburg

Japonaise, 1997, aluminum, fiber, 16' x 6' x 5"   Photo by Ron Luxembu

Barbara Cade

262 Hideaway Hills Drive
Hot Springs, AR 71901
TEL 501-262-4065
E-Mail: cade@ipa.net

Collectible rocks, luscious vegetation, textured trees and dramatic skies — sculptural landscape elements inspired by your geographical location designed specifically for your space. Used together or individually.

Barbara Cade continues to be inspired by themes in nature, constructing two- and three-dimensional work in woven and felted wool. She welcomes commissions for specific areas of the country.

Her work has been in museum-juried shows for 25 years, is represented in many corporate collections and is part of the permanent collection of the Tacoma Art Museum.

Pieces are easy to install; some are framed with wood.

Wool felt is easily cleaned and repaired with minimum maintenance.

Also see these GUILD sourcebooks: *Designer's: 8, 9, 10, 11, 12*

SHOWN: *In My Own Backyard*, triptych of rocks, sunset and dogwood, © 1999, hand-felted wool, 45"H x 48"W x 8"D

Shari Cornish

625 South Hauser Boulevard #402
Los Angeles, CA 90036
TEL 323-422-5887
FAX 323-937-6688
E-Mail: Artcarpets@aol.com

Shari Cornish's art carpets are each developed as an interpretation of her original paintings. The premium quality rugs are created by working in collaboration with production artisans in the U.S. to achieve the lush texture and rich color that complement either private or public spaces. The carpets are hand knotted using 100% New Zealand wool.

Information regarding costs and commissions is available upon request.

A *Pie & Coffee* painting, pigment on industrial felt, 36"H x 28"W

B *Pages of Envy* painting, pigment on industrial felt, 46"H x 28"W

C *Pie & Coffee* carpet sample, wool, sized to order

D *Pages of Envy* carpet sample, wool, sized to order

E *Auntie's Apron* carpet, wool, 6.5' x 6.5'

A   Photo by Bradley Miller

B   Photo by Bradley Mille

C   Photo by Bradley Miller

D   Photo by Bradley Mille

E   Photo by Bradley Mil

Suzanne Gernandt

108 Welwyn Lane
Asheville, NC 28805
TEL   828-299-4889
FAX 828-299-7430
E-Mail: jgernandt@aol.com

Bold graphic designs along with rich color textures and patterns bring vitality to Gernandt's work, attracting the viewer's attention and encouraging repeat viewing. Working only with natural fibers, she uses advanced surface design techniques to layer the colors on the cloth, creating depth, complexity and increased surface texture. Finished pieces can be presented in several formats: quilted, stretched or framed.

Gernandt has numerous works in corporate and private collections. Commissions are welcomed; photos, slides and resumé are available upon request.

Also see these GUILD sourcebooks:
Designer's: 12

SHOWN: *Balancing Act*, quilt, 36" x 54"

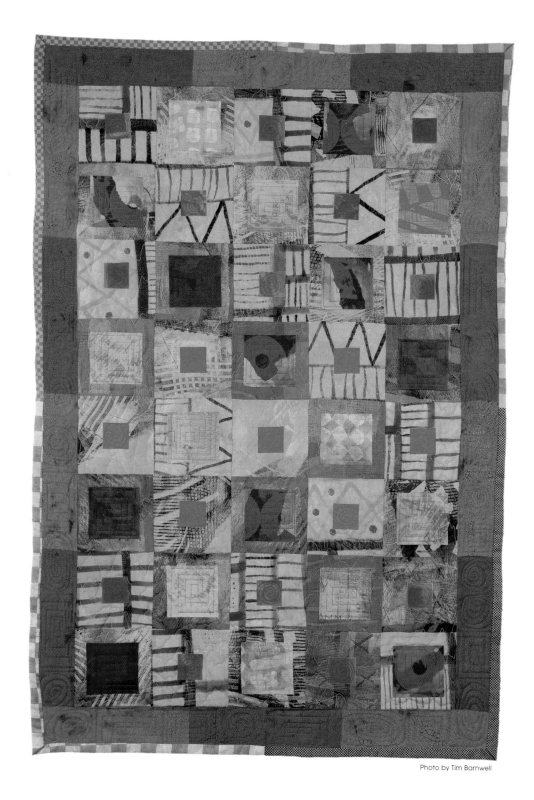

Photo by Tim Barnwell

Christi and Mark Carter, owners of Hotel Carter in Eureka, California, contacted me. They had received my portfolio, which included six tear sheets from my advertising with GUILD Sourcebooks over the past ten years. I worked with Mark after Christi reviewed my prototype. Their extensive traveling and knowledge of bed-and-breakfasts throughout the United States encouraged them to individualize their own lovely hotel with custom artwork for the wall, as well as textiles.

These bed canopies softened the edges of the room, adding color, light and fantasy to the setting through the use of unique textiles. Since this project started, the Carters have commissioned 28 canopies. Each room has different hues with which the canopies coordinate. As this project continues, there will be additional painted and appliquéd aro-matherapy pillows to balance the overhead design work and carry the visitor's eye down to the bed. We've also discussed adding slipper chairs and ottomans.

This project began four years ago and includes all rooms in the hotel except those with poster beds. This was not the initial plan. Mark and Christi originally imagined canopies only on the bottom floor. However, the response of guests requesting "canopy rooms" encouraged them to finish the other floors also. The canopies average 60" wide and 108" long. They are comprised of handpainted silks and linens appliquéd and hand stitched onto cotton canvas. Wrought iron curtain rods, finials and brackets hold them in place.

— JM

Photo by Robin Robin

Jennifer Mackey

COMMISSIONING AGENT: Mark and Christi Carter

DESCRIPTION: 28 bed canopies, handpainted silks and linens on cotton canvas

SITE: Hotel Carter, Eureka, CA

Sandra Golbert

Designs Unlimited
2 Washington Lane
Tappan, NY 10983
TEL/FAX 914-365-6093
E-Mail: sgolbert@tco.com
Web: www.guild.com

Sandra Golbert has worked in fibers for more than 35 years, using mostly handmade paper, hand-dyed silk and mixed media. She creates her pieces so that light, movement and shadow will be integral parts of the artwork.

Her paper pieces are usually in neutral shades, but when she works in silk or banner cloth, the work explodes with color and life. Her work was recently included in an exhibit at the American Craft Museum in New York City and can be found in the permanent collection of the Zimmerli Art Museum's National Association of Women Artists Collection at Rutgers University.

Contact the artist for more information on her large banners, sculptures and hangings. Prices from $200.

Commissions include:
San Juan Hotel, Puerto Rico
Bacardi Corporation, Puerto Rico

Awards include:
National Endowment for the Arts, Instituto de Cultura, Puerto Rico
Pollock-Krasner Foundation

Colores, 9"H x 9"W x 3"D

Anaphe, 110"H x 28"W x 38"D

A

Photo by James Dee, New York City

B

Photo by Olga Alicea, Puerto Rico

Arlene Levey

1020 West Ardmore Avenue
Chicago, IL 60660
TEL 773-271-7446
FAX 773-271-7426
E-Mail: aleveyarts@21stcentury.net

These works are painted, dyed and layered silk organza, fused and treated with acrylic. This original process creates a leathery translucent material that is lightweight, durable, low-maintenance and exceptionally lightfast.

From lamp shades and folding screens to large atrium hangings, natural or artificial backlighting reveals multiple layers, changing both the color and imagery. As in life, what you see depends on where you stand.

A *Next?*, 34" x 42"

B & C *Choose*, 44" x 42"

A

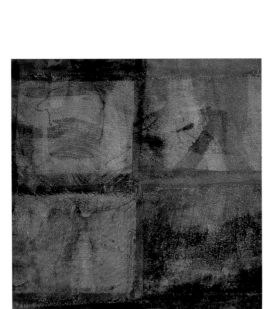

B

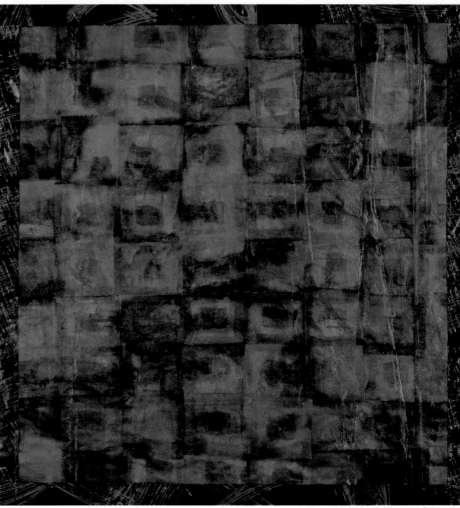

C

Arlene Levey

020 West Ardmore Avenue
Chicago, IL 60660
TEL 773-271-7446
FAX 773-271-7426
E-Mail: aleveyarts@21stcentury.net

With this translucent material, natural light from windows or skylights is especially effective: the work will change in appearance as the day progresses.

Levey's works have been shown in galleries and public spaces, and are in corporate and private collections nationally. She offers experience and reliability in working individually or as part of a design team to create site-specific designs or to place existing work.

Pricing available upon request.

SHOWN: *Rain*, 72" x 72"

GRAPHICS IN WOOL, INC.

Anna Vojik
PO Box 382
292 Nuttall Road
Riverside, IL 60546
TEL **708-447-1746**
FAX **708-447-5867**
E-Mail: **interarts@aol.com**

GRAPHICS IN WOOL, INC., is a collection of incredibly detailed contemporary tapestries handwoven by prominent Polish artisans. Master weavers ingeniously render the artist's design in tapestry. Each piece is created entirely by hand, preserving 17th- and 18th-century traditions in an era of advancing technologies.

The wool is hand spun and hand dyed using a process that imbues every tapestry with a surprisingly distinct personality. As a result of special yarn treatments, tapestries are colorfast and mothproofed. Each weaving is a testament to the art and craft of exceptional design.

Many designs can be made to match a color scheme with a variance in size up to 10 feet wide.

Commissions are welcomed. Pricing available upon request.

Rituals, artist: Dennis Downes

Umbrellas, artist: Piotr Grabowski

Joyce P. Lopez

Joyce Lopez Studio
147 West Ohio Street #304
Chicago, IL 60622-5874
TEL 312-243-5033
FAX 312-243-7566
E-Mail: **JoyceLopez@aol.com**
Web: **www.guild.com**

Joyce Lopez meticulously creates her sculpture out of metal poles and silk-like cotton thread. With over 300 exquisite colors to choose from, color specifications are always met. Her stunning sculptures enrich corporate, public and private interiors.

Collections include the Sony Corporation of America, City of Chicago, State of Illinois, State of Washington, Nokia Corporation, Health South, Jim Beam Brands and many private residences.

These sculptures are easily maintained and usually take between two to four months to complete. Prices start at $3000. Call, fax or e-mail to request a brochure.

Also see these GUILD sourcebooks:
THE GUILD: 1, 2, 3, 4, 5
Designer's: 6, 7, 8, 9, 10, 11, 12, 13, 14
Architect's: 8, 11, 14, 15

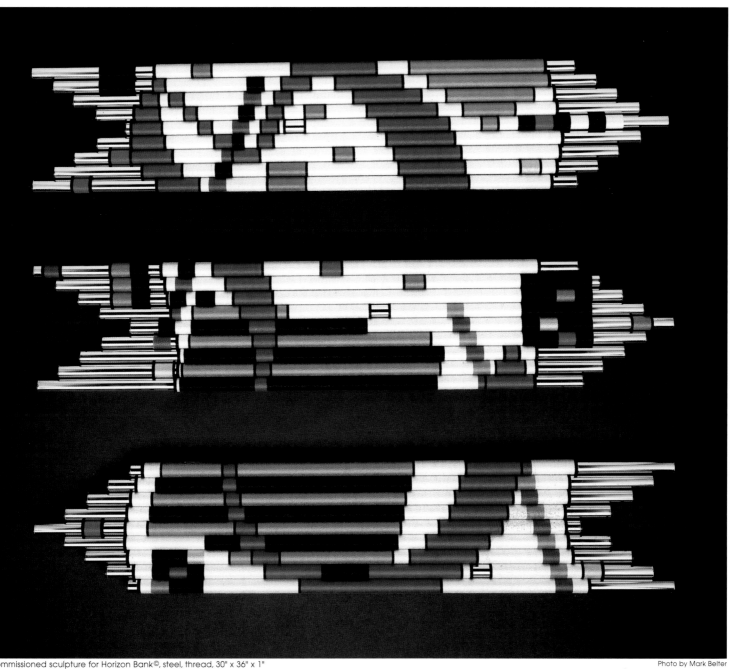

Commissioned sculpture for Horizon Bank©, steel, thread, 30" x 36" x 1"

Photo by Mark Belter

Jennifer Mackey

Chia Jen Studio
2430 Fifth Street, Unit I
Berkeley, CA 94710-2452
TEL **510-841-3930**
FAX **510-841-0949**
E-Mail: **chiajen@hotmail.com**

Jennifer Mackey of Chia Jen Studio uses sponging, painting, screen printing and appliqué techniques to fashion unique designs. Mackey's works blend European, Mediterranean and Eastern influences.

Mackey, who strives for a creative and fresh look, applies her talents to upholstery fabrics, drapery material, floor coverings and hangings. Her clients are in both the design community and the general public.

Chia Jen Studio offers its designs in natural fiber textiles, such as linen, silk, hemp, wool and cotton. Non-toxic, water-based pigments are used; they are colorfast and environmentally sensitive.

Color brochure available.

Also see these GUILD sourcebooks:
THE GUILD: 3
Designer's: 6, 11, 12, 13, 14
Architect's: 6, 12

A Side chairs, gold foil and wash

B Hand-finished bench, foil accents

C Black linen slip chairs, metallic wash inks

A

Photo by Mark Guerra

B

Photo by Robin Robi

C

Photo by Robin Robi

Jennifer Mackey

Chia Jen Studio
2430 Fifth Street, Unit I
Berkeley, CA 94710-2452
TEL 510-841-3930
FAX 510-841-0949
E-Mail: **chiajen@hotmail.com**

Custom signature prints are the forte of designer Jennifer Mackey. Comfortable with collaborations and the endless application possibilities of fiber, the Chia Jen Studio has enjoyed the success of a variety of projects.

Mackey's use of fiber for atriums, interiors and art for the wall can be seen in other GUILD sourcebooks.

Color brochure, slides and references available.

Also see these GUILD sourcebooks:
THE GUILD: 3
Designer's: 6, 11, 12, 13, 14
Architect's: 6, 12

A Licensed to Springs Industries, Inc.

B Permanent collection, College of the Redwoods

A   Photo by Mark Guerra

B   Photo by Mark Guerra

Noelle McGuire

Tapeis Safan
497 Reis Avenue
Oradell, NJ 07649
TEL 201-261-5336
FAX 201-261-3154
E-Mail: NoelleMcGuire@worldnet.att.net

An interior designer for 27 years, Noelle has found in handwoven tapestries a technique that really expresses her vision. In it, she combines her love of painting with the tactile qualities of textiles to reflect the diversity of the world around her.

Highly regarded for her ability to design and create custom work to suit specific client needs, whether functional or purely decorative, she can express many different styles and cultural motifs.

She works on a frame loom with cotton warp and a vast variety of wool and other natural fiber weft materials, even incorporating found objects for greater texture and dimension.

Prices range from $95 to $145 per square foot with pieces available from stock or as commissions. McGuire is a professional member of the American Crafts Council.

A *Georgia's Doorway*, cotton warp, wool weft,
   30" x 32"

B *Breakers at Malin Bay*, cotton warp, wool weft,
   27" x 36"

A

B

Nana Montgomery

Blue Shark Design
PO Box 3873
Santa Cruz, CA 95063-3873
TEL 831-423-6804
FAX 831-423-5466
E-Mail: nana@bluesharkdesign.com
Web: www.bluesharkdesign.com

Nana Montgomery's original art quilts draw upon a wide vocabulary of shapes and colors. Figurative themes are inspired by merging archetypal imagery with the personal. The strong traditional techniques of machine and hand sewing are used in construction; long experience with textiles and paint assure a surface that is durable and vibrant. Both residential and corporate environments are enhanced by her softly painted, densely quilted works.

Inquiries about completed works and commissions are welcome.

Also see this GUILD sourcebook:
Designer's: 14

Mason, 20" x 30"   Photo by Richard Johns

Marriage Quilt, 33" x 35"   Photo by Richard Johns

Big Cat, 74" x 50"   Photo by Richard Johns

Barbara McQueeney

McQueeney Designs
2415 Converse Street
Dallas, TX 75207
TEL **214-630-4955**
FAX **214-630-1023**
E-Mail: **barbara@mcqueeneydesigns.com**
Web: **www.mcqueeneydesigns.com**

Barbara McQueeney's textiles are an exploration of making simple shapes into complex cloth. Circles, squares and triangles are found repeatedly throughout her art. Use of these universal symbols, which have occurred in every culture throughout history, lends an ancient and everlasting quality to her work.

Working mainly in silk, her pieces emphasize the unique energy and sensuality of the medium. While many of her pieces reflect an ethnic influence, she remains fluid in her ability to interpret the parameters of each individual project.

Commissions are welcomed. Portfolio and pricing available upon request.

Also see these GUILD sourcebooks:
Designer's: 13, 14

A *Primitive Geometries I,* dyes on silk, 30" x 43.5"

B *Primitive Geometries II* (detail), dyes on silk, 29.25" x 43.25"

A

Photo by Robb Debenpo

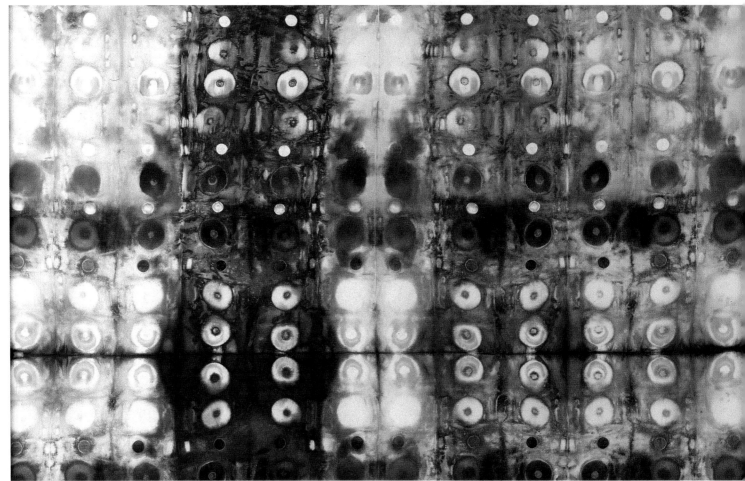

B

Photo by Robb Debenpo

Nancy McRay

Woven Art
320 Southlawn
East Lansing, MI 48823
TEL 517-351-5205
Web: **www.guild.com**

Inspired by music, architecture and people,
Nancy McRay uses the techniques unique
to weaving to interpret these influences. The
elements of form, pattern and structure are
combined with color and texture to create
new images. Commissions are welcome. Slides,
resumé and prices available upon request.

Also see this GUILD sourcebook:
Designer's: 14

A *Constellations,* © 1999, 6' x 4'

B *100 Hour Weaving/100 Hour War,* © 1991, 48" x 70"

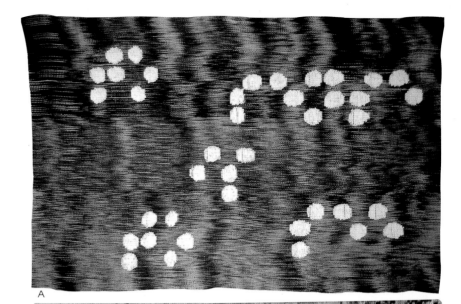

A

B

Gretchen Morrissey

Gretchen Morrissey Hand Printed Textiles
PO Box 0099
Havre de Grace, MD 21078-0099
TEL/FAX   **410-942-0071**
E-Mail: **gmorrissey@hotmail.com**

"I am intensely intrigued with the potential of transforming the visual images of natural forms into fiber compositions. I use various materials, means and techniques in manipulating the surface to achieve a sophisticated balance and rhythm between natural elements and natural fibers."
Gretchen Morrissey

For more than a decade, Gretchen Stormer Morrissey has been creating exquisite hand-dyed and hand-printed textiles. Working with natural fibers, she transforms each piece into an individually conceived work of art. Her artwork includes sumptuous pillows and wall hangings.

Morrissey's work is represented in private gallerie and has been featured in museums throughout the United States. What distinguishes her art is the richness of material, the depth of hue, and a passion to explore the work at hand.

A   *Africa-Blue,* 1999, oil pastels, hand-dyed silk, handmade paper, wire and nails, 20" x 14"

B   *Coral Reef I,* 2000, hand-dyed and hand-printed silk charmeuse, silk dupioni border and backing, pieced and stitched, 51" x 33"

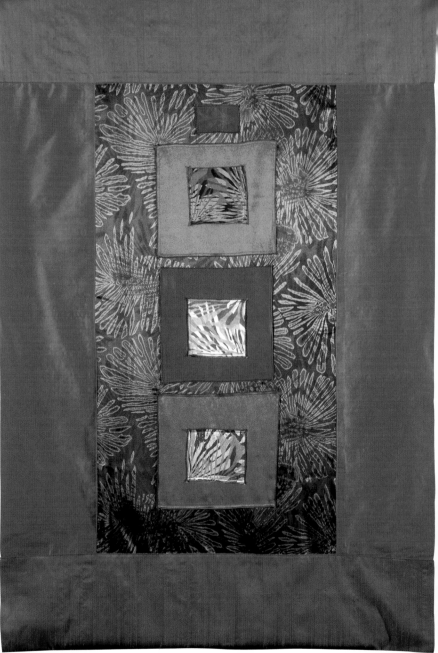

A   Photo by David Lightner   B   Photo by Karen Mauch

Caroline Rackley

Design Unlimited
C68 Box 23A
Apello, NM 87745
TEL 505-425-6092
E-Mail: **designultd@newmexico.com**

Design Unlimited currently offers a full spectrum of handwoven fabrics by the yard or in restful imagery quilted for the bed or wall, cushions, table linens, unforgettable baby blankets and tapestries. This is a woven cloth strip series inspired by work from looms belonging to the designer's pioneer ancestors.

Fabrics produced in collaboration using a designer's preferred materials can act to harmonize elements of color and texture in the overall decor. Limited-edition yardage assures clients a unique textile commission.

Drawn by the romance of color and pattern, Rackley's 30-year adventure in the fiber world has deepened her commitment to ethical textile engineering. Her pieces, inviting and relaxed as they are, have structural integrity meant to last for generations.

Also see this GUILD sourcebook:
Architect's: 12

Teal Hourglass, twin-size quilt for wall or bed, cotton, blends, rayon, 73"H x 54"W

Kaleidoscope Quilt, The Iris and *Iris Mats* (details), cotton, blends, rayon

Bernie Rowell

Bernie Rowell Studio
250 Hookers Gap
Candler, NC 28715
TEL/FAX   828-667-2479
E-Mail: rowellstudio@earthlink.net

Rowell's *Computer Scrap Quilt* series combines painted canvas with sewn construction. Embroidered forms, recycled circuit boards and metallic elements add rich three-dimensional detail to strong underlying compositions.

Durable materials and innovative construction techniques create tactile fiber art with the easy care qualities of acrylic paintings. Custom colors are available.

Rowell has produced site-specific commissions for more than 20 years. Her art is included in corporate and private collections throughout the United States.

Clients include:
Hewlett Packard
MCI WorldCom
Mitsubishi Semiconductor America
Morgan, Stanley, Dean, Witter
Kaiser Permanente
SAS Institute
Fairfield Processing

Also see these GUILD sourcebooks:
Designer's: 10, 13, 14

SHOWN: *Techno Tango 99, Computer Scrap Quilt* series, sewn canvas, paint, circuit boards, 58" x 62"

Photo by Tim Barnwell

an Schlieper

Design
0 Grandview Place
anitou Springs, CO 80829
L 719-685-3157
Mail: janschlieper@excite.com

an Schlieper's hooked-thread paintings are
eated with a rare technique in which a one-
ch needle, a single strand of thread and a
agnifying glass are used to create thousands
f tightly packed loops of cotton pile which
semble a hand-hooked rug in miniature. Each
ece is finished with a bead border, then is
amed and matted under acrylic. The approxi-
ate framed size is 20" x 23". Larger images can
e obtained in polytych format in the same
ame. Multiple pieces also can be utilized
ogether to accommodate any wall space.

chlieper's work has been exhibited nationally,
cluding a show juried by Kenneth Trapp,
urator-in-charge of the Renwick Gallery of the
mithsonian. She was also one of 500 artists
hosen out of 5,500 for *The International
berArts Design Book Six.*

isuals of completed works are available.

lso see this GUILD sourcebook:
esigner's: 14

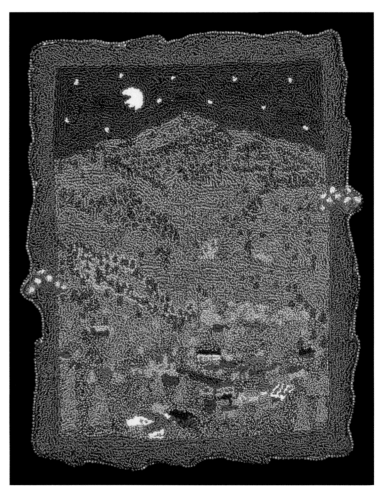

Mountain Village, framed hooked thread, 20" x 23"

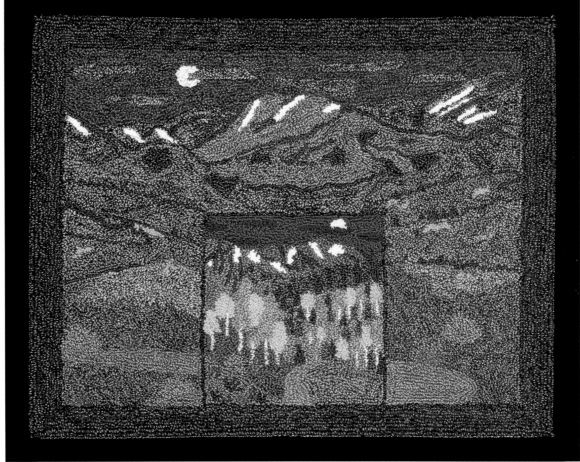

Mountain Roads, framed hooked thread, 20" x 23"

Laurie Post of Corporate Art West in Bellevue, Washington, saw my work in *The Designer's Sourcebook 13* and sent me an e-mail in January 1999. I have been working with this company ever since.

Recently, Corporate Art West commissioned me to produce digital prints (iris and inkjet on paper and canvas) as variations of several images of my slides, which they have on file. All of our communication is done via e-mail. Laurie tells me the image she's chosen, the media she wants used, and the image size. I do the work and ship it off to her.

Turtle Man, the work that appeared in *The Designer's Sourcebook 13,* has been reproduced digitally more often than others. I've recreated it as a print of the original collage, cropped, rotated it to a vertical image, and printed it on paper, as well as on canvas. I also add collage elements to the print paper or canvas so that each work is unique.

Creating and producing work on demand via digital imaging is incredibly exciting. I never imagined that I would be doing commissions that way.

— **NEN**

Nancy Egol Nikkal

COMMISSIONING AGENT: Corporate Art West, Bellevue, WA

TITLE: *Turtle Man*

DESCRIPTION: Collage and acrylic, 22" x 30"

SITE: Various sites

Karen Urbanek

4 Blair Avenue
dmont, CA 94611-4004
L 510-654-0685
X 510-654-2790
Mail: KrnUrbanek@aol.com

Since 1984, Karen Urbanek has been creating unusual "paper" textiles. She builds image and textile simultaneously by hand layering dyed silk fibers compacted by streams of water, later solidified with an adhesive solution. For sites with high lightfastness demands, flax fiber is instead painted with pigments.

Her painterly images have drama, subtlety and spareness. Individual forms and multilayered pieces may encompass openwork, translucent, dense and highly textured areas. These strong, crisp textiles need not be framed and may be easily cleaned.

Work includes wall pieces as well as standing and hanging sculptures. Commissions are welcomed. Visual materials and pricing are available upon request.

Also see these GUILD sourcebooks:
Designer's: 13, 14

SHOWN: *Garden*^{3}, 1999, natural dyed silk fiber, polymer; nine images, each: 15"H x 15"W

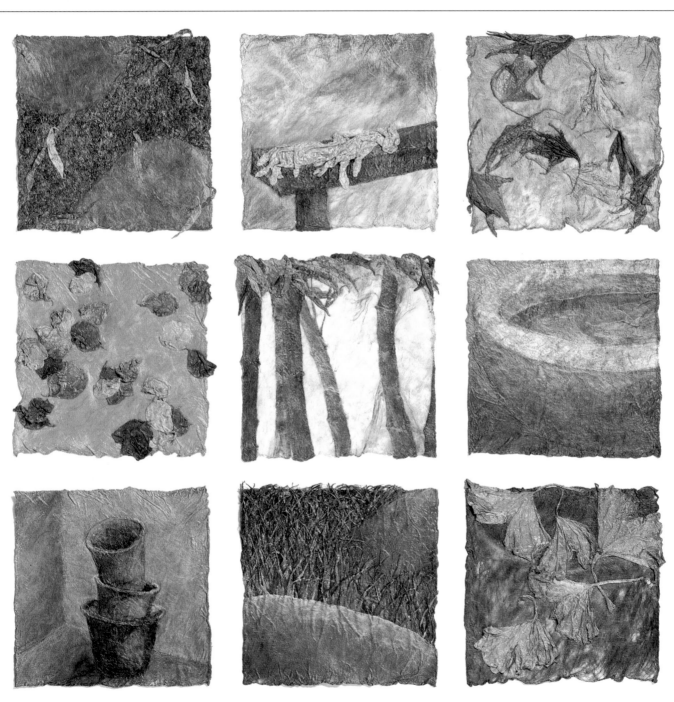

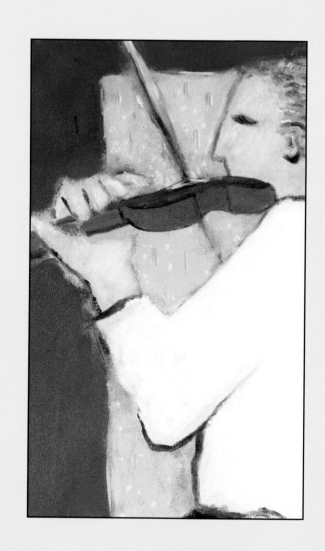

THE CARE AND MAINTENANCE
OF FIBER ART

Handcrafted works in fiber have enriched the lives of both royalty and peasantry since the beginning of humankind. Persian brocades, Indian chilkats, Indonesian ship cloths, Asian ikats, Turkish rugs — the artistry and craftsmanship of textiles from centuries past are kept alive in countless museums around the world. And it's a marvel that they exist at all for us to enjoy today. Homage is paid first to the artists who toiled over these works and second to the conservators who have preserved them for safe passage into this century.

Likewise, today's fiber art deserves our thoughtful attention to care and maintenance. Regarding contemporary textiles as the heirlooms of tomorrow is the best way to ensure their preservation for future generations to enjoy.

You don't have to be a museum curator to purchase and display contemporary textiles, but you do have to remember that they are perishable works of art. While a designer's most important function is to choose the right art or artist for a client's taste, project and budget, in this medium

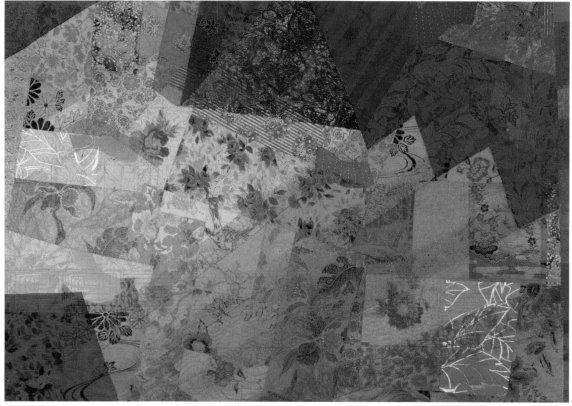

Heather Allen, *98 Broadway* (detail), dye, textile ink, cotton, linen, silk, 91" x 49", see page 252

Photo by Tim Barnwell

there is also an important role to be played in several pragmatic areas. The most exquisite art in the world will be diminished by inappropriate positioning, lighting and overall maintenance. Aesthetics and conservation should get equal consideration.

Presentation

Successful presentation begins with selecting the right environment — a space, position and illumination that shows off the ultimate quality of a piece. On an artistic level, attention must be given to spatial considerations, proportions, focal points. On a practical level, solutions must be found for safely showcasing fiber art.

If the art is commissioned as part of the overall design process and the installation plan thought through in the conception stage, this task is easier. But if a work has been commissioned or purchased for an existing space, solutions need to be found for lighting that will neither diminish the piece aesthetically nor destroy it physically. Because fiber is somewhat fragile, these questions of endurance and care are important. Fiber art that has become shabby or soiled, with its color faded, is an all-too-familiar and disheartening sight.

Jean West, former director of the Center for Tapestry Arts in New York City, brings home the point with a reminder of the short-lived craze of the 1960s and 1970s. Jute and sisal, many clients learned the hard way, are extremely fragile — if unprotected, they deteriorate rapidly. Because there was little history in this field, and scarce information on protection was available, a large body of this work has been lost to the elements. Harsh light and moisture took their toll.

Fiber art has long been recognized as a springboard for explorations in a variety of media; this is a field that continues to evolve through the use of new materials. Peruse the pages of GUILD Sourcebooks and you'll find works in metallic yarns, new lustrous cottons, silk, wools, handmade papers, synthetics, bamboo and wire. Often you'll read in the artists' descriptions of their works assurances that they are "custom-dyed, lightfast, mothproof, treated with fabric protectant, fireproofing available." Our contemporary fiber artists have become knowledgeable in areas of durability and maintenance. Conservation gets a good start with their expertise, but ensuring textiles a long-term existence takes an ongoing effort, one in which designers and art consultants play an important role. In addition to the advice offered here, there are a number of other resources available regarding the care and conservation of textiles (see sidebar, *Textile Conservation Resources*).

OVERCOMING GLARE

Artwork that is covered with glass or plastic can reflect light into people's eyes. The potential for glare can be determined even before the artwork is hung as long as you know where lights will be placed in relation to the art. The angle of light reflecting off the glass or plastic always equals the angle of the light hitting the glass or plastic.

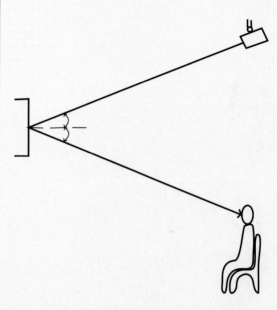

Here are some solutions to the problem of glare:

- **Add parabolic louvers to light fixtures to provide a 45-degree shielding angle.**

- **Set the ceiling lights at a sharper angle: move the lights closer to the wall where the art is displayed.**

- **Use floor canisters that shine light upward onto the art.**

- **Remove the glass or plastic from the work.**

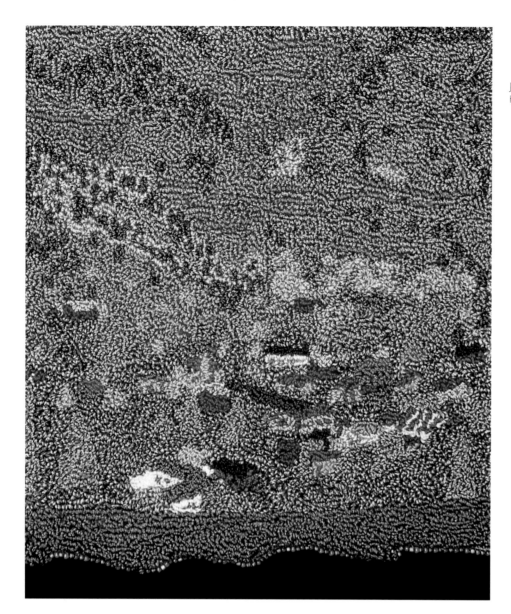

Jan Schlieper, *Mountain Village* (detail), framed hooked thread, 20" x 23", see page 275

Positioning

Too-close or too-intense lighting presents not only physical harm to fiber art, but will diminish these works aesthetically as well. Intense bright light destroys the textile's colors, which have, quite naturally, been painstakingly and masterfully chosen for the ultimate effect. Work lit too brightly can be totally distorted, the colors washed out in the beam. Works with subtle transitions in color, and those in which light plays on fibers and in which spatial depth is critical, must also be lit very carefully.

Laurence Korwin, in his book *Textiles as Art*, provides an extensive guide to optimum lighting combinations, including suggestions on positioning of lights (see sidebar, *Overcoming Glare*). Korwin presents many lighting solutions for the problems facing the installation of a fiber piece: adding lenses to a fixture to soften potential bright spots; using up-lights from a floor canister; lighting from across the room; choosing between incandescent and halogen bulbs. He also suggests talking to major lighting distributors in your area. Many of them have showrooms where lighting solutions can be tested.

Korwin details the color spectrum enhancement properties of different sources of light. The choice of halogen, incandescent or daylight is critical in preserving the color quality intended by the artist. Cool colors are enhanced by daylight; incandescent lighting is high on the red, or warm, end of the spectrum; halogen light is visually less blue than daylight, less red than incandescent and has a crisp, almost icy whiteness. The lighting should be compatible with the mood of the work. Is it dramatic, moody, romantic, cheery? Choosing the right light source will enhance, not contradict, the aesthetics.

Framing

There are many considerations in framing textiles as well. While glass protects against humidity, dust, insects, and touching, it is important, advises West, to allow an air space for the work. It is essential to back with adhesives that won't discolor the fibers. Spacers that keep the glass from coming in direct contact with the material are also critical, since the acidic quality of glass can adversely alter the fibers. While there are plastics on the market today that offer protection from ultraviolet rays, these, as well as glass, may present glare problems.

Installation

Hanging presents another set of challenges. West says the Center for Tapestry Arts has used the solution of hand-stitching a four-inch wide twill tape (used in upholstering) onto the backs of tapestries. A strip of Velcro was attached to the tape and another stapled to a board (shellacked so no acids can leach out) that was covered in muslin. Screw eyes secured the board to the wall, giving the piece adjustability.

While many artists block their work before installation, in some instances gravity can take its toll. The Center has solved problems by reshaping works in a squaring up frame. They tacked the work down, ironed with the use of damp towels, and then let the piece dry overnight. Heavily textured pieces that could not endure the press of an iron were simply wetted down in blocks, squared out, and left to dry.

Cleaning

While the new fabric protectors solve many of the problems associated with soiling, insect infestations and humidity, periodic cleaning may still be needed. Some pieces can be carefully vacuumed, with a mesh screening placed over the work to avoid fibers being either disturbed or extricated from the piece. Dry cleaning, though, by anyone other than a well-versed conservator, can be dangerous business.

There are textile conservators around the country who specialize in cleaning. The new fabric protectors are much better, but it's helpful to be aware of these resources should the need arise.

When it is appropriately cared for, contemporary fiber art will endure long after its original purpose. Good care from the beginning will guarantee that the best of our textile treasures will be passed on within the family or to museum archives for future generations to enjoy.

TEXTILE CONSERVATION RESOURCES

Considerations for the Care of Textiles and Costumes, Harold F. Mailand, Indianapolis Museum of Art, 1980. A general handbook on textile and fiber care.

Preserving Textiles: A Guide for the Nonspecialist, Harold F. Mailand and Dorothy Stites Alig, Indianapolis Museum of Art, 1999. A guide on how to properly store, clean and display textiles.

The Textile Conservator's Manual, Sheila Landi, Butterworth Architecture, 1998. An in-depth review of practices and materials used in textile conservation.

Textiles as Art, Laurence Korwin. A layman's book with easy-to-understand, basic instructions; includes diagrams such as ideal lighting angles. Available through the author, Laurence Korwin, 333 N. Michigan Ave., Chicago, IL 60601.

The Textiles Conservation Laboratory of Cathedral Heights is a working textile laboratory that advises on specific questions. 212-316-7523

The Smithsonian Center for Materials Research and Education provides workshops on the preservation and care of textiles and fiber art. 301-238-3700

USING THE GALLERY
AS A RESOURCE

AN ORIENTATION FOR DESIGNERS

Editor's Note: When is a gallery more than a place to shop? Leslie Ferrin, co-owner of Ferrin Gallery in Northampton, MA, gives a guided tour for design professionals.

When it comes to finding a specific object to complete a space or a certain artist with a particular skill, working with a gallery is a lot like using GUILD Sourcebooks — the gallery is a resource.

Like GUILD Sourcebooks, a gallery is a resource center, and like the sourcebooks, you can browse for ideas or come prepared with your own. Like chapters in GUILD Sourcebooks, most galleries have a specialty. And just like everyone involved in a creative pursuit, each gallery has its own personality that is expressed through the choice of artists represented and the mode of operation. Every gallery has its own broad range of sources drawing from years of experience, and a library of magazines, books and slides. Like all relationships, when the chemistry is right, working with a gallery can result in great collaborations. For you, the unofficial partnership can become a part of the services you offer to clients.

Defining Your Ideas

As intermediaries, galleries provide credibility for you and your projects when they recommend or introduce you to an artist or an artist's work. If they help to negotiate a project or fees, their ability to communicate with an artist can save time; they may be able to speak more frankly or directly with you and with the artist. Galleries can be especially helpful in steering you away from artists who might not be available or

appropriate because of prior commitments, problems with deadlines or the requirements of your project. If the budget is predetermined or limited, a gallery can also identify excellent artists whose work is affordable.

If you have an idea of what you are looking for, it will be easier to identify which galleries you should be contacting. Are you searching for a certain type of object? Are you

What scale?

What style?

What price range?

Are you seeking an artist who has a specific skill or uses a certain technique? Do you want an artist known for his or her ideas or style, or are you looking for someone to breathe life into your ideas?

The answers to these questions will help determine which artists a gallery might recommend. Some artists work only from the client's ideas, while others are only interested in creating from their own ideas. Most projects will fall somewhere in between. Once an idea is explored, the artist creates an object to fit a client's needs, balancing creative expression with the requirements of the site.

Finding a Gallery

The yellow pages for your area probably has a listing like "Art or Craft Galleries." Often, one primary street or neighborhood can be identified, and a quick visit will provide an overview of the offerings. Be prepared to find a wide range of work, because often the word "gallery" is used to describe everything from a framing shop to a retail store. A true gallery presents changing exhibitions and represents a stable of artists, but other venues, such as showrooms and stores, have much to offer as well.

Local galleries tend to have special knowledge of the area's artists. Working with a local or regional artist can often save you time and money by eliminating travel and shipping costs. In addition, supporting a regional community of artists may be desired by private clients; it can also be a positive statement for a local business to make.

Working with nationally known galleries outside your area opens up specialties of a different sort. Finding a gallery with strong ties to a particular medium sometimes means the option of working with artists who would otherwise be inaccessible. Additionally, a gallery's knowledge may save time in identifying the most appropriate artists for a project. These galleries generally have strong relationships with the artists they represent, and the relationships may prove helpful in gaining cooperation and avoiding problems.

How to Begin

Once you have located the galleries you would like to approach, identify the appropriate contact person and make an appointment to meet in person or talk on the phone. It is as much the contact person's job to talk with you as it is your job to seek out him or her. Whether to the trade or the public, the gallery's role is the same: to present an artist's work, explain the techniques involved and the artistic statement expressed and, through this process, sell an existing object or create a commission opportunity.

Once you have identified the artists you are interested in, you might want to set up a time to bring in your client. Sometimes seeing actual objects is the best way to introduce the concept of working with an artist or purchasing artwork. If this is not possible, ask for printed materials such as color cards, articles on the artist, resumés, statements and slides of existing pieces or installations.

The gallery may not have all of these materials on hand, especially when the most current material is needed. If the project's timeline permits, the gallery can contact the artist for appropriate materials. If time is short, the gallery will probably allow you to photograph an object. Just keep in mind that while a snapshot can provide a quick image, the quality may be poor. If your client is not familiar with reading quality into a photograph, it may be wise to wait for more professional materials to arrive from the artist.

Cost Structures

The price of a piece of work depends upon a variety of factors: the time involved in design and production, the degree of difficulty of the process used, the cost of materials and studio overhead, how well known an artist is, and the price he or she can command for current work. Most people are surprised to discover just how wide the range of prices is for works they consider comparable. You should definitely ask gallery personnel to explain what you're looking at and why it costs what it does; you're likely to get a terrific education in handcrafted

work. Also tell them if you need to stay within a certain budget. That will simplify your search.

If you identify several possibilities that you feel would interest your client, it may be possible to take a number of objects on an approval basis. I've found that once placed in the site, an object can either sell itself or definitely prove to be the wrong choice. Our gallery asks that the borrower take full responsibility for an object's retail value, guaranteed through a credit card number. (Even slight damage like a chip or a tear would result in a purchase.) Although galleries have insurance, the deductible is very high and no one really wants to make claims. The timing on "borrowing" work should be clearly determined.

Borrowing a piece from an exhibition overnight may be possible. However if lengthier arrangements are necessary, the loan will probably not be possible until the show is over.

Ask if a gallery has a standard system of working with the trade; this should set everyone at ease from the beginning. With our gallery, if someone approaches us who is actively working to "sell" our artists' work to their client, we feel it only fair to share the sales commission. Assuming that the gallery is working on a 50/50 relationship with artists, and selling is equally shared between you and the gallery, the arrangement could be made to split the sales commission evenly. If the gallery is more involved through making presentations, visiting sites, billing, etc., the commission to you might be as a "referral," or around 10%.

If your project requires the actual commissioning of site-specific work, customized financial arrangements will be necessary. Establishing how the gallery would like to work with you ahead of time will prevent any misunderstandings at a later date.

Everyone Can Win

Every gallery and each person you encounter are going to have different offerings and ways of working, and not every gallery is set up to work with the trade. There are no rules and there are no set systems. Each artist, gallery and client will find their own ways of working together and, likewise, the results will be unique collaborations. When the chemistry is right — the artist makes a great piece, you place it in the right setting, and all concerned get paid fairly and promptly — what could be better?

The listing on the next page provides information on galleries whose artists are featured on GUILD.com. Browse their work at www.guild.com, and be sure to visit the galleries themselves whenever you're near their locations.

SELECTED GALLERY LISTINGS

Each of the galleries listed below is a showcase of fine craftsmanship and exceptional design.
Make a point to drop by when you're in their location, or visit them at the GUILD.com website: www.guild.com.

ART MECCA
1101 W. Webster
Chicago, IL 60614
773-529-2669

AUSTRAL GALLERY
4236 Lindell Boulevard #LL14
St. Louis, MO 63156
314-371-9100

CRAFT ALLIANCE
6640 Delmar Boulevard
St. Louis, MO 63130
314-725-1177

ELLIOTT BROWN GALLERY
619 N. 35th Street #101A
Seattle, WA 98103
206-547-9740

FERRIN GALLERY
179 Main Street
Northampton, MA 01060
413-586-4509

GALLERY: FUNCTION ART
21 N. Saginaw Street
Pontiac, MI 48342-2111
248-333-0333

GALLERYMATERIA
4222 N. Marshall Way
Scottsdale, AZ 85251
480-949-1262

HANDSEL GALLERY
112 Don Gaspar
Santa Fe, NM 87501-2120
505-988-4030

HIBBERD MCGRATH GALLERY
101 N. Main Street
Breckenridge, CO 80424-7638
970-453-6391

HOLSTEN GALLERIES
3 Elm Street
Stockbridge, MA 01262
413-298-3044

JOHN ELDER GALLERY
529 W. 20th Street
New York, NY 10011-2800
212-462-2600

KATIE GINGRASS GALLERY
241 N. Broadway
Milwaukee, WI 53202
414-289-0855

KENTUCKY ART & CRAFT
609 W. Main Street
Louisville, KY 40202-2951
502-589-0102

LAKESIDE GALLERY
15486 Red Arrow Hwy.
Lakeside, MI 49116
616-469-3022

LINDA RICHMAN JEWELRY
241 N. Broadway
Milwaukee, WI 53202
414-289-0886

MARY WOODMAN GALLERY
PO Box 1456
Kennebunkport, ME 04046
207-967-0789

MOSTLY GLASS
3 East Palisade Avenue
Englewood, NJ 07631
201-816-1222

PORTIA GALLERY
207 W. Superior
Chicago, IL 60647-5509
312-932-9500

R. DUANE REED GALLERY
215 W. Huron
Chicago, IL 60610
312-932-9828

R. DUANE REED GALLERY
1 N. Taylor
St. Louis, MO 63108
314-361-8872

SITTA FINE ART
PO Box 251
Millis, MA 02054
508-376-2676

SYLVIA WHITE GALLERY
2022 E. Broadway
Santa Monica, CA 90404
310-828-6200

THE BULLSEYE CONNECTION GALLERY
1308 NW Everett Street
Portland, OR 97209
503-227-2797

THE RACHAEL COLLECTION
433 E. Cooper Avenue
Aspen, CO 81611-1831
970-920-1313

THE SOCIETY OF ARTS & CRAFTS
175 Newbury Street
Boston, MA 02116
617-266-1810

THOMAS MANN GALLERY
1804 Magazine Street
New Orleans, LA 70130
504-581-2113

TRINITY GALLERY
315 E. Paces Ferry Road
Atlanta, GA 30305
404-237-0370

WALTER WICKISER
568 Broadway #104B
New York, NY 10012
212-941-1817

WEST END GALLERY
12 W. Market Street
Corning, NY 14830
607-936-2011

WILLIAM HAVU GALLERY
1040 Cherokee Street
Denver, CO 80202
303-893-2360

WILLIAM ZIMMER GALLERY
PO Box 263
Mendocino, CA 95460-0263
707-937-5121

ORGANIZATIONS

AMERICAN ASSOCIATION OF WOODTURNERS

3499 Lexington Avenue N., Suite 103
Shoreview, MN 55126-8118
TEL 651-484-9094
FAX 651-484-1724
Mary Lacer, Administrator

The American Association of Woodturners (AAW) is a non-profit organization dedicated to the advancement of woodturning. Over 130 chapters throughout the United States provide education and information for those interested in woodturning. Members include hobbyists, professionals, gallery owners, collectors, and wood and equipment suppliers. Contact AAW for information on their annual symposium.

AMERICAN CRAFT COUNCIL

72 Spring Street
New York, NY 10012-4019
TEL 212-274-0630
FAX 212-274-0650
E-Mail: council@craftcouncil.org
Web: www.craftcouncil.org

The American Craft Council is a national, non-profit educational organization founded in 1943 by Aileen Osborn Webb. Its mission is to foster an environment in which craft is understood and valued. The council programs include the bi-monthly magazine *American Craft*, eleven annual craft shows and markets, a special library on 20th-century craft, workshops and seminars, as well as services to professional craftspeople. Membership in the council is open to all.

AMERICAN TAPESTRY ALLIANCE

PO Box 2768
Fort Bragg, CA 95437
TEL 707-964-5279
FAX 707-964-6698
Jackie Wollenburg, President

(listing continued)

The American Tapestry Alliance was founded in 1982 to: (1) promote an awareness of and an appreciation for tapestries designed and woven in America; (2) establish, perpetuate and recognize superior quality tapestries by American artists; (3) encourage greater use of tapestries by corporate and private collectors; (4) educate the public about tapestry; and (5) coordinate national and international juried tapestry shows, exhibiting the finest quality American-made works.

ARCHITECTURAL WOODWORK INSTITUTE

1952 Isaac Newton Square
Reston, VA 20190
TEL 703-733-0600
FAX 703-733-0584

The Architectural Woodwork Institute (AWI) is a non-profit organization devoted to the education and development of the architectural woodwork field. The AWI provides a number of services, including brief informational publications and research of various aspects of the industry. It also coordinates meetings of professionals within the woodwork realm. Membership is available to manufacturers and suppliers in the woodworking field interested in helping to further public knowledge.

ARTIST-BLACKSMITHS' ASSOCIATION OF NORTH AMERICA

PO Box 816
Farmington, GA 30638-0816
TEL 706-310-1030
FAX 706-769-7147
E-Mail: abana@abana.org
Web: www.abana.org
LeeAnn Mitchell, Executive Secretary

Artist-Blacksmiths' Association of North America (ABANA) is a non-profit organization devoted to promoting the art of blacksmithing. ABANA serves to help educate blacksmiths, acts as a central resource for information about blacksmithing, and publishes two quarterly journals — *The Anvil's Ring* and *The Hammer's Blow* — for blacksmiths. These publications are included as a part of ABANA membership.

CREATIVE GLASS CENTER OF AMERICA

1501 Glasstown Road
PO Box 646
Millville, NJ 08332-1566
TEL 609-825-6800
FAX 609-825-2410

The Creative Glass Center of America, established in 1983, is a resource center for contemporary glass artists, educators, students and collectors to join together in an environment of creativity and interaction. The center provides artists with the support necessary to develop individual ideas and talents and establish a body of work, regardless of personal financial limitations. The Creative Glass Center of America is a division of Wheaton Village, a non-profit organization.

THE EMBROIDERERS' GUILD OF AMERICA

335 W. Broadway #100
Louisville, KY 40202-2105
TEL 502-589-6956
FAX 502-584-7900
E-Mail: egahq@aol.com
Web: www.egausa.org
Mary Lou Storrs, President

The Embroiderers' Guild of America, Inc. (EGA) has more than 20,000 members and over 350 chapters across North America and Canada. EGA is a non-profit, educational organization founded in 1958 to foster high standards of design, color and workmanship in embroidery, to teach the embroidery arts, and to preserve our needle arts heritage. *Needle Arts* is the magazine of the organization. The national headquarters in Louisville offers an extensive lending and reference library, a historic needlework collection and a needlework exhibit gallery.

THE FURNITURE SOCIETY

Box 18
Free Union, VA 22940
TEL 804-973-1488
FAX 804-873-0336
E-Mail: Furniture@avenue.org
Web: www.avenue.org/Arts/Furniture
Dennis FitzGerald, President

(listing continued)

SELECTED ORGANIZATIONS AND PUBLICATIONS

The purpose of the Furniture Society is to advance the art of furniture making by inspiring creativity, promoting excellence, and fostering understanding of this art and its place in society. The Furniture Society is open not only to professional furniture makers, but to all who have an interest in the art of furniture making including galleries, arts professionals, collectors, and amateur furniture makers. The Furniture Society encompasses furniture making in all media.

GLASS ART SOCIETY

1305 Fourth Avenue #711
Seattle, WA 98101-2401
TEL 206-382-1305
FAX 206-382-2630
E-Mail: glassartsoc@earthlink.net
Web: www.glassart.org
Penny Berk, Executive Director

The Glass Art Society (GAS), an international non-profit organization, was founded in 1971 to encourage excellence and advance appreciation, understanding and development of the glass arts worldwide. GAS promotes communication among artists, educators, students, collectors, gallery and museum personnel, art critics, manufacturers and others through an annual conference and through the *Glass Art Society Journal* and newsletters.

HANDWEAVERS GUILD OF AMERICA

Two Executive Concourse #201
3327 Duluth Highway
Duluth, GA 30096-3301
TEL 770-495-7702
FAX 770-495-7703
E-Mail: 73744.202@compuserve.com
Web: www.weavespindye.org
Sandra Bowles, Executive Director/Editor-in-Chief

For more than 30 years, the Handweavers Guild of America, Inc. (HGA) has had the mission to encourage excellence, creativity, and preservation of our fiber heritage. HGA provides a forum for education, as well as opportunities for networking, inspiration and encouragement of handweavers, handspinners, dyers and basketmakers. *Shuttle Spindle & Dyepot*, the award-winning quarterly magazine, is one of the benefits of membership and the HGA-sponsored "Convergence" is a biennial conference that brings together fiber artists from all over the world.

INTERNATIONAL SCULPTURE CENTER

14 Fairgrounds Rd
Hamilton, NJ 08619-3447
TEL 609-689-1051
FAX 609-689-1061
E-Mail: ISC@Sculpture.org
George Eager, President

The International Sculpture Center (ISC) is a non-profit membership organization devoted to the advancement of contemporary sculpture. Members receive listings of job and commission opportunities, access to conferences, workshops, discounts on services and tools used by sculptors, and much more. The ISC also seeks to educate the public at large about contemporary sculpture and advocates for including the arts in the life of communities throughout the world. The ISC publishes *Sculpture* magazine.

INTERNATIONAL TAPESTRY NETWORK (ITNET)

PO Box 112229
Anchorage, AK 99511-2229
TEL 907-346-2392
FAX 907-346-2216
E-Mail: itnet@alaska.net
Web: www.alaska.net/~itnet

ITNET (International Tapestry Network) is a non-profit organization in support of contemporary tapestry worldwide. ITNET organizes international juried exhibitions for display on the Internet as well as displaying tapestry collections and exhibitions curated by other individuals or organizations. The organization intends to create a resource for curators, collectors, architects, art professors, museums, gallery owners and anyone else interested in contemporary tapestry.

NATIONAL COUNCIL ON EDUCATION FOR THE CERAMIC ARTS

PO Box 158
Bandon, OR 97411
TEL 800-99N-CECA
FAX 541-347-7076
Regina Brown, Executive Secretary

(listing continued)

The National Council on Education for the Ceramic Arts (NCECA) is a professional organization whose purpose is to stimulate, promote and improve education in the ceramic arts. NCECA accomplishes this by providing a forum for the exchange of stimulating ideas and vital information about ceramics throughout the creative studies community. NCECA teaches its members and the arts community through an annual conference, publications, exhibitions and other educational services.

NATIONAL ORNAMENTAL & MISCELLANEOUS METALS ASSOCIATION

532 Forest Pkwy., Suite A
Forest Park, GA 30297
TEL 404-363-4009
FAX 404-366-1852
E-Mail: nommainfo@aol.com
Web: www.nomma.org
Barbara Cook, Executive Director

The National Ornamental & Miscellaneous Metals Association (NOMMA) is the trade organization for those who produce ornamental gates, railings, furniture, sculpture and other fabricated metal products. NOMMA publishes a professional "glossy" magazine, newsletter and various sales aids. The association also holds an annual awards competition, trade show and convention. During the convention, NOMMA provides an intensive education program.

NATIONAL WOODCARVERS ASSOCIATION

PO Box 43218
Cincinnati, OH 45243
TEL 513-561-0627
FAX 513-561-0627
E-Mail: nwca@chipchats.org
Edward F. Gallenstein, President

The National Woodcarvers Association promotes woodcarving and fellowship among its members; encourages exhibitions and area get-togethers; publishes *Chip Chats*, a bimonthly magazine; and assists members in finding tool and wood suppliers, as well as markets for their work. Distinguished professional woodcarvers in the United States and abroad share their know-how with fellow members.

SOCIETY OF AMERICAN SILVERSMITHS

PO Box 704
Chepachet, RI 02814-0704
TEL 800-584-2352
TEL 401-567-7800
FAX 401-567-7801
E-Mail: sas@silversmithing.com
Web: www.silversmithing.com
Jeffrey Herman, Executive Director

The Society of American Silversmiths (SAS) was founded in 1989 to preserve the art and history of contemporary handcrafted hollowware, flatware and sculpture. SAS also provides its juried artisan members with support, networking and greater access to the market, partly through its annual traveling exhibitions. The public is welcome to consult SAS with all silver-related questions, including those regarding silversmithing techniques, history and restoration. A referral service commissions work from artisan members for collectors, corporations and museums.

STAINED GLASS ASSOCIATION OF AMERICA

PO Box 22642
Kansas City, MO 64113
TEL 800-888-7422
FAX 816-361-9173
Kathleen Murdock, Executive Secretary

The Stained Glass Association of America is a non-profit national organization founded to promote the finest in stained and art glass. In addition to publishing *Stained Glass* magazine, it sponsors educational programming and public awareness programs.

SURFACE DESIGN ASSOCIATION

PO Box 300286
Kansas City, MO 64130
TEL 816-836-0913
FAX 816-254-8521

The Surface Design Association promotes surface design through education; encouragement of individual artists in all areas of textile/fiber; communication of technical information and information concerning professional opportunities; and the exchange of ideas through conferences and publications.

TILE HERITAGE FOUNDATION

PO Box 1850
Healdsburg, CA 95448
TEL 707-431-8453
FAX 707-431-8455
Joseph A. Taylor, President

The Tile Heritage Foundation is a national non-profit organization dedicated to promoting awareness and appreciation of ceramic surfaces in the United States. In addition to maintaining a reference and research library, Tile Heritage publishes a biannual magazine and a quarterly newsletter, conducts annual symposiums, and supports research in the field of ceramic history and conservation.

WOODWORKING ASSOCIATION OF NORTH AMERICA

PO Box 478
Tamworth, NH 03886
TEL 603-323-7500
FAX 603-323-7500
Laura Bonica, Managing Director

The Woodworking Association of North America (WANA) serves as a networking agency for both hobbyists and professionals who engage in woodworking as an industry, as a hobby or as an art. WANA publishes a quarterly newsletter which includes special purchases, project plans, and numerous opportunities for contacting fellow woodworkers.

PUBLICATIONS

AMERICAN CERAMICS

9 E. 45 Street #603
New York, NY 10017
TEL 212-661-4397
FAX 212-661-2389
$28/year

American Ceramics, an art quarterly, was founded to enhance the preservation of ceramics' rich heritage and to document contemporary developments in the field. Articles feature the best and brightest ceramists: rising stars and established luminaries, as well as those early pioneers who transformed ceramics into a genuine art form.

AMERICAN CRAFT COUNCIL

72 Spring Street
New York, NY 10012-4019
TEL 212-274-0630
FAX 212-274-0650
E-Mail: amcraft@craftcouncil.org
$40/year

American Craft, a bimonthly magazine, focuses on contemporary craft through artist profiles, reviews of major exhibitions, a portfolio of emerging artists, a national calendar and news section, book reviews, and illustrated columns reporting on commissions, acquisitions and gallery/museum shows.

CERAMICS MONTHLY

The American Ceramic Society
735 Ceramic Place
PO Box 6102
Westerville, OH 43086-6102
TEL 614-523-1660
FAX 614-891-8960
$28/year

Ceramics Monthly offers a broad range of articles — including artist profiles, reviews of exhibitions, historical features, and business and technical information — for potters, ceramic sculptors, collectors, gallery and museum personnel, and interested observers.

DESIGN SOLUTIONS

Architectural Woodworking Institute
1952 Isacc Newton Square
Reston, VA 20190
TEL 703-733-0600
FAX 703-733-0584
$18/year

Design Solutions, a quarterly magazine, focuses on architectural woodwork, including explanations of techniques, materials, installations and restorations.

FIBERARTS MAGAZINE

50 College Street
Asheville, NC 28801
TEL 800-284-3388 (Orders)
TEL 828-253-0467
FAX 828-253-7952
$22/year

Five annual issues of *Fiberarts Magazine* focus on contemporary textile art, including clothing, quilts, baskets, paper, tapestry, needlework and surface design. Features include artist profiles, critical essays, book reviews, and extensive listings of opportunities, exhibits and resources.

FINE WOODWORKING

The Taunton Press, Inc.
PO Box 5506
Newtown, CT 06470-5506
TEL 203-426-8171
FAX 203-426-3434
$32/year

Fine Woodworking is a bimonthly magazine for all those who strive for and appreciate excellence in woodworking — veteran professional and weekend hobbyist alike. Articles by skilled woodworkers focus on basics of tool use, stock preparation and joinery, as well as specialized techniques and finishing.

GLASS CRAFTSMAN

64 Woodstock Drive
Newtown, PA 18940
TEL 215-860-9947
FAX 215-860-1812
E-Mail: gcmagazine@aol.com
Web: www.glasslibrary.com
$25/year

Glass Craftsman is a full-color bimonthly publication featuring articles on the creative use of the glass arts and crafts. In addition to how-to information and artist and studio profiles, each issue contains book reviews, career tips, a home-studio section, and a complete calendar of glass-related events.

GLASS: THE URBANGLASS ART QUARTERLY

Urbanglass
647 Fulton Street
Brooklyn, NY 11217
TEL 718-625-3685 x222
FAX 718-625-3889
$28/year

Glass, a full-color quarterly for design professionals, artists and collectors, features profiles of contemporary artists, an educational directory, and critical reviews of national and international exhibitions.

GLASS ART

Travin Inc.
PO Box 260377
Highlands Ranch, CO 80163-0377
TEL 303-791-8998
FAX 303-791-7739
$30/year

Glass Art, published bimonthly, includes business articles geared toward glass retailers and professional studios, as well as features on hot and cold glass techniques and artist profiles.

METALSMITH

SNAG/Metalsmith Business Office
710 E. Ogden, Suite 600
Naperville, IL 60563-8603
TEL 630-579-3272
FAX 630-369-2488
E-Mail: Info@SNAGmetalsmith.org
$29/year North America
$41/year foreign

Metalsmith, the award-winning publication of the Society of North American Goldsmiths (SNAG), is the premier publication of the metal arts in the United States. Recurring features include in-depth profiles of contemporary artists; commentary from leading provocateurs of the art world; historical essay; technical articles; and reviews. The annual Exhibition in Print is a special venue that enables guest jurors or curators to add a unique voice to the field.

ORNAMENTAL & MISCELLANEOUS METAL FABRICATOR

National Ornamental & Miscellaneous Metals Assn.
532 Forest Pkwy., Suite A
Forest Park, GA 30297
TEL 404-363-4009
FAX 404-366-1852
E-Mail: nommainfo@aol.com
Web: www.nomma.org
$24/year

Printed bimonthly, *Ornamental & Miscellaneous Metal Fabricator* is a resourceful guide to metalwork techniques, business tips, new products and book reviews.

PRESERVATION

National Trust for Historic Preservation
1785 Massachusetts Avenue NW
Washington, DC 20036
TEL 202-588-6388
FAX 202-588-6266
$20/year

Preservation, published six times a year, is the magazine of the National Magazine Award-winning publication (for general excellence, 1998) of the National Trust for Historic Preservation. It includes full-color feature articles on historic places, architecture, travel, landscape, and people, and a special news section focusing on issues, people and trends in historic preservation.

PUBLIC ART REVIEW

Forecast Public Artworks
2324 University Avenue W. #102
St. Paul, MN 55114
TEL 651-641-1128
FAX 651-641-0028
E-Mail: forecast@mtn.org
$17/year

Public Art Review is a semi-annual journal which explores the many dimensions of public art. Each issue focuses on a theme — such as graffiti, first amendment issues, or monuments and memorials — and offers information about recently completed projects and artist opportunities, as well as critical reviews of books, exhibits and conferences. *Public Art Review* is a unique resource for anyone interested in the ongoing evolution of public art.

SELECTED ORGANIZATIONS AND PUBLICATIONS

SCULPTURE

International Sculpture Center
14 Fairgrounds Road
Hamilton, NJ 08619-3447
TEL 609-689-1051
FAX 609-689-1061
E-Mail: ISC@Sculpture.org
$50/year

Sculpture, published ten times a year, focuses on established and emerging sculptors and contemporary sculpture. Each issue includes profiles, feature articles, interviews, reviews, and technical information. *Sculpture* also includes listings of opportunities for sculptors, including competitions, residencies, workshops and other information.

SHUTTLE SPINDLE & DYEPOT

Handweavers Guild of America Inc.
Two Executive Concourse #201
3327 Duluth Highway
Duluth, GA 30096-3301
TEL 770-495-7702
FAX 770-495-7703
E-Mail: 73744.202@compuserve.com
Web: www.weavespindye.org
$35/year

Shuttle Spindle & Dyepot (SS&D) is one of the benefits of membership in the Handweavers Guild of America, Inc. (HGA). SS&D is an award-winning, four-color quarterly journal, featuring articles of historical and technical interest, artist profiles, book reviews, articles in support of HGA-sponsored activities and events, a "Gallery" section highlighting work of contemporary fiber artists, and a calendar of events and opportunities.

STAINED GLASS MAGAZINE

Stained Glass Association of America
6 SW Second Street #7
Lee's Summit, MO 64063
TEL 800-438-95815
FAX 816-524-940
Web: www.stainedglass.org
$30/year

Since 1906, this quarterly publication has focused on expanding the use of stained glass as an architectural element. *Stained Glass Magazine* features descriptions of materials and techniques, artist profiles, trade news and source information.

SURFACE DESIGN JOURNAL

Surface Design Association
PO Box 360
Sebastopol, CA 95473
TEL 707-829-3110
FAX 707-829-3285
$45/year

Surface Design Journal, a full-color quarterly magazine, is published by the Surface Design Association (SDA), a non-profit educational organization of artists, educators, designers and lovers of beautiful textiles and quality design. Subscription to the *Surface Design Journal* is provided as a benefit of membership in the SDA.

TILE HERITAGE

Tile Heritage Foundation
PO Box 1850
Healdsburg, CA 95448
TEL 707-431-8453
FAX 707-431-8455
$20/year

Tile Heritage: A Review of American Tile History, a biannual publication, features informative articles on both historic and contemporary ceramic tiles, written from a humanistic perspective and enhanced with large black-and-white photographs. From the time of the earliest cave paintings and molded clay forms, people have sought to conceptualize themselves and inspire others through this decorative art form that today is thoroughly integrated into our daily lives.

WOODSHOP NEWS

Soundings Publications, L.L.C.
35 Pratt Street
Essex, CT 06426
TEL 860-767-8227
FAX 860-767-1048
E-Mail: woodshopnews@worldnet.att.net
$21.95/year

Woodshop News, published monthly, includes features and descriptions of new woodworking tools and technology, profiles and techniques, trade news and source information.

FROM THE GUILD.COM COLLECTION

The **GUILD**.com website debuted in the spring of 1999.
After 15 years of ink and paper, we were intrigued with
the opportunities presented by the Internet. Electronic
publishing has allowed us to expand our audience, our
services and our pool of artists.

As we go to press, the collection of artworks available
through **GUILD**.com approaches 10,000 pieces. Most of
the artists represented sell on a retail basis. Many also
undertake commissions; you'll find examples of their
work in a special area of the website called The
Commission Center.

In the first year of **GUILD**.com, we announced our presence through a series of ads featuring works from the
website. One of these ads appears on the facing page.
We hope you're intrigued, and that you'll drop by to see
the rest of the collection.

Day or night: www.guild.com.

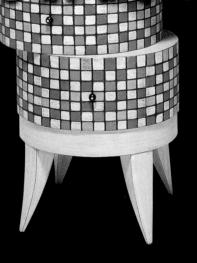

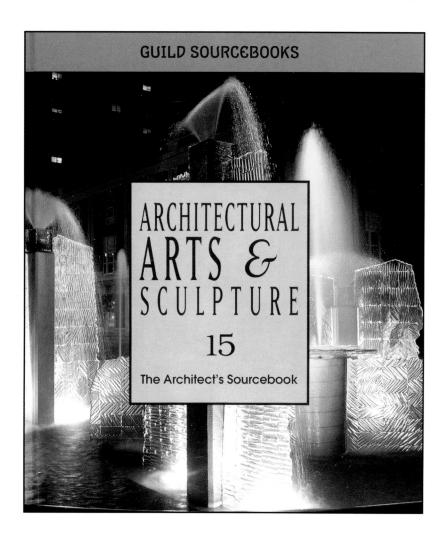

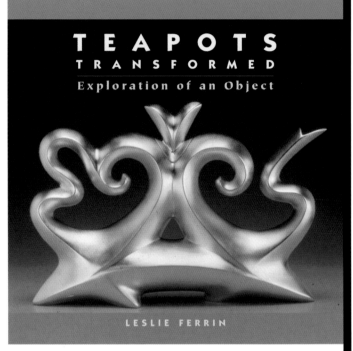

Introducing... **GUILD PUBLISHING**
a new imprint from **GUILD.COM**

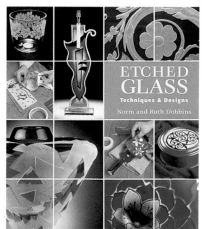

Etched Glass
Techniques & Designs

Inspiration, instruction and stunning showpieces, from plates to picture windows.

Jewelry
Fundamentals of Metalsmithing

Instruction with a perfect balance of insight and enthusiasm. Lavishly illustrated.

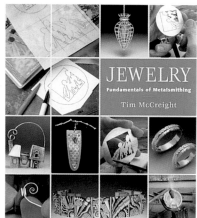

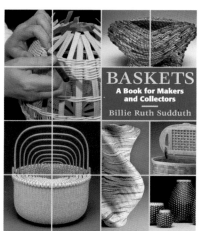

Baskets
A Book for Makers and Collectors

Instruction from a master teacher — and an extraordinary gallery tour.

Needle Lace
Techniques & Inspiration

Stitches, techniques and a gorgeous gallery of needle lace from around the world.

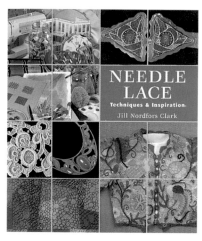

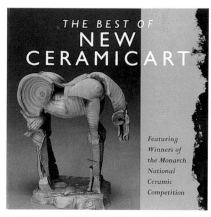

Best of New Ceramic Art

Glorious full-color plates celebrate the beauty of contemporary ceramic art.

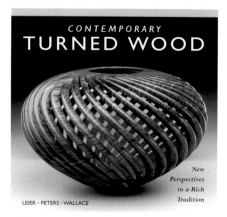

Contemporary Turned Wood

A major survey of a field rich in talent, beauty and innovation.

Available at bookstores, or order directly. Call 1-877-344-8453.

GUILD PUBLISHING

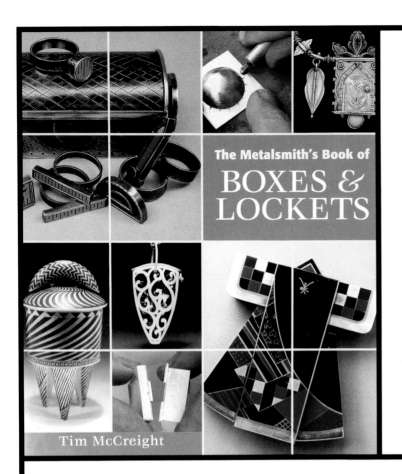

INDEX OF ARTISTS BY LOCATION

INDEX OF ARTISTS AND COMPANIES